Making the Right Moves

PETER DALBY

Making the Right Moves

authorHOUSE®

AuthorHouse™
1663 Liberty Drive
Bloomington, IN 47403
www.authorhouse.com
Phone: 1 (800) 839-8640

Published by AuthorHouse   10/16/2015

ISBN: 978-1-5049-5335-1 (sc)
ISBN: 978-1-5049-5348-1 (e)

I would like to express my sincere thanks to U.S. Figure Skating for granting me permission to re-produce the Moves-in-the-Field descriptions and diagrams in this book.

Contents

Part One
1

Part Two
31

Part One

Introduction

WHEN 'MOVES IN THE Field' were first introduced in 1996 I was somewhat skeptical about their usefulness, but, after making a detailed study of them, I can assure skaters that they can do nothing but good.

Since I started writing this book, the structure of Moves in the Field has undergone some worthwhile changes. Some new moves have been introduced, and some existing ones revised or deleted. The improvements made are praiseworthy and exciting, and the Moves in the Field Task Force are to be congratulated on completing what must have been a monumental task. We now have a new set of challenges, which can only raise the standard of skating.

Sadly, the 'Moves in the Field' test structure has its detractors, and there are those who would like to see it eliminated. Many of us feel this would be a step in the wrong direction because it's important, for the advancement of ice skating, that there is a method of testing a skater's ability to perform certain tasks, and the 'Moves in the Field' discipline fulfills that need admirably.

My original version of 'Making the Right Moves Vol.1' only covered the moves up to Intermediate level, but this new revised edition covers all levels.

Competitive skaters need to pass Moves in the Field, freestyle, and pair or dance tests in order to qualify for competitions, but skaters of all levels can benefit greatly by mastering these moves, and, by doing so, will find that they have increased skills at their disposal. Therefore, it's important that you think of them as a means of improving your skating.

Each level has its own difficulty, but the skills you learn in mastering one level will serve you well when you move on to the next, even though the new moves you'll encounter may be very different to the ones you've just passed. By passing a test, you will have learned new ways of controlling your skating, and probably have developed more power. In fact, it's ultimately a good thing that, on many of the moves, you can't cheat. If you don't skate them properly, they just don't work.

Young skaters will, no doubt, find that Moves in the Field are not as exciting as freestyle skating, so it's important that they understand that these moves *will* make them better skaters, because they'll be learning new skills.

Unlike studying for an examination, or memorizing the lines of a play (where the brain does most of the work), ice skating is a physical endeavor that presents many challenges, not the least of which is the need to control the whole body. And the human body has a lot of movable parts! In addition to this, it also requires courage, good posture, an understanding of what makes things happen on the ice, and, most importantly, a keen sense of balance. So my point is, be proud of yourself, whatever level you achieve.

In order to achieve consistency, it's essential to think ahead when you're preparing for a turn or setting the direction of an edge, and to make sure that your body is in the same position each time you perform them. You also need to have the same consistent flow during a move to be able to skate lobes and circles the same size. It's the same when you're skating freestyle. By thinking ahead you'll be able to put yourself in the correct take-off position for a jump every time, and this will give you consistency. You'll be leaving less to chance, and won't have to rely on that unique ability a cat has, whereby it always lands on it's feet by wriggling itself into position in the air before it lands.

Even if you don't need to take Moves in the Field tests, you'll find that many of the moves can be useful as warm-up exercises. Adult skaters, too, are finding that they provide new and interesting challenges, with each move helping them to develop a new skill.

I would like to explain that I will often use the words 'circle' when I'm talking about a lobe (which usually looks like a semi-circle), and 'torque', which is defined as 'a force that produces a twisting effect'. I will also use the word 'tracing', which is the line the skate makes on the ice, and 'square', which refers to the position of the hips and shoulders when they are ninety degrees to the tracing, with neither side of the body leading.

Many wonderful books have been written about learning to skate - and the technique of ice skating - so there is no need for me to add to the already rich supply of literature available on those subjects. My intention is merely to help skaters and their coaches understand the pros and cons of this relatively new discipline. Even if you only find some small measure of help from this book, I shall consider that the six years I have spent researching and writing it have not been wasted.

To the best of my knowledge, there are no books out there on the market that deal specifically with Moves in the Field in the way that I'm trying to, and I now realize why. It's not so easy to put in writing what a skater should do, as opposed to being with them on the ice, where I would be able to position their bodies, demonstrate the moves, and instruct them on a one-on-one basis.

On many of the moves I'll be going into great detail, so bear with me, and I hope that you won't find my advice and recommendations too difficult to understand.

If I've been successful as a coach, it's because I don't just tell the skater *what* to do, but *why* they should do it. I believe a skater should understand what makes things happen.

At this point, I would like to thank my students who, unwittingly, have helped me in the preparation of this book. Each one of them - through their body language and comments - told me a different story in their lessons, and, in doing so, helped me compile the important points I wanted to get across to my readers. At various places in this book I'll be saying a 'thank you' to the student who made me aware of a particular problem and helped me find the solution, but I must also add my apologies to those students of mine whom I may have omitted. You have all helped me greatly.

My students are just a small cross section of the skating world, but I'd like to make the point that no two people skate exactly alike, although 'Synchronized Skating' coaches may well take exception to that last remark! What I mean, is that each one of my skaters experienced different problems with their moves, because everyone is different. Instruction that works for one skater may not work for another because we're not machines, we're human beings. Therefore, it's important for coaches to recognize the individual needs of each one of their skaters.

In the following pages I shall first express some thoughts on ice skating before I address each move in turn, and explain how I feel they are best performed. I will be making suggestions based on methods I have found to be successful, but your coach may have other methods that will prove equally effective. As far I am concerned, no coach should ever say, 'This is the only way to do it. Everyone else is wrong.' As is so often the case, there is usually more than one way to achieve the desired result.

I will also point out problem areas, and, wherever possible, suggest 'tricks of the trade' that will help the move.

Remember, skaters, judges want to pass your test, so try not to think of them as a firing squad. They don't get paid, so judging, for them, is a labor of love. With this in mind, try to make their experience a little more pleasant by adding something extra to your performance.

One of the ways you can make your moves more enjoyable for the judges is by adding meaningful, stylish arm movements. As long as they are not done to excess, they will enhance your performance. There are many moves where the use of the arms and free leg are left up the discretion of the skater, so let it show that you are enjoying skating for the judges, and not just going through the motions. If you can think of your move as a performance, you will make a much better impression. When you look at a picture on a wall, you either like it or you don't. It's the same for the judges. When you perform in front of them it's the picture *you* present that they're either going to like, or not like so much.

DEVELOPING GOOD HABITS

There is something else you need to consider. In most walks of life it pays to develop good habits, and it's no different with ice skating.

When we start skating we invariably look down to see what's going on, and we also attach no importance whatsoever to pointing the toe of our free foot when we extend our free leg. Why should we? Who cares? But as we progress into more serious skating, we need to become far more aware of the refinements that help make champions. So, get into the habit of holding your upper body nicely, and holding up your head so that it becomes second nature. You also need to get into the habit of holding up your arms gracefully so that they don't look like the wings of a tired penguin (thank you, Keeyana, for making the necessary improvement). And, get into the habit of always pointing your toes (except in some parts of the Yankee Polka) when your free leg is extended.

PUSHING CORRECTLY

Another very important aspect of Moves in the Field that must not be overlooked is the push, or strike, onto an edge.

You must turn out your pushing foot and push from the inside edge of the blade when you are pushing onto basic forward outside or inside edges, or stroking down the ice (I'm not talking about crossovers or cross strokes, etc. where the blade also pushes from the outside edge). The blade needs to turn about forty-five degrees so that you don't push with the toe pick. Make sure you your weight is on the pushing foot and that you bend your ankle slightly so that you can feel the inside edge of the blade gripping the ice. You also need to bend your pushing knee to get the thrust against the ice. (Thank you, Hannah S. for understanding this, and making the necessary improvement).

ALIGNMENT

On many of the Moves in the Field you're going to be making movements that change your body position during the course of an edge. Among other things, you'll be rotating and counter-rotating, as well as bending and rising on your skating knee. You'll also be making strong movements with your free leg, but you mustn't let any of these movements throw your body out of alignment.

The problem is that even if you start off in complete alignment over your skate, there's no guarantee that you'll stay that way as you make the aforementioned movements. Therefore, take great care to keep in alignment over your skating hip and foot, especially going into a turn.

As an example, Move No. 5 in the Novice test (Backward Rocker/Choctaws) has some places where over-rotation of the upper body can cause you to twist yourself off your skating hip, so that you end up not being aligned over your skate. You're still going around the ice, but you're not really in alignment over your skate.

These are just a few of the good habits you should develop, but I now need to continue with my advice about 'Moves'.

Make sure that the first move of your test is strong, because you never get a second chance to make a first impression. Keep in mind, also, that speed is impressive. Whether it's a car, airplane, racehorse, or athlete, speed draws attention. Many of the moves require speed (flow) – gained through powerful stroking and good use of the skating knee - and judges like to see a skater who can get going, which brings me to an interesting point.

In most walks of life you'll find that the faster you travel, the more dangerous things become, and the more likely you are to hurt yourself, but this isn't always the case in ice skating. If you're riding a bicycle slowly, and fall off, you'll probably just roll over. But if you fall off when you're going much faster, you're going to have a few cuts and grazes, if not some broken bones. And, a more serious example would be if you were traveling in a car at eighty miles per hour and got into a head-on collision. Well...we'll remember you fondly.

Rollerblading, too, is a sport that loses much of its charm when you take a nasty fall at speed, but traveling fast across the ice doesn't usually present the same dangers, unless, of course, you've fallen over and are sliding towards the barriers at high speed. Then, speed will take its toll. But in a rink, you'll mostly be traveling up or down the ice, so the point I want to make is that you shouldn't be thinking that you're at a greater risk of hurting yourself if you skate faster, because, unlike on the aforementioned activities, if you fall when you're ice skating, you're going to *slide*. In fact, the slippery nature of the ice is your best friend, so the chances are you won't be at a greater risk of hurting yourself if you skate faster.

I can remember, a few years ago, I was chasing around the ice, following my student with a 'boom-box' so that she could hear her music in a public session. All of a sudden, I caught my toe pick and went flying, sprawling across the ice, with the boom-box going one way, and the batteries and various other parts going the other. I slid about thirty feet, but didn't hurt anything but my pride.

Conversely, one of the worst falls I ever had was when I was standing still on the ice, gossiping with friends. I must have rocked back on my blades a little, because both feet went out from under me, and I remember finding myself completely horizontal for a split-second before slamming down onto the ice, flat on my back. The culprit? No momentum! But enough about those painful memories.

Remember, too, that when you progress from one level to the next, you will not just be moving on to a new set of moves, you'll also be expected to raise the *standard* of your skating to a new level. Posture, control, speed, presentation, and edge quality, will all have to be skated to a higher degree. It's also important to understand that if you can master the elements at the level on which you're working, you will be that much better prepared to skate those elements again at the higher levels, where they are sometimes repeated in a different format.

If you prepare well, you should be able to go into your test with no question marks in your mind about any part of it, and, as a result, be able to perform with confidence. Remember, it's better to be a warrior than a worrier! Try, also, to get enough sleep, and eat sensibly. Skating is hard enough when you're feeling well and strong, but if you're sleep-deprived and eating a lot of junk food, you're not helping yourself.

In the days leading up to your test, try simulating the test conditions by skating the whole test in correct order, with about thirty seconds between each move. This is the approximate time the judges need to write down their comments and marks, and should also be enough time for you to regain your breath.

When you arrive at the test session, be sure to do plenty of warm-up exercises and stretches. That way, you won't be caught out if you only have five minutes to warm up your moves on the ice, which is usually the case. And, although you may be scheduled to skate at a certain time, you may be required to skate earlier if other skaters have withdrawn from the test session, or if the session is running ahead of time. So, check with the test chairperson to see if you need to get ready earlier.

MAKING THE BEST USE OF YOUR OFFICIAL WARM-UP

At most test sessions, there is usually a five minute warm-up - although it could be as little as three minutes if the session is full, and time is at a premium - so it's important that you make every minute count.

The Pre-Preliminary test consists of only four moves, so you should have enough time to go through each one of them, but the remaining tests have five or six moves, so it's important that you discuss with your coach which moves you most need to warm up. You may find that there isn't enough time to practice all of them.

At the higher levels, where you are required to skate turns on different feet on each side of the rink, you probably won't have enough time to skate the full pattern of each move. In these tests, if warm-up time is at a premium, I recommend that you only skate the half of each move you most need.

SOME MORE THOUGHTS BEFORE WE COMMENCE WITH OUR 'MOVES IN THE FIELD'

It has been said that the simple definition of ice-skating is 'keeping a pair of skates between yourself and the ice'. In essence this is very true, but, of course, there is much more to it than that.

Good posture is an essential part of skating, and, if you work at it, it will eventually become 'second nature'. But, until you are an experienced skater who feels completely at home on the ice, it's essential that you are aware of your body alignment (center) over your skate.

When you walk through a shopping mall or a park, good posture is probably not very high up on your list of priorities, but the moment you step onto the ice you should feel as though you've flicked a switch in your brain that now makes you...*a performer,* 'carrying' yourself properly, and wanting to make a good impression.

Between the rib cage and the hips there is – as I like to put it – a lot of 'mush'. This is the core of the body, and if you let it wallow around like a plate of Jello, you're never going to be able skate consistently well. I can't imagine trying to do some of these moves with this part of the body feeling loose. If you don't maintain a certain amount of muscular tension in this, and other parts of your body, you will never be able to control and co-ordinate your movements.

Considering that the human body has so many movable parts - and more than *six hundred* muscles - I think it's remarkable that we're able to hold all these bits and pieces together in order to keep our balance. So, *only move what's necessary. Keep the rest of your body still.*

This brings me to '*GOLDILOCKS AND THE THREE BEARS*'. (No, don't worry. I'm not going to lapse into a children's story!)

Just as Goldilocks found out that it's not a perfect world, and that some things are either too much or too little, so we find, in skating, that it becomes a problem if you do something too much, or too little.

For example, it's important that we prepare the rotation of the upper body before a turn, but, if you rotate too much, you may have trouble checking out of the turn by having to make excessive movements of the arms, shoulders and hips. By the same token, if you don't rotate enough before a turn, your body position is effectively 'blocking' your foot from completing the turn. A blade has to turn 180 degrees from forward to backward, or vice versa, but it will turn much more easily than you think if everything above it is positioned correctly, and pre-rotated to the right degree. You shouldn't have to force your blade to turn.

Another example is the skating knee on twizzles. It should be fairly straight, but not with the knee locked rigid. A strongly bent knee doesn't work too well either, because you will rotate quicker if all parts of the body are drawn close to the straight vertical axis that runs through the body. This means that the skating knee should be fairly straight.

A further example is the movement of the arms on power pulls. If you swing your arms wildly backwards and forwards, you may actually throw yourself off balance, but if you don't move them at all you won't benefit from the natural, and necessary, coordinated movement of hips against shoulders. There should be just enough movement for control.

There are many more examples of 'too much or too little', so, on some of the moves, I'll point out the compromises we must make in order to skate them successfully.

Talking of compromise, in most ice rinks you will see quite an assortment of skaters. There will be the pretty, graceful skaters who need to show a little more 'attack' and a higher energy approach to their skating, and then, at the other end of the spectrum, there are those who have abundant power, but need to add some finesse and style to their skating. No-one ever said this business of compromise was going to be easy.

In my thirty-eight years of coaching, I've found that many people skate like their personalities. Now, this can be both a help and a hindrance. Generally, the perky types, with bubbling personality, are the ones who take to the ice with an almost frightening amount of energy. At the other end of the scale are the dreamy, ethereal skaters who seem to be in another world. No harm in that, but remember that the judges are judging you in *this* world, so, if you can look at yourself honestly, you may have to try to make some adjustments. Sometimes, we need to be a little less 'Swan Lake', and a little more 'Sabre Dance'.

These are a few examples of compromise, but there is one more that is extremely important, and that is the use of the skating knee during turns. Although I like to see a skater rise a little on the skating knee to use the rocker of the blade into a turn, you must be careful not to do it too energetically, because if you spring up too sharply you can end up 'jumping' the turn off the bottom toe pick on a forward turn. The evidence is on the ice. If you see a gap between the entry and exit edge of the turn, and toe pick marks in between, you need to be a bit more subtle about the use of your skating knee. I see this a lot on forward counters and rockers. On back turns, you need to be careful not to hop off the back of the blade by pressing up on the skating knee too strongly.

TO BEND, OR NOT TO BEND?

Skaters are always hearing that time-honored demand, "BEND YOUR KNEES!", and, in most cases, it's necessary. Many of the moves require strong knee bend in order to achieve power, and to skate on steep edges, but there are many instances where you are better off being 'up' on the skating knee, with the knee only slightly bent.

Examples:

PRE-PRELIMINARY TEST
Basic Consecutive Edges
Forward Right and Left Foot Spirals
Waltz Eight (especially on the back edge, and final edge of each circle)

PRELIMINARY TEST
Consecutive outside and inside spirals
Alternating forward three turns
Forward circle eight

PRE-JUVENILE TEST
Backward circle eight

INTERMEDIATE TEST
Spiral sequence (on the actual spirals)
Brackets in the field sequence
Forward twizzles

NOVICE TEST
Backward twizzles (on the actual twizzles)

Spirals, on all moves, need to be skated on a straight skating knee.
The above advice also applies when the aforementioned elements are skated in the Junior and Senior moves tests.

THE CHANCE TO BENEFIT BILATERALLY

Moves in the Field are not just a necessary and worthwhile discipline, they may also be a blessing in disguise. They have come into being at a very crucial time, chronologically, because never before have skaters needed to develop bilaterally as they do now. The Moves in the Field tests may well be instrumental in helping skaters develop an overall strength that will help prevent injuries that were previously caused by only having developed their muscles unilaterally.

I don't think anyone knows the reason why, but it's a plain fact that most 'racing' sports move in a counter-clockwise direction. Look at speed skating, athletic track events, motor racing (NASCAR, Indianapolis, etc.), horse racing (in North America), and indoor bicycle racing, to name but a few. Even the chariots racing in the movie '*Ben Hur*' kept turning to the left!

The point is, that if you watch skating championships and high-level competitions, you'll see that most skaters skate backward crossovers in both directions in their programs, and forward crossovers in a counter-clockwise direction, but from Preliminary up to Olympic level you will almost *never* see them skating forward crossovers in a *clockwise* direction. And, when they get on the ice for their warm-up, which way around the rink do they start skating? Counter-clockwise.

So, at least the Preliminary test Forward Crossovers, and Juvenile test Forward Power Circle, make a start in helping the skater to develop bilaterally.

These days, skaters are required to skate with more speed and power, and are using much more force to take off and land multi-rotational jumps. As the demands on their bodies increase, foot, knee, back, and hip problems are becoming commonplace.

I firmly believe that we are very near to the limit of how much the human body can withstand, when it comes to the stresses it is subjected to in ice skating, and, indeed, many sports. I'm very concerned that I see so many *young* skaters (sometimes as young as eight or nine years old) complaining of hip, knee, and foot problems. The least we can do, as coaches, is to encourage our skaters to build the muscles on both sides of their bodies equally. We have two feet, two knees, and two hips. Let us try to develop our skater's muscles evenly so that they don't stress any one joint more than its counterpart.

At the time of writing this paragraph (Dec. 2013) I have just heard about a skater I used to teach Moves in the Field lessons - now thirteen years old - who has just undergone spinal surgery for a vertebrae problem caused by practicing the contortionist spin positions skaters now have to master in order to be competitive. This is very sad, and I beg all of you to do some loosening up exercises before you attempt to contort your bodies into these un-natural positions.

Those of you who ice-dance will have noticed that, apart from a few exceptions like the *Reverse Waltz* in England, compulsory dances always move in a counter-clockwise direction, and nearly all forward progressives are skated counter-clockwise.

Although skaters should be getting equal power from both legs on counter-clockwise crossovers and progressives, it's generally accepted that we get a more powerful push from the right leg. Can you imagine, then, the stress on the right knee as the full weight of the body is taken upon it as you push against the ice. Additionally, as the foot is finishing the stroke it's also turning out a little as it leaves the ice, which means there is a slight twisting (torque) of the pushing knee at the same time. This is not how nature intended our knees to move.

Counter-clockwise progressives don't affect the left knee as much because that foot isn't turning out as it pushes. If anything, it turns *in* very slightly in relation to your body, or is in a neutral position if the blade stays parallel. This means that the right knee is under greater stress than the left knee.

I'm bringing this fact to your attention because it's more than coincidence that I know of so many skaters who have suffered the same deterioration of their right knees, especially ice dancers. The right knee is also the landing knee for most freestyle skaters, and it can take quite a jarring until a skater learns how to absorb the landing of a jump through their knee and ankle. My left knee is still like a teenager's. It's strong, and there's not a bit of pain, but the stresses on my right knee - firstly from my brief career as a singles skater, and then from my longer time as an ice dancer - have caused it to deteriorate badly. I have almost no cartilage left. Therefore, work your clockwise crossovers and progressives as much as your counter-clockwise ones, so that you are not always stressing that hard-working right knee.

POINT OF BALANCE ON A BLADE

There are differences of opinion as to where a skater should balance on the blade. I have always found it best to be just behind the middle of the blade when skating forwards (with a little more weight on the heel than the ball of the foot), and in front of the middle of the blade (the ball of the foot) when going backwards. If you can do this, you'll find that the blade will sit solidly in the ice, rather like a speedboat going through the water. If you are already on the front part of the blade when skating forwards, you will not be able to use the rocker of the blade correctly to make a turn to backwards.

TURNS

The subject of turns could fill a whole book, so I'm only going to touch on some basic principles of turning, but, before I get onto this subject, I want to stress that *you don't have to be a contortionist to make a turn on the ice!* You just have to keep in mind that you can help your foot make correct and easy turns by preparing your body to be in the right position before the turn. It's the same for jumps. If you prepare your body in the right position before a jump, you give yourself a much better chance of taking off correctly, and doing the jump more consistently.

The four basic one-foot turns are: Three Turn, Bracket, Counter, and Rocker.

Three turns turn *into* the circle, with the natural rotation of the body. The cusp of the turn points into the circle. The blade turns into - and continues on - the same circle. Brackets turn *out* of the circle, requiring a counter-rotation of the upper body before the turn. The cusp of the turn points out of the circle. The blade turns out of the circle but still continues on that same circle. Counters turn like a bracket, but change direction onto a new circle as you exit the turn on the same edge. Rockers turn like a three turn, but change direction onto a new circle as you exit the turn on the same edge.

One of the reasons three turns and brackets are considered easier turns than counters and rockers, is that the skate continues around the same circle after the turn. The body lean remains the same, unlike counters and rockers, where the body lean has to change as you go onto a new circle and direction.

There are two basic two-foot turns: Mohawks and Choctaws.

The purely technical definitions of the turns are as follows:

A Mohawk is a turn, from forwards to backwards, or backwards to forwards, on edges of the same character. That is, inside to inside, or outside to outside. So, when the edges are the same going in, and coming out of the turn, it's a Mohawk.

A Choctaw is a turn from forwards to backwards, or backwards to forwards, on edges of a different character. That is, outside to inside, or inside to outside. So, if your edges are different going in, and coming out of the turn, it's a Choctaw. You should also notice that a Mohawk continues on the same circle (or same direction), whereas a Choctaw changes direction when you turn, onto a new circle.

I don't want to sound old-fashioned, but, when it comes to turns, those of us who have spent some time skating school-figures have an advantage over those who haven't. They really are the basis of so many things we do in all branches of our skating, and really help us to understand about the preparation for a turn, and how to check out of it.

I think it's *very* important to understand that, when making a turn, *we are only trying to turn the foot* and not the whole body, which you'll be able to do if you pre-rotate your upper body the right amount. I see so many skaters 'whipping' their bodies around, unable to control the exit edge of a turn. You *can* go into a turn this way, but can you hold a controlled position of your body after you come out? This is especially noticeable on back three turns. When you turn to forwards on a basic back three turn, you don't need to end up with your body facing where your skate is going. Your upper body should actually be facing out of the circle.

Once again, there are many different theories on the subject of turns, but I have found that, when preparing the rotation for a turn, your shoulders need to rotate further than (or 'against') the hips, thus creating a slight 'twisting' feeling at the waist. What we are actually doing is rotating the rib cage, or upper body, but no more than necessary. This rotation must be completed *before* the turn, so that you are able to check *when* you turn. Now, you will be able to check out of the turn by reversing this rotation.

It's all about preparation. Preparation of the body position for what is to follow. The upper body pre-rotates in the direction the foot is going to turn, while the hips are kept still, which helps to keep the edge steady. Because our body parts are all joined together, the hips will turn a little with the foot, but should only turn enough to allow the foot to complete the turn. The moment the foot has completed the turn, the hips must not rotate any further, and must be checked, along with the arms and shoulders.

There are several moves where you need to hold a checked position until you get back to the long axis, but you shouldn't have to perform a feat of strength to do this.

In simple terms, you will find that, when you turn, the foot must turn 180 degrees, the hips turn about half as much, and the shoulders hardly turn at all if you've prepared well. In fact, you should find that your upper body stays facing the same place before and after the turn. This is my '0 – 90 – 180' theory.

USING THE BLADE CORRECTLY ON TURNS

Judges can usually see, and sometimes hear, when a skater scrapes or skids through a turn, so it's important that you use the rocker of the blade correctly. When turning from forward to backward, make sure that you lift from behind the middle of the blade to the front as you enter the turn(but not as far as the toe-pick), and then back to the ball of the foot as you exit. When turning from backward to forward, go from the ball to the heel as your skate enters the turn, and then back to just behind the middle as you exit.

Unless you're traveling fast across the ice, let your blade go into, and out of, a turn without rushing it. I have seen some skaters who think they must turn their blades very quickly, and 'whip' their turns around. Admittedly, though, the faster you travel across the ice, the faster your blade must turn. The rule is: The speed your blade must turn is relative to the speed you're traveling across the ice. After all, a blade runs forwards and backwards very well, but not sideways! It must turn 180 degrees.

NATURAL LEAN

There are certain similarities between ice-skating and riding a bicycle. When we ride a bicycle in a straight line, we, and the bicycle, are completely perpendicular to the ground with no lean, but when we ride around a curve the body has to lean into the curve with the bicycle, in order to stay in alignment with it.

It's the same with skating. Our bodies must 'go' with the edge (or circle), and be in alignment with the blade. Remember, all edges are part of a circle. The amount of the lean will depend on the depth of the curve, and the speed of the skater.

GENERAL TIPS

- If you're on an edge, on a bent knee, you can get a good push.
- When pushing, make sure you have your weight on the pushing foot long enough before you transfer your weight onto the new foot. After all, you can't push against the air. We want 'grip', not 'slip'. I see so many skaters 'kick' their foot off the ice because they have been told to get a nice free leg extension. Unfortunately, it didn't get there as the result of a correct stroke.
- Even on those moves where power is the sole focus, try to be aware of the picture you present to the judges, and not just demonstrate sheer power at the expense of style. The line of your arms, your overall posture, your free leg extension and head carriage, should all contribute toward a pleasing performance.
- Know you are in total control by making yourself hold *any* position, on *any* edge - especially before or after turns - for as long as *you* want to. Do this as an exercise.
- In most cases, the free foot position - regarding turn-in (closed) or turn-out (open) - should be dictated by the free hip position.

- Although I don't play golf, I know that golfers are taught to 'follow through' with the club once they've hit the ball, and not cut short (or check) their swing. So, in much the same way, as you finish the 'length' of your stroke, let your free leg continue to extend after it leaves the ice.

- An extended free leg not only looks good, it's also a useful aid to balance.

- Pushing doesn't necessarily mean rushing. Many coaches find that when they tell their skaters to push harder, they invariably speed up the tempo of their strokes. When you are required to push harder, in order to gain speed, it means you need to get more out of your stroke by applying more energy through your leg muscles to push against the ice. This is what propels us across the ice, and demonstrates what we learned in Physics, *'Every action has an equal and opposite reaction.'*

- When we walk, march, or run, it is natural for our arms to move 'opposite' to our legs in order to feel coordinated, but when stroking (especially skating crossovers), try not to let the powerful movement of the legs 'transmit' through the body to the arms and shoulders. On crossovers it's necessary to keep the arms still (unless you have specifically choreographed arm movements), and isolate the movement of the legs from the upper body by holding the torso area (core) in control. Nothing needs to move from the hips upward. Therefore, stroking is essentially 'leg work'.

- There are many instances where an increase of knee bend helps your momentum, power pulls being an obvious example. Once again, the laws of Physics come into play. By pressing up on a curving edge, against the ice, you gain speed.

- When skating backwards onto a wide step, make sure that you transfer your body weight onto a well-bent skating knee on an inside edge. You will then be able to gain momentum by pushing from that bent knee as you shift your body weight back over to your other foot.

- When skating three's, double three's, brackets, etc., on semi-circles (lobes), think 'circle first'. You don't want to push onto a straight line, and then have to turn a corner. Your prime concern should be to get your body in alignment over your skating hip, and then start preparing for the turn. So, remember, CIRCLE FIRST! Especially on single three's and brackets. You have half the lobe to skate before you turn.

- Lastly, if something isn't working properly, look back and see if what you did beforehand is causing the problem.

CHALLENGE YOURSELF WITH THESE TESTS

BALANCE TEST

From a standstill, take one small push, and skate forward in a straight line, on the flat of the blade, with the intention of traveling twenty feet or so. The skating knee should be straight. The free foot should be held behind the heel of the skating foot, over the tracing, toe pointed, and turned out. The arms can either be held out to the side of the body, or, if you want test yourself even more, relaxed at your side.

The object is to see how long you can keep your balance on your skating foot *after you have slowed down to a standstill*, without having to put your other foot down or twist on your skate.

You will have no trouble balancing while you have some speed, but, the more you slow down, the more you'll be aware of how perfectly aligned you need to be over your blade in order to keep your balance. The slower you go, the harder it becomes. When you come to a standstill, try not to cheat by twisting around on the blade. This defeats the object of the exercise. Your skating foot needs to keep facing forward.

On this exercise, I have found it really helps to feel 'tall', holding up the upper body nicely, while relaxing the shoulders down.

Have some competitive fun with your friends by counting how long each one of you can balance, once the skate has come to a standstill. I have seen skaters stay balanced for as long as *seven* seconds!

ARMS CAN HELP...AND HINDER.

Skaters rely on their arms far too much, especially when it comes to skating around a curve, or changing direction. (Thank you, Karen, for bringing home the same point when you took my ski poles away from me, many years ago!)

As a test, try eliminating the help you get from your arms by folding them in front of you, leaving them relaxed at your side, or holding them behind your back. You'll immediately become more aware of the need to control your hips and core in order to skate around a curve, or change direction. The core area of a skater's body is what I call the 'Control Center'.

Try skating 'change of direction' forward strokes (like the Forward Perimeter Strokes in Pre-Juvenile Moves, Pattern 1) with your arms folded. This will greatly improve your hip control, because you will have to rely almost entirely on your hips and core to control the direction of your edges. Generally, where the hips go, the skate follows.

There are many instances where the arms should be considered an extension of the shoulders because having an arm in a certain position doesn't guarantee that the shoulder is in the right position. So, when you need to skate forward crossovers, just rotate your upper body to get your outside arm in front of you on the circle. You will have a much more natural - and comfortable - line through your arms and shoulders.

POWER PULL VARIATION

Try skating Power Pulls with the free foot held behind on forward pulls, and in front on backward pulls. It's much harder because your free foot is not leading the way, and you have to rely on using your knee action, and a controlled movement of the hips against the shoulders, to maintain momentum.

ACCELERATION TEST

Even before Moves in the Field came into existence, I would have my skaters turn a three turn from a standstill, and then see how much speed they could achieve after skating four or five back crossovers, finishing in a jump landing position (both ways around). It's important to be able to do this. Judges won't be very impressed with your freestyle program if you need seven or eight crossovers to get up speed after coming out of a jump or spin.

ADDING A TURN AFTER THE INTENDED TURN

At the risk of having my readers cringe at this terrible pun, there is an old saying that goes, 'One good turn deserves another!'

There is a very useful turning exercise whereby a turn is followed by a second turn in order to see if the skater is checking the first one correctly. It doesn't matter if the first turn is a one, or two foot, turn. The point is, if you check the first turn correctly, you should be able to execute the second turn (*continuing on the same circle* if you're combining threes with brackets for example, or vice versa) without any further preparation. The torque will be there. The movement you make checking the first turn prepares your rotation for the second. And the way you rotated to check should tell you which way you can make another turn. As you check the first turn, and go into the second, you should feel 'twist-twist'.

Here's an easy example. If you check a forward inside bracket properly, on a circle, you should be able to immediately turn a back outside three turn, staying on the same circle.

Here are some more examples where the second turn continues on the same circle. You should be able to figure out even more examples for yourself.

One-foot turn to one-foot turn:

Forward Outside Three to a Back Inside Bracket
Forward Inside Three to a Back Outside Bracket
Back Outside Three to a Forward Inside Bracket
Back Inside Three to a Forward Outside Bracket

(You can also reverse this, and skate bracket to three-turn, etc.)

Outside Rocker (forward or backward) to Outside Three
Inside Rocker (forward or backward) to Inside Three

Outside Counter (forward or backward) to Outside Bracket
Inside Counter (forward to backward) to Inside Bracket

Two-foot turn to one-foot turn:

Forward Outside Mohawk to Back Outside Three
Forward Inside Mohawk to Back Inside Bracket

Forward Inside Choctaw to Back Outside Three
Back Outside Choctaw to Forward Inside Three

'MOVES' PATTERNS

It's good for skaters to have to turn both ways, and skate in both counter-clockwise and clockwise directions, but, unfortunately, the flow of skaters on freestyle and public sessions is nearly always counter-clockwise, so, for safety reasons, we don't get to practice clockwise movements as much as we need to. This is unfortunate, because most skaters need twice as much practice their unnatural way around. Therefore, take advantage of when the ice surface is not very crowded, and use that time to practice your clockwise patterns.

I may be asking for trouble by saying this, but I'm not much of a hockey fan. Having said that, I must say that I'm grateful the sport exists because, without it, we wouldn't have all those useful hockey markings on the ice to help us lay out our moves. They are invaluable as guidelines and reference points. We can, and should, take advantage of them whenever possible. All five circles, the blue and red lines, and the four red 'dots' that go down each side of the ice, are a great help in setting out our patterns correctly.

A good example of how you can use the red dots to your advantage is when you skate the Eight Step Mohawk Sequence, and Backward

Power Three turns, in the Juvenile moves test. I like to have the skater start on the red line near the barriers, skate the introduction steps along the red line up to the blue dot in the center of the rink, and then use the red dots to establish the size of the circle. They will be at the quarter, and three-quarter marks of the circle.

The four red 'dots' down the length of the ice surface also make a perfect long axis for so many moves.

Examples are:

Pre-Preliminary Spirals
Preliminary Consecutive Spirals
Preliminary Forward Power Three Turns
Pre-Juvenile Power Change of Edge Pulls
Juvenile Cross Strokes
Juvenile Forward Double Three Turns
Intermediate Brackets in the Field
Novice Counters
Novice Backward Twizzles
Junior Rockers
Junior Backward Loop Pattern

I realize, of course, that some ice rinks have no hockey markings, so if you test in one of those rinks you'll have to use your own judgment on where to place the long axis for many of the moves.

ICE SURFACES

Although most ice surfaces are oblong-shaped, it's not uncommon to come across some that are square, and even triangular shaped! But, for the purposes of this book, I'll talk about regular oblong ice surfaces, where the barriers not only form a straight line down the sides of the rink, but across the ends, too. You need to keep this in mind when you are planning how to skate the end patterns of your moves.

Some moves still incorporate crossovers around the ends of the rink, so it's crucial to set up the end pattern correctly. How you set up your approach to the end of the rink can make or break the move. Help yourself to do this by arranging the lobes down the side of the ice surface so that they don't put you too close to the end of the rink. That way, you'll be able to skate the end patterns on an arc, even though it's a shallow one. If you stretch your lobes too much down the side of the rink by skating weak edges, you'll end up having to skate across the end of the rink on a straight line. Crossovers are much more difficult to skate when you're not on an edge.

You will notice that some rinks have rounded corners, while others are more 'square', but, irrespective of how the corners are shaped, if you skate too much *into* the corners you will end up having to skate a straight line across the end of the rink.

Remember, too, that as ice rinks come in all shapes and sizes, it is *very* important that you go to the rink where you will be testing to see if your moves will fit the ice surface. If you train on a smaller than regulation-size rink, you will have to gain more speed and flow to satisfy the judges that you can cover a larger ice surface with the correct pattern. Conversely, if you have been training on a large ice surface, and will be testing at a smaller rink, you will have to 'compress' the length of your lobes along the side of the rink, so that you don't find yourself too close to the ends of the ice surface. Judges will usually take it into consideration when a rink is considerably smaller than regulation size (200x85 N.H.L). Also, take into account that the ice may be slower or faster than the ice on which you usually train.

Another thing to keep in mind is that the size of the ice surface is not going to get any bigger, so, if you find yourself skating faster and stronger, you'll have to use more of the ice to fit in your moves. Judges have no problem with this.

Remember: Unless otherwise specified, from a standing start you are allowed SEVEN introductory strokes when starting a move. In many moves you will not need this many, but use these steps effectively so that you start your move at the ideal speed. On moves where you need to repeat the other way around (often a mirror image) you're not confined to seven steps between the two halves, but try not to skate too many more as you build flow for the second half of the move. A good skater will not need very many strokes to build the necessary flow.

It's also important to know *where* you are on the ice surface, in which direction you're heading, where the tops of the lobes are on the moves that incorporate them (because so many turns are placed there), and where the long axis is on moves that use a long axis.

When you have completed the first move in any test, go to the start of the next move, but wait for the Judge-in-Chief's signal to start. The judges need a few moments to write down their mark and make any comments they deem necessary, so, by waiting for their signal, you'll make sure they won't miss seeing you begin the next move.

If, after your test, you see that the judges have circled 'Retry', it's natural to feel disappointed, but you must try to take their comments as *constructive criticism,* and not take them personally. They will tell you in which areas you need to improve, and, with some diligent practice you'll give yourself the best chance to pass the test the next time you take it.

You will, of course, want to get all the moves in a test up to a passing standard, but there is one more thing to consider that may take a little of the pressure off you. In order to pass a test, you don't have to have a passing mark on each of the moves. It's the passing *total* that's important. For example, in a test with six moves you could be one tenth below the passing average on one, or even two moves, but if you're above the average mark on two other moves, and the remaining moves are on the passing average, you'll still pass the test through having enough total marks to achieve the passing total.

One last piece of advice about test sessions. If you fall, and are not hurt, get up and finish the move. That way, the judges can give you a mark for it, and give you the chance to re-skate it after you complete the remaining moves. If the fall is the result of an equipment failure (broken or undone lace, blade coming loose, etc.), or caused by debris on the ice, then go over to the judges and explain the situation.

Finally...

NERVES, AND WAYS TO HANDLE THEM

I could go on, at length, about the subject of 'nerves', or to put it more correctly, nervousness, but I'll confine myself to some simple comments about this important aspect of our sport.

First of all, don't be too hard on yourself. It's *normal* to feel nervous – or at least a little 'keyed up' – when you're going to perform in front of an audience. This is why actors sometimes forget their lines on stage, but not so much in rehearsal. Therefore, I want to repeat something I mentioned earlier in this book. *The judges want to pass your test.* You just have to prove to them that you can.

It's *normal* to be a little apprehensive about whether you can perform the moves you are going to skate, or the elements in your freestyle program. That's why it's important to train yourself to be 101% ready in practice, thereby allowing for a little margin of nervousness when the big moment arrives.

NERVOUSNESS COMES FROM NEGATIVE THOUGHT

You don't just become nervous. In many instances, mere *thought* can make you nervous. If you start getting that nervous feeling, it means that you're losing control of the way your mind thinks, and allowing negative thoughts to take over and dominate. Therefore, it's not the moves test – or the competition you're skating in – that makes you nervous, *it's your thought process about that event* that makes you nervous. Control your thinking, and you'll go a long way to controlling your nerves, and skating confidently.

Nervousness can cause us to skate very differently from the way we normally do in our daily practice. For example, it causes many skaters to suddenly develop stiff knees when they test. I believe this is because – sub-consciously – we have the feeling that if we bend them, they'll give way, and we'll fall down. So, we stay up on our knees because we feel more secure, and less likely to fall. You *must* tell yourself that your leg muscles are quite strong enough to support your body weight on a well-bent knee, and you will certainly be more secure skating strong edges if you bend your knees and get 'into the ice'.

So, there are many natural reasons why you might feel nervous. For example, the thought that:

- You're going out in front of judges or an audience.
- You won't be able to do the things you need to do.
- You might fall down.
- You're going to make a fool of yourself.
- You might forget your routine or moves.

Negative thoughts like these are your worst enemy. They can cause you to lose mental control and take over your emotions, thus making you doubt your ability to perform the required task.

In order to combat these worries, try to prepare a mental 'shield', a powerful image in your mind, made of strong, pleasant thoughts that can't be easily erased. Something positive. A picture in your mind of something re-assuring and inspiring. Something that makes you feel good, and brings a smile to your face. Something that you can keep in reserve, ready to fend off any negative thoughts that may try to enter your head. That way, the moment you feel the slightest hint of a negative thought coming into your head, you can bring that positive picture into your mind and banish any negative thoughts. Better still, have those positive thoughts already *in* your mind, *so that no other thoughts can enter*. And that's the whole point.

Most people can't think of two things at exactly the same time. When the mind is concentrating on one thing, other thoughts take a back seat. For example, if you're reading this very sentence, the chances are you're not thinking about something else.

Here's another example. If you concentrate on counting backwards – counting forwards is too automatic - maybe seven numbers at a time (or really test your concentration by deducting, say, thirteen at a time), starting at two or three hundred, it will take your mind off whatever else you were thinking about. You won't be able to think about something else if you're *concentrating* on the counting.

To give you one more example, have you ever noticed how time flies when your mind is occupied? You don't notice the time passing because your mind isn't thinking about it. It's occupied with other thoughts, so it doesn't think about the time.

I hope you can now understand that if you can occupy your mind with positive thoughts, you'll be able to block out any negative thoughts from coming into it. It's just like the Sheriff and the bad guy in those old Hollywood movies. There isn't room in the town for both of them!

When I was competing I genuinely looked forward to skating in front of an audience, and would have the thought in my head, 'I can't wait to get out there!' I may have been sub-consciously brainwashing myself, but with that thought in my mind there wasn't a chance that a negative thought like, "Oh my God! I've got to go out there!" could ever enter my head.

Additionally, my coach used to tell me that she would never send me out onto the ice to do anything that she didn't think I could do really well. I found this very re-assuring, and it gave me great confidence. Hopefully, your coach will have similar words of advice to make you feel the same.

So, remind yourself that all you are going out there to do is what you've done hundreds of times before. *It's just one more time.* And, enjoy the luxury of knowing that no-one's going to get in your way.

Here's another small tip I learned from someone many years ago. If you control your breathing, you can go a long way to controlling your nerves. Nervousness often causes a person to feel 'butterflies' in the stomach, and this exercise is a proven way to get rid of them:

Breath in deeply, filling your lungs. Then, control how you exhale by letting the air out very slowly through a tiny hole between your lips. You should try to make this last about ten seconds. Repeat two or three times. It has an amazingly settling feeling on that fluttery stomach.

Part Two

Moves In The field
Let's Get Started!

Pre-Preliminary Moves in the Field Test

1. Forward perimeter stroking The skater will perform four to eight straight strokes depending on the length of the ice and the strength of the skater, with crossovers around the ends, using the full ice surface and for one full lap of the rink (in both directions). Introductory steps are optional. Focus: Power and extension

2. Basic consecutive edges: Forward outside edges Forward inside edges Backward outside edges Backward inside edges Starting from a standing position the skater will perform four to six half circles, alternating feet, using an axis line such as a hockey line. The skater may start each set on either foot, but they must be skated in the order listed. Focus: Edge quality

3. Forward right and left foot spirals The skater will perform right foot and left foot spirals down the length of the rink maintaining a spiral position on each foot for approximately four seconds with extended leg held at the hip level or higher. The skater may be on flats and may start on either foot. Introductory steps are optional. Focus: Extension

4. Waltz eight The skater will perform the Waltz Eight, using large circumference circles, completing two patterns on each foot, and performed with control. This move may start on either foot. Introductory steps are optional or may begin from a standing start. The skater may mark their center. Focus: Edge quality Revised 7/1/2010

Pattern 1

FORWARD PERIMETER STROKING (COUNTER CLOCKWISE AND CLOCKWISE)

Primary Focus: Power

Secondary Focus: Extension

Forward Perimeter Stroking

The skater will perform four to eight strokes depending on the length of the ice and the strength of the skater, with crossovers around the ends, using the fill ice surface and for one full lap of the rink (in both direction). Introductory steps are optional.

Focus: Power and extension

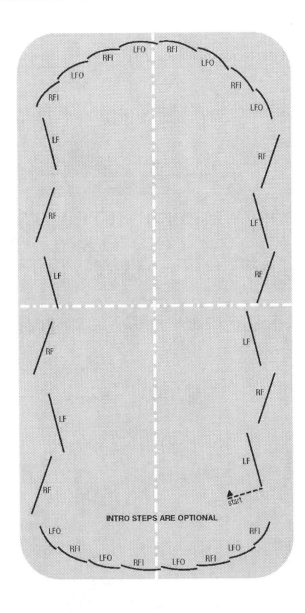

COMMENT

The first step of the ladder. And, if it seems like a very long ladder, just think of the view from the top!

This is the first of forty-four Moves in the Field, so relax, and keep in mind that the judges are not expecting miracles at this level. Just try to demonstrate good posture, balance, a nice stroking movement with good power, and an extended free leg.

Generally, I would not advise holding the arms any higher than the shoulders. If you do, they may look forced, or 'scarecrow-like'.

An old Chinese proverb says, 'The longest journeys begin with a single step', so be encouraged by the fact that many United States champions started off with this very move, and went on to greatness.

RECOMMENDED INTRODUCTION STEPS:

From a standing start, skate across the end of the rink with five strokes (Left, right, left, right, left), and then skate one crossover to be facing down the rink to start the move. For the clockwise direction, you could just add another stroke before the crossover. Alternatively, you could start at the end of the rink - already facing down ice - and skate a couple of strokes to get moving.

THE MOVE

Hold your head up nicely, and skate four to eight long strokes down each side of the rink, but increase the tempo on the crossovers around the ends of the rink so that you skate at least three of them. Use more if you need to. Try to extend your free leg on these crossovers, and remember to skate them across BOTH ends of the ice, completing one full circuit of the rink.

Even at this beginner level you should try to avoid toe-pushing, so get into the habit of turning out your pushing foot on the basic left, right, strokes down the ice, and pushing from the inside edge of the blade. If you can do this, you'll get a more efficient and correct push, and your free leg will extend at a nice angle to the tracing. Not too wide, and not right behind you as the result of a toe push.

Maintain good knee bend as you skate the crossovers across the end of the rink, and lead with your right arm and shoulder (it will be your left arm and shoulder when you skate in the clockwise direction). As you finish the crossovers, square off your arms and shoulders for the left, right, strokes down the second side of the ice.

To finish, either come to a controlled stop, or perform a glide in a nicely presented position before bringing your feet together to skate back to the start of the clockwise lap. Start at the same end of the rink, but facing the other way so that you can repeat this move skating clockwise around the rink. Give yourself enough room to skate some introduction strokes across the end of the rink, and skate a crossover to bring you around to face down ice, but first, *wait for the judge's signal to start.*

You can also start the clockwise direction already facing down ice.

PROBLEM AREAS:

- Rushing the strokes down the side of the ice, instead of achieving some glide with an extended free leg.
- Skating knee too stiff.
- Looking down at the ice instead of looking ahead of you. (To my students who look down at the ice when they are skating, I ask the question, "What's so interesting about frozen water?")
- Arms held too high.
- Toe pushing

TRICK OF THE TRADE:

It's not expected for the skater to skate around the edge of the ice surface, so, for those smaller and less powerful skaters, why not take advantage of the red hockey 'dots', and skate just outside of them, all the way around the rink. This will still make quite a presentable pattern.

Pattern 2

BASIC CONSECUTIVE EDGES

Primary Focus: Edge Quality

Basic Consecutive Edges

- Forward outside edges
- Forward inside edges
- Backward outside edges
- Backward inside edges

Starting from a standing position the skater will perform four to six half circles, alternating feet, using an axis line such as a hockery line. The skater may start each set on either foot, but they must be skated in the order listed.

Focus: Edge quality

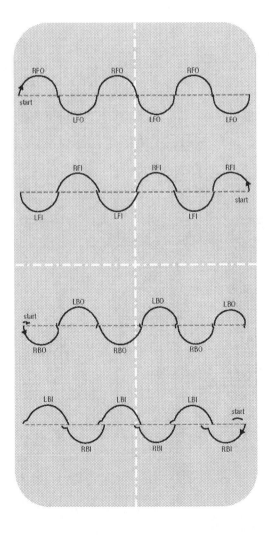

COMMENT

I was fortunate in having the great Arnold Gerschwiler as my figure skating coach. He trained many European and world champions, and I base a lot of my basic figure skating teaching on his methods.

These four basic edges are the foundation of ice skating, and I can't stress enough how important it is to master them. In this test, they all start on the right foot.

On all four edges, you're going to be skating a series of semi-circles (lobes) across the rink, alternating on each foot, and starting each edge on the long axis. The blue and red hockey lines are usually used as the long axis for this move, and four to six lobes are required.

I like to see a skater demonstrate two basic positions on each of these edges; a set starting position, rotating to a controlled finishing position. It's not a crime if you rotate in a continual manner at this level, but it helps if you can define these two positions. If you can master the eight basic positions on this move, you are well on your way to becoming a good skater.

RECOMMENDED INTRODUCTION STEPS:

There are no introduction steps on this move. These edges start from a standstill, on the right foot.

THE MOVE

FORWARD OUTSIDE EDGE

Stand on one of the hockey lines with your right foot on the short axis, 90 degrees to the long axis, and align your body over your skating hip. Rotate your shoulders about 45 degrees so that your skating arm will be leading on the circle, and your free arm will be held slightly behind you (in line with your shoulders).

This should be a very comfortable position, with nothing forced. Turn out your left foot so that you can push off from the inside edge of the blade without toe-pushing, and press your skating ankle over slightly to feel the outside edge of your blade before you move off.

When you push onto your edge, try not to rotate immediately. First, find your balance and position over your skating hip, straighten the skating knee slowly, and *then* start to change position. I prefer the skater to change the free leg position first, and then the arms and shoulders, but you *can* do it the other way around. Both methods work equally well.

The free foot should pass close to the skating leg and move to the front with the free leg nicely extended. Then, start changing your arm position. To do this, lower your arms slightly to allow them to pass near to your body as you change from the first to second position, ending up with the free arm and shoulder in front of you, and the skating arm slightly behind you. Start changing the arms first, and let the shoulders follow, ending up with the free arm now leading. This will now be your leading arm for the start of the next lobe, on the left foot. Passing your arms close by the body (but not touching) makes the change of position feel less 'swingy'.

At the end of each edge, bring the free foot back to the skating foot, and turn out the skating foot to push onto the next edge.

PROBLEM AREAS:

- Starting to rotate the body too soon, and too quickly, causing the shoulders and hips to over-rotate. This makes it difficult to hold on to the edge.
- Toe pushing

TRICK OF THE TRADE:

Try holding that first position (skating side leading) for a full circle, thus proving that it's the natural inclination of the body over the skating hip and circle that makes the edge curve, and not the rotation of the body.

FORWARD INSIDE EDGE

To get the perfect starting position, stand on the line with your shoulders and hips parallel to the long axis (facing down the rink), feet together, arms extended out to your side. Then, turn out your left foot just behind the heel of your right foot, at the same time moving your left arm (free arm) in front of you on the circle (lobe). Your skating arm can remain held out to your side. This movement should rotate your right hip forward so that it is ready to lead when you stroke onto the RFI edge.

Push off in this position, and extend the free leg back, toe pointed and turned out, heel near the tracing. Slowly straighten the skating knee. Then start to bring the free foot through, 'brushing' it close past the skating foot. You will have to bend the free knee a little to do this, before it straightens again as you extend your free leg in front, keeping the toe pointed all the time. At the same time, reverse your arm position so that you end up with your skating arm over the circle in front of you, and your free arm slightly behind you. Your arms are now in the correct position to strike onto the LFI edge. Just before you reach the long axis, bring your free foot back beside the skating foot, and turn out the skating foot to push from the inside edge of the blade onto the next lobe (LFI). Repeat the same technique of passing the free foot through, and reversing the arm position for the remaining lobes.

PROBLEM AREAS:

- Rotating the upper body too much, causing the skater to feel 'twisted'.
- Toe-pushing at the start of the edge, caused by the skater not turning out their foot to push from the inside edge of the blade.
- Skating lobes too big or 'U' shaped, meaning that the skater has to come back to the axis on a straight line (therefore not on an edge)

Once again, try holding that first position all the way around a circle.

BACKWARD OUTSIDE EDGE

The body position on a backward outside edge is a little more comfortable - and natural - than on a backward inside edge, because the skating hip is toward the *inside* of the circle. This makes it easier to feel the alignment of the body over the skating foot, and the natural lean over the circle.

Start near the barrier, with your body facing across the rink and down the long axis (red or blue hockey line), arms extended to your side. Move your right arm in front of you to make an 'L' shape of your arms, at the same time shifting your body weight over to the left foot, on a well bent knee, in readiness to push.

Bring your right foot in close to your left foot, with the toe turned in (pigeon-toe) to place it on the short axis with the heel facing in the direction you'll be skating, and then 'swizzle' push with your left foot, shifting your weight back over to your right (skating) hip by the end of the push. Rise up on the skating knee as you start the edge – this move needs very little knee bend - and *get your balance before you start changing position.*

Although it may be a little more difficult, try to face your upper body *into* the circle at the start of the edge by bringing your free arm and leg in front of you as you push, and *then* change position by passing your arms and free leg close by the body to end up with your free arm and leg behind you over the circle. Look *inside* the circle to start with, and then turn your head with your shoulders so that you end up facing outside the circle, able to see the long axis where your lobe will finish.

I see so many skaters start to rotate their bodies the moment they push onto the edge, with their free leg already passing behind their skating leg. This usually causes them to end up over-rotated, and unable to hold onto their edge for the rest of the lobe.

Just before the long axis, bring your free foot beside your skating foot to place it on the short axis, and turn out the heel of your skating foot to swizzle push onto the next edge. As you bend to push on these edges, keep your weight on the ball of the pushing foot, and then press up to the toe as you finish the push. This will make the free toe nicely pointed as it leaves the ice.

Using the blue or red hockey lines, skate four to six lobes across the width of the ice surface. If there is room for one more lobe, then skate it, provided that you don't exceed six lobes in total. If there isn't enough room, there isn't any point in squeezing in a tiny lobe.

PROBLEM AREAS:

- Rotating the body too soon, or too quickly, making it hard to hold a steady position to the end of the lobe.
- Not being able to stay in alignment over the skating hip as you rotate the body.

TRICK OF THE TRADE:

Practice holding your upper body in that first position for at least half a circle. You're going to need it when you start learning your loop jump, back outside brackets and counters.

BACKWARD INSIDE EDGE

Back Inside edges are nearly always the hardest to skate and control. One reason is because the skating hip is the outside hip, and skaters find it more difficult to get balanced and aligned over their blade on a back inside edge than they do on a back outside. Also, the body has more of a tendency to fall into the circle on a back inside edge than it does on an outside edge. Therefore, try to hold your upper body up over your skating hip to have good alignment over your skate. Another difficulty you may encounter on this move is that the body also has to counter-rotate against the circle in order to assume the second position, instead of rotating naturally *with* it, as it does on the backward outside edges.

To start, stand in the same position as you did for the back outside edges, but this time facing the barrier, and use the same method to push.

Transfer your weight onto the left (pushing) foot, and pigeon-toe your right foot to place it on the short axis with the heel facing in the direction of travel. Take care to place the blade on the inside edge, near the ball of the foot.

At the same time you push, bring your free arm in front of you, over the tracing (edge). Then, immediately after you finish your swizzle push, bring your free leg in front of you. You should now find your free leg under your free arm, directly over the edge. By the time you have finished the push, your weight should have transferred back over to the skating hip, thus enabling you to pick up your free foot, and not 'trail' it on the ice.

Try not to pull your skating arm too far back at the start of the edge, because it may make your shoulders rotate too much out of the circle. Instead, make an 'L' shape of your arms with the free arm in front of you on the tracing, and the skating arm held out to the side. This is your first position. It may feel a little awkward, but if you can master this position, it will help you when you come to skate backward inside three-turns on the Pre-Juvenile test, where the upper body will need to rotate a little more before the turn.

It's so important for the body to be aligned over the hip and the circle before you even think about changing position. You have time to change, so don't panic. Skaters usually rush to get to the second position, and want to rotate their shoulders and hips too soon, before they have their balance over the skating hip. (Thank you, Vivian, for showing me that a skater has time enough to change position before the end of the edge.)

While your free arm steadies you, start moving your free foot back first, passing it fairly close to the skating foot, just before you rotate your free arm and shoulder back, but they should all end up in the second position at the same time. This just means that you need to move your free leg slightly before you start changing your arm position.

Just before you reach the long axis, draw your free foot in close to your skating foot, and turn the heel of your skating foot to swizzle push onto a left back inside edge. As you push, set your arms in the same first position as the previous edge, free arm in front over the free leg, and skating arm held out to the side. Repeat the lobes across the rink.

PROBLEM AREA:

- Over-rotating the shoulders at the beginning of the edge, with the free arm too far across the chest, causing the skater to feel stuck when they try to rotate into the second position.
- 'Trailing' the pushing foot on the ice, instead of picking it up once the weight has been transferred to the new foot.
- Not enough flow
- Lobes too small
- Not placing the foot on the short axis, resulting in very shallow edges.

TRICK OF THE TRADE:

This is a basic exercise to start getting you aligned over your skating hip, whereby you skate backwards on a straight line down the ice, in the two positions you'll need. First, with the free arm, shoulder, and leg in front of you, over the tracing, then with the free arm, shoulder, and leg behind you, over the tracing. This will help you learn to align your body over the skate *before* trying to get on edges, and give you a chance to practice the two positions I recommend.

Pattern 3

FORWARD RIGHT AND LEFT FOOT SPIRALS

Primary Focus: Extension

Pre-Preliminary 3

Forward Right and Left Foot Spirals

The skater will perform the right foot spirals down the length of the rink maintaining a spiral position on each foot for approximately four seconds with extended leg held at the hip level or higher. The skater may be on flats and may start on either foot. Introductory steps are optional.

Focus: Extension

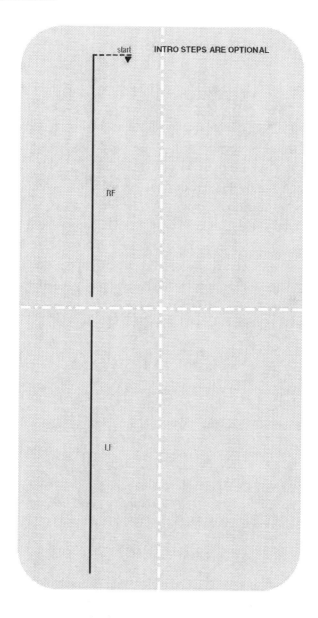

RECOMMENDED INTRODUCTION STROKES:

Skate across the end of the rink with four strokes (left, right, left, right), and then one crossover to bring you facing down ice. Bring your feet together in readiness to push onto the right spiral.

Alternatively, start at the end of the rink, already facing down ice, and skate two strokes to get to the right spiral. You may, however, start on either foot.

THE MOVE

Make sure you are facing down the ice before you get in the spiral position. I see so many skaters start off at an angle, and then have to curve their edge to get back onto a straight line down the ice.

Get into spiral position as soon as possible, so that you have at least four seconds in that position. Skate on a straight knee, and raise your free leg as high as possible behind you, at least hip height. Keep your free leg straight, and turn out your free foot, with your toe pointed. Arch your back a little, and keep your head and arms held up.

Change onto your left foot spiral at the red line (halfway down the rink) and hold for at least four seconds. I usually recommend staying in this second spiral position until you are inside the red circle at the end of the rink. (Thank you, Natasha, for showing how beautiful forward spirals can be).

PROBLEM AREAS:

- Free leg held too low, or off the side.
- Edge curving, instead of being in a straight line.

TRICK OF THE TRADE:

Practice your spiral positions off the ice, and at home. Your legs don't know whether you're on the ice or not!

Pattern 4

WALTZ EIGHT

Primary Focus: Edge Quality

Waltz Eight

The skater will perform the waltz eight, using large circumference circles, completing two patterns on each foot, performed with control. This move may start on either foot. Introductory steps are optional or may begin from a standing start. The skater may mark the center.

Focus: Edge quality

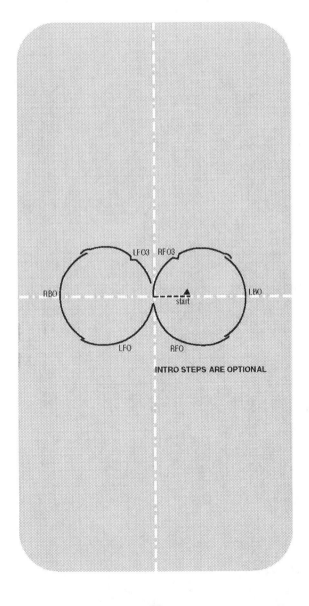

COMMENT

This is quite a difficult move for this beginner level, and easily the hardest of the Pre-Preliminary moves to perform well.

Most skaters do not use introductory steps on this move, but choose to start by stroking straight onto the outside three turn from a standstill. This is alright as long as you can get a good enough push. If you don't, you run the risk of not having enough flow, and skating a circle that is too small to start with. An alternative method is to skate one stroke up to the long axis, and then stroke onto your first three turn. This will enable you to skate at the same speed throughout the move.

This move incorporates some basic positions that will be helpful in preparing you for your jumps. It features a Salchow three-turn, followed by a back outside edge that starts off with the arms and shoulders in the position for a loop jump take-off, and, after rotating the body, a step forward that prepares the skater for a waltz jump or axel take-off.

As with all moves, it's so important to be over your skating hip on all three of these edges, but especially on the step forward from the back edge to the forward outside edge. That way, you will be over your edge, and be able to stay on a circle back to the center (the place where the two circles join together).

The size of the circles should be proportionate to the size of the skater. The diameter of the circle should be approximately three times the height of the skater. If a small skater skates too large a circle, it may result in loss of speed, and problems in placing each edge in the correct place.

RECOMMENDED INTRODUCTORY STEPS:

This move is usually started from a standstill, but you could skate one stroke up to the long axis to have some initial speed.

THE MOVE

I like to see two positions on each edge.

There are two different starting positions for the arms, and either one is acceptable. I prefer to start with the skating arm leading, and then switch the arms in preparation for the turn. There is just enough time to do this. The alternative method is to already have the free arm in front as you push onto the circle. Whatever method you use, you need to make sure that you check your free hip and shoulder when you turn, otherwise you'll keep rotating, and probably have to step early onto the 2nd (back) edge in order to steady yourself. Remember, when you turn the three turn you are only half way through the first edge, so try not to 'whip' the turn around, or you won't be able to hold the back edge of the turn long enough. I like to see the skater hold their free leg extended back through the three turn, but it's also alright to draw the free foot in close to the skating foot. You should be on each edge for a third of a circle.

Apart from stroking onto a slightly bent knee when starting each circle, I would recommend rising a little on the three turn, and then skating the following two edges on fairly straight knees. There is nothing to be proved by skating these edges on well-bent knees.

Waltz music has a count of three beats per measure, and this move has six beats per edge, so try to skate three beats in each position. Therefore, on the three edges, skate with this timing: Push, two, three, turn, two, three, push, two, three, rotate, two, three, step forward, two, three, change arm and free leg position, two, three. If you *are* counting, the turn occurs on beat four.

More often than not, skaters rotate their bodies far too much, or too fast, on these three edges, causing them to end up with their arms and free leg swinging around out of control.

If you can check the three turn properly, then you will be able to push onto the back edge still facing into the circle, with the free arm and leg in front at first, before rotating your upper body over the skating hip in preparation to step forward.

At the end of the back edge you should be aligned over your skating hip with your free arm and shoulder rotated back on the circle, looking in that direction, and with your free foot turned out, held behind you over the tracing. Your skating arm will be just outside the circle. If you are in this position, you will be able to step forward with your foot, and not have to turn your whole body to do so.

Step forward with your upper body over your new skating hip, skating arm in front of you on the circle, and free foot behind. At first, leave your arms still and bring your free foot through to be held in front of your skating foot, *then* change your arm and shoulder position, passing your arms fairly close to your body so that they don't swing around.

PROBLEM AREAS:

- Whipping the turns around, causing the skater to put down their free foot to steady themselves.
- Putting too much energy into the turns.
- Rotating the body as soon as you start an edge. On all three edges, there is time to set the edge and body position, and *then* rotate (change position).

Preliminary Moves in the Field Test

1. Forward and backward crossovers The skater will perform forward crossovers in a figure eight pattern. It is expected that the skater will perform the transition between circles on one foot. Four to six crossovers per circle are recommended. Upon completing the forward figure eight, the skater will perform a swing roll and change of edge to an open mohawk in order to turn from forward to backward and continue the figure eight pattern with four to six backward crossovers per circle. This move may start in either direction. Introductory steps are optional. Focus: Power

2. Consecutive outside and inside spirals The skater will perform right foot and left foot spirals. The outside edge spirals will be skated for the first length of the rink. Forward crossovers may be utilized (optional) around the end of the rink. Forward inside edge spirals will be skated for the second length of the rink. The exact number of spirals will depend on the size of the rink and the strength of the skater, however a minimum of four spirals down each length of the rink must be skated. The extended leg in the spiral should be held at hip level or higher. Introductory steps are optional. Focus: Extension and edge quality

3. Forward power three-turns The skater will perform forward outside three-turns to a balance position followed by a backward crossover. Three to six sets of three-turns will be skated depending on the length of the ice surface. Skaters may begin this move with either right or left foot three-turns. On the second length of the rink, the three-turns will be skated on the opposite foot. Introductory steps and backward crossovers around the end of the rink are optional. Focus: Power

4. Alternating forward three-turns Starting from a standing position the skater will perform alternating forward outside three-turns for the width of the rink. The skater will then perform forward inside alternating three-turns for the second width of the rink. The size of the rink and strength of the skater will determine the number of three-turns skated. This move may start on either foot. Focus: Edge quality

5. Forward circle eight The skater will push from a standing start onto a FO edge and complete one FO figure eight. Upon returning to center at the completion of the second circle, the skater will perform a FI figure eight by pushing onto a FI edge, thereby repeating the previously skated circle. The circles should be equal in size and approximately three times the skater's height. The skater may mark their center. This move may start on either foot. Focus: Edge quality and continuous flow

6. Alternating backward crossovers to backward outside edges The skater will perform alternating backward crossovers to backward outside edges in consecutive half circles for one length of the rink. Four or five lobes should be skated. Introductory steps are optional. Focus: Power and extension Revised 7/1/2010

COMMENT

Most skaters have no difficulty in passing their Pre-Preliminary test, but now we get down to business! This test has six moves, and, from the Preliminary level upwards, the judges are going to expect progressively better skating. It's *so* important that you start feeling 'into' the ice, with good knee-bend when necessary. The last thing you want is to be seen skimming around on top of the ice, stepping out your edges.

There are two moves in this test that involve forward outside three turns, but take note. They need to be treated very differently.

Pattern 3 is about power, and I advise skating the three turn as though you were going into a Salchow jump, with the free leg extended. Pattern 4 is about edge quality, and the three turns need to be skated a little more conservatively. On these turns, my advice is to draw the free foot in close to the skating heel, and skate with very little body lean.

Pattern 1

FORWARD AND BACKWARD CROSSOVERS

Primary Focus: Power

Forward and Backward Crossovers

The skater will perform forward crossovers in a figure eight pattern. It is expected that the skater will perform the transition between circles on one foot. Four to six crossovers per circle are recommended. Upon completing the forward figure eight, the skater will perform a swing rill and change of edge to an open mohawk in order to turn from forward to backward and continue the figure eight pattern with four to six backward crossovers per circle. This move may start in either direction. Introductory steps are optional.

Focus: Power

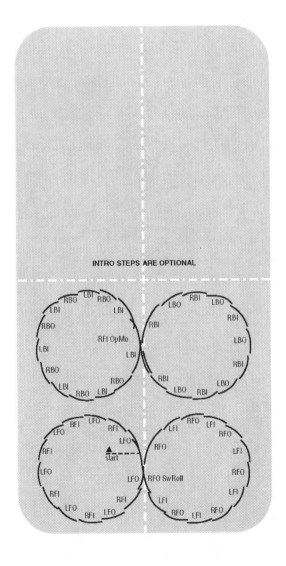

60

RECOMMENDED INTRODUCTORY STEPS:

I like to position this move in the center of the rink, and skate four introductory strokes along the red line to the beginning of the first circle. I usually have the skater perform the counter-clockwise forward circle first, but this move may be started on either foot.

If a test session is full, and time is at a premium, the judges may require two skaters to test at the same time, so you may have to set out your figure-eight pattern at the end of the rink. Be prepared for this.

If you choose to skate this move at the end of the arena - or are requested to - keep in mind that the hockey circles are not joined together, and do not form a true figure eight because they are so far apart. Therefore, use them as a rough guide, but try not to skate diagonally from one circle to another.

If you *do* use the hockey circles at the end of the rink, try to skate a little larger than those circles so that you will make more of a true 'eight' pattern.

THE MOVE

This move is all about showing that you can stroke powerful forward and back crossovers, and even gain speed as you are doing them. Reasonably good posture is expected, so don't let the power of the strokes make your arms move about too much, and try to isolate the powerful movement of your legs from your upper body by keeping your core under control. Get into the ice, and skate each edge on a well-bent skating knee, getting good free leg extension at the end of each stroke.

Remember, the edge you're skating on is the one you'll be pushing from onto the next edge, and this push comes from being able to exert pressure against the ice from a well-bent knee. You should feel your pushing knee straightening as you finish your stroke.

On the clockwise forward crossovers - both on this move, and the Accelerating Forward Power Circle in the Intermediate test - there is a tendency for the skater to cross over with the free foot turned out, which doesn't help the continuity of the circle. You need to be aiming the toe of your crossover blade in the direction your body is traveling, and at least parallel to the blade on the ice, if not turned in a little, which is the technique I recommend.

For some skaters, performing clockwise forward crossovers is almost like having to learn to skate all over again, and that's because we almost never need them except for Moves in the Field tests. So, if nothing else, these tests make you a more bilateral skater. To help feel a correct and efficient push from the left foot, check my suggestion in 'Tricks of the Trade' at the end of this description.

Keep skating crossovers until you are near the end of the first circle, switch your arms while finishing the circle on your left foot so that your outside arm is now leading for the new circle, bend your knees, and push onto your new circle.

If you position this move in the center of the rink you should keep skating the crossovers until you get inside the blue center hockey circle, then prepare for the new circle.

At the end of the forward figure eight (once you have completed both forward circles, and are inside the blue hockey circle) you will need to perform a swing roll and change of edge to an open Mohawk.

As you skate the last outside edge of the circle, swing the free leg forward and counter-rotate the shoulders against it at the same time, still keeping over your skating hip and the circle. Then, bring the free leg back and change edge to turn an open mohawk onto a back inside edge to start the first backward circle. Stretch the free leg back after you turn, and check your arms and shoulders, making sure that you keep looking in the direction you're skating - forward on the forward edge, and back on the back edge.

Make a nice big movement on this mohawk by showing how nicely you can extend your free leg before and after the turn, before continuing with the back crossovers. Now, continue with powerful back crossovers, reaching into the circle with your inside leg, and stroking that leg under you on the crossover.

Just before the end of the first backward circle, extend your free leg back on the last back outside edge, much like a jump landing position, before transitioning onto the new circle. Be careful not to open the free side of the body too much on this edge, because it could pull you into the circle you've been skating on, and make it difficult to get onto the new circle. At the center, bring your feet together and then skate the back crossovers on the second back circle. When you get back to the center, finish backwards with a nice stretched position, or step forward into a similar position.

PROBLEM AREAS:

- Not getting power from both feet on the forward crossovers.
- Skating diagonally across the center on the swing Mohawk, instead of staying on a circle as you swing the free leg before the Mohawk.
- Being scratchy on the back crossovers because of rocking too far forward on the blade.

TRICKS OF THE TRADE:

1) From my observations, this exercise will be more needed on the clockwise forward crossovers, but, obviously, it applies to both directions.

Skate a curve on a left forward inside edge, up on your knee, with your right foot held near the left ankle, off the ice. Your weight is now one hundred per cent on your left blade. Position your upper body as you would for the forward clockwise crossovers, with the left arm and shoulder leading, right arm and shoulder held back. Now, bend both knees, still keeping your right foot off the ice, and feel the inside edge of the left blade gripping the ice.

With the muscles above your left knee supporting all your body weight, push hard against the ice with the inside edge of the blade and *then* transfer your weight onto your right foot. This should give you the feeling of how to stroke, and not just let you pick up your left foot off the ice.

2) If you position this move in the center of the rink, use the red hockey dots as landmarks for the sides of your circles. They will be, approximately, at the quarter and three-quarter marks on the circle.

Make sure you switch your arm position at the end of each circle *before* you start the new circle.

Pattern 2

CONSECUTIVE OUTSIDE AND INSIDE SPIRALS

Primary Focus: Extension
Secondary Focus: Edge Quality

Preliminary 2

Consecutive Outside and Inside Spirals

The skater will perform right foot and left foot spirals. The outside edge spirals will be skated for the first length of the rink. Forward crossovers may be utilized (optional) around the end of the rink. Forward inside edge spirals will be skated for the second length of the rink. The exact number of spirals will depend on the size of the rink and the strength of the skater; however a minimum of four spirals down each length of the rink must be skated. The extended leg in the spiral should be held at hip level or higher. Introductory steps are optional.

Focus: Extension and edge quality

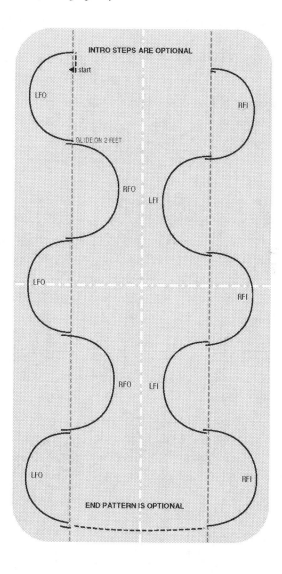

RECOMMENDED INTRODUCTORY STEPS:

Left, right, left, right, across the end of the rink to the long axis.

You are required to skate outside edge spirals the first length of the rink, and then inside edge spirals the second length of the rink.

THE MOVE

Start your spiral edge on the long axis, but make sure you place your foot on the *short* axis, on an edge. That way, you give yourself the best chance to skate a correctly shaped lobe (semi-circle).

Make sure you turn out your pushing foot as you stroke onto the edge, and try to get into spiral position as soon as you can. Look in the direction you are skating, arch your back slightly, and hold your arms up nicely. The body, from the head to the free leg, should form an arched line, with the hips being the lowest point of that line. Try to hold your spiral position for at least three quarters of the lobe, being careful not to let your shoulders turn into the circle. Use your quad muscle to raise your free leg to at least hip level, but much higher if you can, and keep your weight solidly over your skating hip.

Allow just enough time at the end of each edge to bring your free leg down so that you can glide on two feet, before you get to the long axis. That way, you'll be able to start the next spiral *on* the long axis, and be in spiral position long enough to satisfy the judges. This move is, basically, all about a good spiral position, so don't waste time getting your free leg up into position.

The position of the body and free leg are basically the same on inside edge spirals, but there are variations in the way the arms are held.

As you start the inside spiral, lead slightly with the skating hip. It's a little harder to control the hips on these spirals, so keep them very still as you lower your free leg at the end of the spiral. Skaters often drop their free leg down too quickly in order to steady themselves. Once again, it's very easy to toe-push on these inside spirals, so try to avoid that by turning out your foot, and feeling the inside edge of your blade grip the ice to push. At the end of each spiral, skate the required two-foot glide before pushing onto the next one.

There are no set arm positions on spirals, but I usually have the skater lead with the skating arm on the inside spirals, with the free arm held back, a little higher than the other arm.

Problem areas:

- Free leg too low, and not turned out well enough.
- Head not held up nicely, and arms too low.
- Not enough natural lean on the edge.
- Toe pushing on the forward inside spirals.
- Not controlling hips when lowering free leg on the inside spirals.
- Coming out of the spiral too late, causing you to start the next spiral halfway around the new lobe.

Pattern 3

FORWARD POWER 3-TURNS

Focus: Power

Forward Power Three-Turns

The skater will perform forward outside three-turns to a balance position followed by a backward crossover. Three to six sets of three-turns will be skated depending on the length of the ice surface. Skaters may begin this move with either right or left foot three-turns. On the second length of the rink, the three-turns will be skated on the opposite foot. Introductory steps and backward crossovers around the end of the rink are optional.

Focus: Power

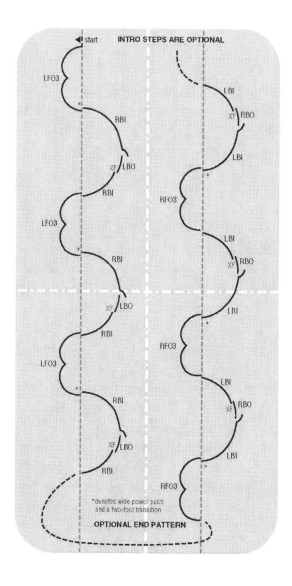

COMMENT

On this move, the judges will be looking to see how well you can push from one edge onto the next, and whether you're taking advantage of the power that can be gained from shifting your weight onto the wide step, and back again to the next edge. If you have knee-bend, you can push. The only time to rise a little is into the three-turns. Otherwise, stay 'into' the ice.

Skaters may start this move with either right or left foot three turns.

RECOMMENDED INTRODUCTORY STEPS:

I am describing this move starting with the left three turns.

Starting across the end of the rink, I recommend skating four strong strokes to build up the necessary speed (left, right, left, right). This should get you to the long axis you will be using down the rink.

THE MOVE

For the power three, push onto a good outside edge with strong knee bend and an extended free leg, and then rise on the knee to turn the three when you are half way around the lobe. Just rising up on the knee, alone, will allow your foot to turn to backwards quite easily. Your extended free leg will also help as a balancing aid, and you should only bend it as you transition onto the wide step. Make a clear transference of weight onto this back inside edge. If you pull in your free foot as you turn, it may cause you to 'whip' your turn around too quickly.

As for arm positions, I would leave the skating arm in front until after you skate the wide step, and then, as you shift your body weight back over to your other knee, start changing your arms in preparation for the step forward. Towards the end of the back crossover edge, start turning out your free foot for the step forward into the next turn. Make sure you are on a well bent knee on the crossover so that you can get a push from that back inside edge as you step forward onto the three turn edge. This should give you a nice transition from one edge to the other. Good use of the knees can make this transition very effective, and this can be a very helpful power stroke.

Each time you step forward make sure you get your upper body well over your new skating hip, because there is quite a strong lean on these threes, and the three turn lobe should be smaller than the lobe with the back edges.

There are different ways you can start into the right threes. You could skate forwards across the end of the rink and then turn a right forward inside Mohawk around the corner, followed by a right back outside edge, and a crossover. Then step forward into your first right three.

Another method, which I now prefer, is to skate across the end of the rink, hockey-glide (two-foot glide, bending the left knee) around the corner to bring you to the long axis, bring your feet together, and then push onto your first right three. From here to the end of the rink, use the same technique that you used on the left threes.

PROBLEM AREAS:

- Three turn lobe too large, causing the skater to wait longer than necessary to reach the long axis.
- Rising too quickly for the three turn, causing it to turn early.
- Not making the lobes 'edgy' enough.
- Not skating with enough knee bend.
- Lifting the free leg too high after the turn, causing the body to tip forward.
- Stepping onto an outside edge on the wide step

Pattern 4

ALTERNATING FORWARD 3-TURNS
Focus: Edge Quality

Alternating Forward Three-Turns

Starting from a standing position the skater will perform alternating forward outside three-turns for the width of the rink. The skater will then perform forward inside alternating three-turns for the second width of the rink. The size of the rink and strength if the skater will determine the number of three-turns skated. This move may start on either foot.

Focus: Edge quality

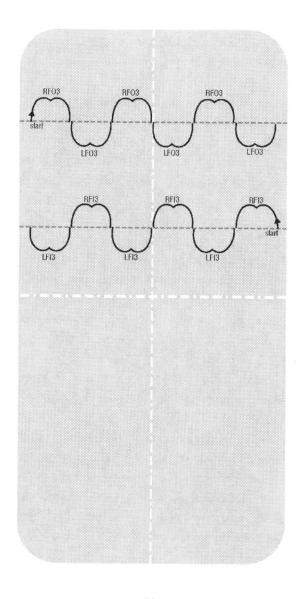

COMMENT

On this move, there are different ways of using the arms and free leg. The turns can be skated with a straight free leg – and extra credit is given if you can do this - but if you find that it's hard to control your body after the turns, try skating with the free knee slightly bent, and the free foot held close behind the skating foot, toe pointed and turned out. This is how a forward three turn is skated in basic figure skating. I find that this keeps better control of the hips, and makes it less likely for the skater to rock forward on their skate after the turns, which can happen if the upper body is trying to counterbalance a straight free leg that may be too high.

There are also different starting positions for the arms.

On the inside threes, it is usually accepted that you start with the skating arm leading, on the circle. That way, you need only rotate the arms a little more to turn the three. On the outside threes, however, two different methods can work equally well. Some coaches have their skaters start with the free arm already in front, which is fine, as long as the skater doesn't feel too 'twisted' when they push off. I prefer to have my skater start with their skating arm leading – the body being in the same position as the basic forward outside edge in the Pre-Preliminary test - and then switch the arms in preparation for the turn. As long as you've made the preparation to turn before you get to the top of the lobe, both methods are effective. Whichever method you use, I would definitely recommend keeping the free hip held back (open), and not try to rotate the hips to make the turn.

At the time of the turn, you should just feel the foot turning, with very little else moving except for the checking movement of arms, shoulders and hips.

If you can hold this position (free arm, shoulder and hip checked back, with the free foot turned out) until you reach the long axis, you will be able to step forward onto your other foot without having to make any movement, because the free arm and shoulder that is held back before you step forward now becomes the leading arm and shoulder on the new edge, for the next three turn.

RECOMMENDED INTRODUCTORY STEPS:

This move is started from a standstill on the long axis (blue or red hockey line), with the skating foot on the short axis (90 degrees to the long axis). Both the outside and inside three turns start on the right foot.

THE MOVE

FORWARD OUTSIDE THREES

Although you are required to turn the three turn on the top of the lobe (half way around), you still need to think first about setting a circle. To do this, start in the same position you would for the basic outside edges on the Pre-Preliminary test, with your right foot on the short axis, and your left foot turned out, heel-to-heel, ready to push. Have your skating arm in front of you, on the circle, and your free arm to the side and slightly back. The angle of the arms is approximately 135 degrees.

Before you push onto each edge, try to visualize your lobe so that you can place your three turn on the top of it, and try to keep the lobes the same size.

There is just enough time to set your edge and body position before you start preparing the rotation for the turn, and you only need to rotate your arms a little in order to turn.

Knowing that you need the free hip checked back after the turn, I strongly recommend skating into this forward outside three with the free foot and knee held slightly open, as this will help you keep your free hip checked back after the turn.

Before you turn, look at the hockey line. This should help you to judge better when you're on the top of the lobe, and, when the skating foot turns the three you must try not to let the free hip rotate around with it. Additionally, try not to make the lobe so big that it takes you too far away from the long axis. It's a long way back if you skate 'U' shaped lobes.

Remember, after the three turn, the skating hip is the OUTSIDE hip on the circle, so hold your body up over that hip to maintain alignment over your skate. This will help you to avoid the feeling that you're 'falling' into the circle.

If you check the turn correctly, the arm, shoulder and hip that you've checked back will become the leading arm and shoulder when you step forward for the three turn on the other foot, but this will only happen if you hold this checked position until you get back to the long axis. This is a good example of where we step forward with the foot, and not by turning the body. Let your feet do the work. You just have to turn your skating foot a little to push from the inside edge of the blade, and at the same time place your new foot on the short axis.

When you start the lobe for the left three turn, you'll have just enough time to make sure that you're over your skating hip before you switch your arms in preparation for the turn.

After you've completed the left turn, continue skating alternating three turns across the width of the arena until you reach the other side. There is no set number of turns, but most skaters will skate at least two turns on each foot.

PROBLEM AREAS:

- Starting off on a straight line instead of setting the semi-circle shape of the lobe. This can take you too far away from the long axis and make it hard to come back on an edge, because you've created a 'U' shaped lobe.
- Not checking the free hip enough as you turn, causing you to end up with your back to the long axis. This makes it very hard to step forward onto the next lobe.
- Three turns becoming too 'swingy', causing the skater to step down before the long axis because of loss of control.
- Struggling to hold the back inside edge back to the long axis after the forward outside three turn.

TRICK OF THE TRADE:

Don't skate the lobes too big. It's a long way back to the axis if you skate too far away from it, and it's hard to hold the free hip and shoulder back long enough at the end of the edge. In addition to this, it can also make your proposed semi-circle look like a 'U', with a long flat edge (an oxymoron if ever I heard one) back to the long axis.

FORWARD INSIDE THREES

Start with your skating arm and shoulder leading (with your skating arm on the circle), and make sure your skating foot is on the short axis so that you start the lobe correctly. Be careful, too, not to let this leading arm make you lean forward. This could cause you not to be in alignment over your skate for the turn unless you re-adjust your posture.

As you are already leading with the skating arm when you start the edge, you need only rotate a little more to prepare for the turn. To do this, move your skating arm a little inside the circle, simultaneously drawing in your free foot close to your skating foot. You should now find your shoulders parallel to the long axis (red or blue line) just before the turn. Forgive the corny rhyme, but try to follow this simple advice when you start the lobe: 'Stand up straight, then rotate'.

Turn the inside three on the top of the lobe, but momentarily check your arms and shoulders so that you are still facing the long axis. After you've made a brief check of the turn to demonstrate control, immediately start rotating your arms and shoulders so that you are now facing out of the circle, with your free arm behind you on the tracing, and your skating arm trailing. Pass your arms close to your body to do this.

When you reach the long axis you'll be on an outside edge, but you now need to push onto the new lobe for the left inside three turn, so turn your skating foot a quarter revolution (your blade will now be parallel to the long axis) and immediately push from the inside edge of the blade. It's almost like doing half a back three turn. Make sure you don't turn your foot completely to forward. You won't be able to push properly, and will end up pushing from the toe pick.

The free arm you held back at the end of the previous lobe will now become the leading arm into the left forward inside three, so at the long axis the feet are doing all the work.

Use the same technique for rotating into, and checking out of, the turn as you used on the right forward inside three, and then continue skating alternating threes all the way across the red or blue line.

When you get near to the other side of the rink, you'll have to decide whether there is space for another lobe, or whether you should come out of the move, and finish.

PROBLEM AREAS:

- Toe pushing onto the forward inside edges.
- After checking the turn, not rotating the free arm and shoulder back enough, making it difficult to step forward on the short axis.
- Rotating the upper body too soon after the push, causing the turn to be early.
- Letting the skating foot turn a back three turn before pushing onto the new lobe. The skate must only turn enough to push from the inside edge of the blade.

Pattern 5

FORWARD CIRCLE EIGHT

Focus: Edge Quality, Continous Flow

Preliminary 5

Forward Circle Eight

The skater will push from a standing start onto a forward outside edge and complete one forward outside figure eight. Upon returning to center at the completion of the second circle, the skater will perform a forward inside figure eight by pushing onto a forward inside edge, thereby repeating the previously skated circle. The circles should be equal in size with each circle approximately three times the skater's height. The skater may mark the center. This move may start on either foot.

    Focus: Edge quality and continuous flow

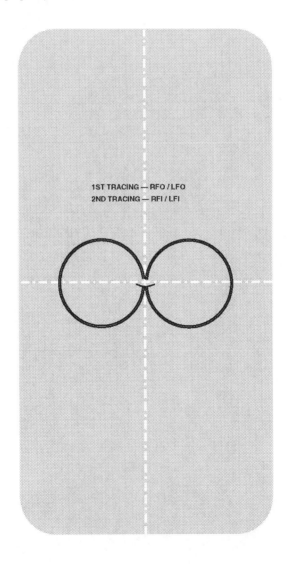

COMMENT

Ideally, the size of the circle should be proportional to the height of the skater, and the diameter of each circle should be about three times the height of the skater.

Although the Forward Circle Eight has only recently been introduced into the Moves in the Field test structure, this move has a lot of 'mileage' on the clock. People have been skating figure eights like this for at least 150 years, on frozen lakes and ponds all over the world.

One of the first things this move teaches us is the fact that we don't have to rotate our bodies in order to make an edge curve to the right or left. The natural lean of the body, being over the skating hip, and having the blade on an outside, or inside, edge is what makes the circle. In fact, you *could* stay in the first position all the way around the circle until you get back to the center, but then you would be in the wrong position to start the next circle.

RECOMMENDED INTRODUCTORY STEPS:

This move is started from a standstill, and can start on either foot. I usually have the skater start on the right foot because I think judges expect this.

THE MOVE

Start this move in the same position you would on the Pre-Preliminary test forward outside edges, with the skating side leading.

When you start the first circle, there is a tremendous temptation to let the body rotate immediately. Try to resist this urge, because you have plenty of time to change position.

Throughout the circle, try to maintain the feeling of being over your skating hip. The natural lean doesn't change from the moment you push onto the edge, until you finish the circle, although, as the body slows down, the lean will naturally decrease toward the end of the circle. Just like when you're riding a bicycle, the amount of lean depends on how fast you are going, and the circumference of the curve (in this case, the size of the circle). It's easy to look good on this move, and there is absolutely no excuse for not having a nicely held free foot, with the toe pointed and turned out.

For your skating positions, I would divide the outside edge circles into four quarters.

For the first quarter, hold your starting position, with your skating arm on the circle in front of you, your free arm held back, slightly outside the circle, and your free foot held nicely behind the heel of your skating foot. During the second quarter, switch your arms smoothly so that you now have your free arm and shoulder in front of you, while still holding your free foot behind. During the third quarter, bring you free foot in front of your skating foot, over the circle, with a nicely extended free leg, and pointed toe. For the remaining quarter just be patient, and hold that position until you come back to the center. Alternatively, you can bring your free leg through first, and then switch your arms and shoulders. Both methods work equally well.

To push properly onto the second circle, keep you weight on your skating foot, and, about a skate's length from the long axis bring your free foot back close to your skating foot (but still off the ice), turn out your skating foot, and push from the inside edge of the blade. Make sure you get your body aligned over the new hip as you skate from circle to circle, and use exactly the same movements at each quarter that you used on the first circle.

After you've completed the second circle, you are now going to skate on the same circle again, but on the inside edge of the other foot. To do this, first draw your free foot close to your skating foot as you approach the center, and, at the same time, switch your arms so that your free arm will be in front of you on the circle as you start the inside edge. *Then*, turn out your skating foot to push onto the new circle.

On the inside edge circles, I would divide the circle into thirds. For the first third, hold that first position with the free foot held gracefully behind the skating foot, the free arm in front, and the skating arm held to the side, slightly back. On these forward inside edges, your skating hip should be slightly leading throughout.

Use the second third of the circle to smoothly change position by switching your arms so that your skating arm is now leading, and, at the same time, pass your free foot close by your skating foot so that it's now in front of you over the circle.

Just before you reach the center, draw your free foot close to your skating foot, and then turn out your skating foot to push from the inside edge of the blade onto the remaining circle on the other foot.

Don't change the position of your arms. Just leave them where they are. The skating arm that's in front of you will now become the free arm leading the way on the new circle.

PROBLEM AREAS:

- Not being aligned over the skating hip
- Pushes made from the toe pick
- Rotating too soon after starting the circles
- Arms too high or too low
- Skating diagonally back to the center from the three-quarter mark, thereby not finishing the circle.

Pattern 6

ALTERNATING BACKWARD CROSSOVERS TO BACKWARD OUTSIDE EDGES

Primary Focus: Power
Secondary Focus: Extension

Alternating Backward Crossovers to Backward Outside Edges

The skater will perform alternating backward crossovers to backward outside edges in consecutive half circles for one length of the rink. Four or five lobes should be skated. Introductory steps are optional.

Focus: Power and extension

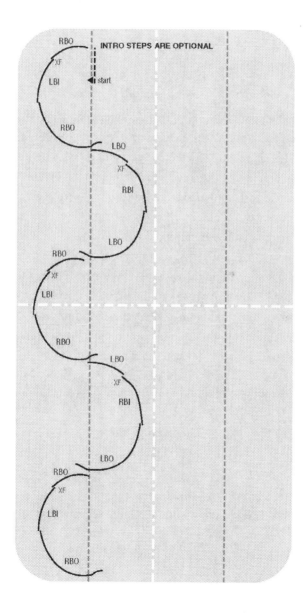

COMMENT

Four or five lobes should be skated. This is a relatively simple move that needs *long flowing edges,* especially if you only skate four lobes.

RECOMMENDED INTRODUCTORY STEPS:

(Across the end of the rink) Left, right, left, RFI Mohawk, to the first RBO edge of the move.

THE MOVE

Although you should have strong knee-bend on the crossovers, allow yourself to rise up a little on the knee after you have pushed onto the long outside edge (the third edge of each lobe). This edge is usually skated in a jump landing position, so stay square to the tracing with your shoulders - just as you would landing a jump - and only let the free shoulder rotate back a little as you bring your feet together at the long axis to start the crossovers for the new lobe.

On the new lobe, skate the crossovers on a well bent knee, and then rise again on the third edge, finishing the lobe back to the long axis.

Extra credit is given if you skate larger lobes, so make sure that you skate into the center of the rink, near the midline, and then back out toward the barriers. If you skate this move with good speed, you should find yourself with a nice natural lean over the circle on the landing position edge, which should help you to finish the lobe. Just be careful not to let your shoulders rotate too much on that edge.

Problem areas:

- Not completing the semi-circle shape of the lobe because of skating 'flat' on the third edge.
- Not holding a nicely extended free leg on the third edge.

Pre-Juvenile Moves in the Field Test

1. Forward and backward perimeter power stroking The skater will perform four alternating forward crossovers separated by strong FI edge transitions. The end pattern consists of two forward crossovers followed by a LFO open stroke; then a RFI open mohawk followed by one or two backward crossovers. All end pattern steps should be performed with an even cadence except the LFO open stroke, which should be held for two counts. The second side of the pattern resumes with four backward crossovers separated by two-foot transitions, also known as a power push. Skaters should take care to perform the transitions on two solid inside edges. The second end pattern consists of three to five backward crossovers. Introductory steps are optional. Forward focus: Power and extension Backward focus: Power and edge quality

2. FO–BI three-turns in the field The skater will perform forward three-turns alternating to backward three-turns covering the length of the rink. One length of the rink will start with RFO-LBI three-turns. The number of sets of three-turns will depend on the length of the rink and the strength of the skater. On the second length of the rink, the skater will perform LFO-RBI three-turns. The end sequence and the introductory steps are optional. This move may start on either foot. Focus: Edge quality

3. FI-BO three-turns in the field On one length of the rink, the skater will perform RFI-LBO three-turns. On the other length of the rink, the skater will perform LFI-RBO three-turns. The number of sets of three-turns will depend on the length of the rink and the strength of the skater. The end sequence and the introductory steps are optional. This move may start on either foot. Focus: Edge quality

4. Forward and backward power change of edge pulls The skater will perform consecutive power change of edge pulls — FIO to FOI — for the full length of the rink followed by backward change of edge pulls — BOI to BIO — for the second full length of the rink. The skater will change feet at the center of the rink. The end sequence and the introductory steps are optional. This move may start on either foot. Focus: Power

5. Backward circle eight The skater will push from a standing start onto a BO edge and complete one BO figure eight. Upon returning to center at the completion of the second circle, the skater will perform a BI figure eight by pushing onto a BI edge, thereby repeating the previously skated circle. The circles should be equal in size and approximately three times the skater's height. The skater may mark their center. This move may start on either foot. Focus: Edge quality

6. Five-step mohawk sequence The skater will perform alternating forward inside mohawks, skated in consecutive half circles. Each series consists of a five step sequence. The skater will skate one length of the ice with four or five lobes. Introductory steps are optional. Revised 7/1/2010

COMMENT

The three turns are a major part of this test, so a skater must learn how to prepare for a three turn, place it correctly on the top of the lobe, and check out of it. I would stress, again, that you should be thinking 'circle first, *then* prepare for the turn'.

The power pulls test the skater's ability to show that they can maintain, or gain, momentum along the ice performing change of edge pulls, while staying well-balanced over their skate. They are also a good leg-strengthening exercise.

The Backward Circle Eight is an interesting, and worthwhile, addition to the Moves in the Field structure. It teaches us so many things, not the least of which is the correct position for skating into a back outside bracket. It also teaches a skater how important it is to get a good, efficient, 'swizzle' push onto these circles. Without this push, you won't be able to skate a good sized circle, and will probably have lots of wobbles toward the end of your circle because of lack of flow.

The other moves on this test are more about basic stroking, extension, and flow.

Pattern 1

FORWARD AND BACKWARD
PERIMETER STROKING

Focus: Forward - Power, Extension

Backward - Power, Edge Quality

Forward and Backward Perimeter Power Stroking

The skater will perform four alternating forward crossovers separated by strong forward inside edge transitions. The end pattern consists of two forward crossovers followed by a LFO open stroke; than a RFI open mohawk followed by one or two backward crossovers. All end pattern stops should be performed with an even cadence except the LFO open stroke, which should be held for two counts. The second side of the pattern resumes with four backward crossovers separated by two-foot transitions, also known as a power push. Skaters should take care to perform the transitions on two solid inside edges. The second end pattern consists of three to five backward crossovers. Introductory steps are optional.

    Forward focus: Power and extension

    Backward focus: Power and edge quality

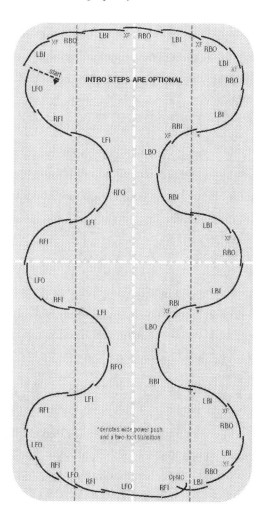

RECOMMENDED INTRODUCTORY STEPS:

Skate left, right, left, right, across the end of the rink, letting the last edge take you to the side of the rink. This gives you the best chance of setting up the first lobe correctly.

THE MOVE

From the side of the rink, follow the red hockey circle in towards the center of the ice on the first forward outside edge and crossover, before starting the big left forward inside edge on the long axis. Skate nice, long, flowing edges, staying on them long enough to complete the lobes.

As the third edge of each lobe (forward inside) is the longer of the three edges, treat it as a two-count edge, whereas the push and crossover preceding it are one-count edges. So you can count 1, 2, and then hold 3, 4 on the long inside edge. Short, quick strokes won't allow you to complete the shape of your lobes. Do the same on the backward edges down the second side of the rink, using a count of one beat on the first edge, one beat on the crossover, and then two beats on the wide step back inside edge. This will give you the opportunity to complete the lobes.

After you've skated the forward lobes, the end pattern starts with two crossovers (one count edges), followed by a longer (two-count) edge that crosses the midline of the rink. Make this edge look nice by extending the free leg, and holding your arms in a nice position.

After you turn the right forward inside open Mohawk, you have two back crossovers to bring you around to the long axis on the second part of this move. Keep curving these edges to finish the lobe so that you are ready to change direction when you step onto the back inside wide step. If you're not far enough around this first back lobe, it could cause you to step wide onto a flat, or outside edge.

It's so important that you feel 'into the ice' on the backward wide step by shifting your weight onto a well-bent knee. Although you need to feel over your skating hip as you skate onto this edge, be careful not to lean too far over the hip because it will cause the edge to run straight, or even go onto an outside edge. Your body weight should actually be slightly inside the edge, even though your weight is mainly on the wide-stepped foot.

When it comes to the position of the arms and shoulders on these back edges, you have to take into consideration the fact that you are changing direction several times, so you don't want to have drastic changes of position. On each lobe, I would recommend having the right arm and shoulder only slightly back on the outside edge, crossover, and wide step into the center of the ice, and the left arm and shoulder only slightly back on the outside edge, crossover, and wide step that go toward the barrier. Switch your arm and shoulder position on the 'rock over' as you push from the wide step onto the next edge.

PROBLEM AREAS:

- Not bending knees enough on the crossovers
- Third edge of each lobe (inside edge) going too straight.
- Skating onto an outside edge on the wide step (backward edges).
- Backward edges too shallow.
- Poor posture.

*P*attern 2

FORWARD OUTSIDE, BACKWARD INSIDE 3-TURNS IN THE FIELD

Focus: Edge Quality

FO-BI Three-Turns in the Field

The skater will perform forward three-turns alternating to backward three-turns covering the length of the rink. One length of the rink will start with RFO-LBI three-turns. The number of sets of three-turns will depend on the length of the rink and the strength of the skater. On the second length of the rink, the skater will perform LFO-RBI three-turns. The end sequence and the introductory steps are optional. This move may start on either foot.

Focus: Edge quality

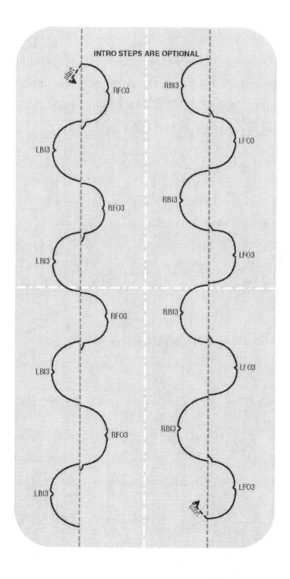

COMMENT

These are basic three turns that need to be learned well.

I like to see an extended free leg on the back turns, but, although you could 'freestyle' the forward turns with an extended free leg, I recommend drawing the free foot in close to the skating foot, and then extending the free leg after you've checked the turn. So, whereas I agree with most recommendations in the PSA Moves in the Field Manual, there are some things on which I will differ.

I want to stress that on these three turns - and, indeed, many other turns - all we should be trying to do is turn the blade from forward to backward, or vice versa. *Not the whole body.* On back three turns, especially, remember not to rotate the arms and shoulders too far before the turn, because it will require a lot of excessive movement to check them back into the right position after the turn.

My general advice for turning these three turns is to keep the hips still, and only rotate the upper body (shoulders and arms) before the turn. By keeping the hips still, your edge should be steadier while you're preparing the rotation of the arms and shoulders for the turn, but when you turn, you will need to check your shoulders *and* hips, because your hips *will* turn a little with your foot. All you need to do during the turn is make a checking movement in order to stop any further rotation of the shoulders and hips. By the time the foot turns, nearly all the hard work is done.

THREE TURN ESSENTIALS:

- Being on an edge
- Being aligned (centered) over the skating hip and foot
- Preparing adequate rotation
- Using the rocker of the blade correctly.

If you take care of these essentials, you should be able to turn good three turns.

You *could* turn on a straight knee, but your turn will be greatly helped if you use the skating knee to help you work the rocker of the blade. Start off with the skating knee only slightly bent, and then, as you finish completing the rotation before the turn, bend a little more, so that you can rise slightly to turn and rock the blade from front to back, or vice versa, as the case may be. It's very important to feel how you use the rocker of the blade when making turns.

Back threes (both outside and inside) are a little more daunting than forward threes, and I frequently see skaters 'break' at the waist when first learning these turns. It's easily done, so try to keep your hips tucked under you as you turn.

RECOMMENDED INTRODUCTORY STEPS:

Two strokes, to get to the long axis. They should be enough to attain the right speed for this move. This move may be started on either foot.

THE MOVE

To start this move, I usually have the skater skate the right forward outside three's first, starting with their back to the barrier, and then skating two strokes to get to the long axis. I would use the red dot hockey markings for the long axis on this move because you can always see one of them, and know where to finish each lobe.

Make sure you place your foot on the short axis when you start this move. This will enable you to skate a properly shaped lobe, and not take a short cut to the top of the lobe by placing your foot diagonally on the long axis.

Think 'circle first, and good body position' when you start the edge. Don't even think about the three turn. There is time to prepare. Start the lobe in the basic forward outside edge position used on the Pre-Preliminary move, and get a good enough push to have enough speed to take you through the lobe without wobbling. After you push onto the edge, draw your free foot in close behind the heel of your skating foot, with the toe pointed and turned out a little.

Switch your arms so that your free arm is now in front, and slightly across your chest, and your skating arm is behind you near the circle.

Building up rotation for a three turn should be gradual, so try to time it so that you are prepared for the turn just before the top of the lobe. One of the requirements of this move is that you place the turns on the top of the lobe, so, by trial and error, you'll know how much (or how little) time you have to prepare.

As your foot turns, check back your free arm, shoulder, and hip. It's very important to not only check the rotation of the shoulders and hips after the turn, but to stay in that checked position until you come back to the long axis. If your hips start moving around you will find yourself fighting to maintain the circle, and could even find your blade changing edge before the push onto the back inside edge.

After you've turned, you can either keep holding your free foot close to your skating foot, or you can show a nice free leg extension, which is my preference. If you do extend your free leg, though, you will need to bring your free foot back close to your skating foot for the swizzle push onto the edge for the back inside three.

To prepare for this push, keep your hips and shoulders still, but release your free arm a little from the checked position as you draw in your free foot. That way, you'll be able to make a synchronized movement of setting your upper body position as you push onto this new edge.

Back inside edges are a little unforgiving, and if you start off this edge with your shoulders and hips too 'square' (at a ninety degree angle) to the tracing, you may well feel 'stuck' and unable to rotate your upper body into the right position for the turn. Therefore, it helps if you use the push to set your arms and shoulders in the right position.

Back Inside three turns feel more awkward than the other three turns, but you will help yourself so much more if you can keep your hips still, and hold your upper body up nicely over your skating hip. This will keep the edge a lot steadier as you rotate your upper body in preparation for the turn. Your hips *will* turn a little with your foot, but try not to let them turn any more than necessary.

When you start the back inside edge, set your skating arm and shoulder back a little, with your free arm on the circle. You should now find your chest facing out of the circle. Your head should be looking in the direction you're skating and, as soon as you've finished the swizzle push, pick up your free foot and hold a nicely extended free leg over the circle.

Once you've pushed onto the new edge, your weight should have transferred onto your new foot, so don't let your pushing foot trail on the ice. You don't want to give the judges the impression that you need to steady yourself by staying on two feet.

As you approach the turn, simultaneously press your skating shoulder back a little, bring your free arm around a little further, and then use a slight rise on the knee to rock the blade correctly from the ball of the foot to the heel into the turn, and immediately back to just behind the middle of the blade as you exit the turn.

As you turn to forwards, check your arms and shoulders so that your skating arm is now on the circle in front of you, with your free arm held back just outside the circle.

Once you're on a steady edge after the turn, you need to start switching your arms and shoulders so that you'll be in the right position for the start of the next forward outside three turn. While you're doing this, keep your free leg nicely extended in front of you, heel over the tracing with the toe pointed and slightly turned out. Switch your arms first, allowing your shoulders to rotate so that you end up with your free arm and shoulder in front, ready to start the next lobe.

You *can* restart the next lobe without switching your arms, but you may find it harder to turn out your foot to push when your skating arm and shoulder is in front.

This move is skated 'the length of the arena', so continue skating lobes until you are near the end of the rink. If there is room for another lobe, then skate it. Otherwise, finish the lobe you're skating on, and then skate across the end of the rink to start the three turns on the other foot.

If you finish on a lobe from a back inside three, then you should only need three strokes (right, left, right) to get across the end of the ice to the long axis for the left forward outside threes.

For the LFO-RBI Three turns on the other side of the rink, apply the same methods for preparing the threes, except now you're skating on the other foot.

PROBLEM AREAS:

- Not checking the forward three turn well enough to keep a steady edge back to the long axis.
- Back inside lobes too small.
- Back inside threes too early, because the upper body is rotated too much at the start of the lobe, forcing the foot to turn before the skater wants it to.
- Trailing the pushing foot after the start of the back inside edge.
- Lack of control after the back three turn, causing wobbles and a change of edge.

TRICK OF THE TRADE:

If you are feeling a bit 'rocky' preparing the rotation of the upper body on one foot, try, at first, to make this preparation on two feet. Then, when you are ready to turn, pick up your free foot and turn.

Pattern 3

FORWARD INSIDE AND BACK OUTSIDE THREE TURNS

Focus: Edge Quality

FI-BO Three-Turns in the Field

On one length of the rink, the skater will perform RFI-LBO three-turns. On the other length of the rink, the skater will perform LFI-RBO three-turns. The number of sets of three-turns will depend on the length of the rink and the strength of the skater. The end sequence and the introductory steps are optional. This move may start in either foot.

Focus: Edge quality

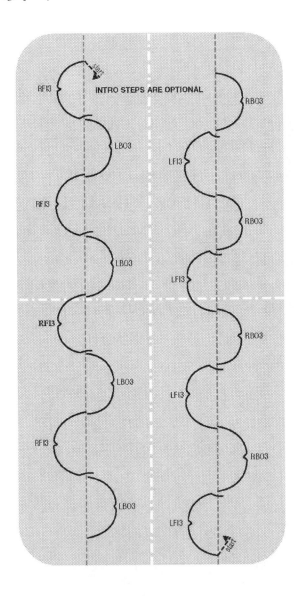

COMMENT

When you push onto these forward inside threes, make sure that you turn out your foot to push correctly from the inside edge of the blade. Judges won't tolerate toe-pushing at this level.

RECOMMENDED INTRODUCTORY STEPS:

Three strokes (left, right, left) across the end of the rink to the long axis of this move. I usually have the skater start with the right forward inside three.

THE MOVE

From the introduction steps, place your foot on the short axis and get a decent push to set a solid edge, with your skating arm leading on the circle. Your free arm should be held back, but slightly inside the circle. At the same time you draw your free foot in close to your skating foot, rotate your shoulders a little more, so that your skating arm is now inside the circle. Make this rotation while keeping your hips still. You should now feel a slight 'twist' at your waist, which is going to help you turn.

Just before the turn, you should find your upper body facing directly into the circle, toward the long axis. When you reach the top of the lobe, it's time to make the turn. Rise a little on the knee, and use the rocker of the blade to go from behind the middle of the skate to the front as your blade goes into the turn, and back to the ball of the foot as you come out. At the same time you turn, check back your skating arm and shoulder, and check your free arm slightly across your chest, while still keeping your line of sight inside the circle.

Once you've checked the turn, you need to change position to prepare for the push onto the back outside three turn. Start lowering your arms and rotate your shoulders so that you're now facing out of the circle, with your free arm and shoulder behind you, and the free hip slightly back. Once again, use the method of passing your arms a little closer to your body as you rotate your shoulders into this new position.

You *can* leave your free foot close to your skating foot until you reach the long axis, but I think it looks nice to extend the free leg, and then bring it back close to the skating leg for the push onto the back outside three.

As you bring in your free foot for the push, release your free arm a little to the side, keeping your hips still for control, and turn out the heel of your skating foot to get a good swizzle push.

Of all the three turns, the back outside three is probably the hardest one on which to keep your body in alignment over the skating hip. It's all too easy to tilt your upper body off your hip as you rotate your shoulders in preparation for the turn.

It's very important to set the body in the right position at the start of the back outside three turn lobe, so use the push to set the skating hip and shoulder back, with your upper body facing into the circle to begin with. By starting off with your hips in this position, you'll have a better chance of keeping your free hip from opening as you rotate your shoulders in preparation for the turn.

As you push, look inside the new circle toward the top of the lobe to judge where you will place your three turn. There will be time enough to rotate the upper body before the turn.

Immediately after the push, start rotating your upper body at the same time you pick up your pushing foot, and move your free foot back in front of you over the circle, or slightly inside, with your free knee slightly bent. Rotate your shoulders so that you're now facing out of the circle, with your free arm and shoulder back on the tracing, and your skating arm a little outside of the circle. Provided that your shoulders are in the right position, you shouldn't need to press your free arm any further behind you to make the turn.

To make the turn, rise slightly on the skating knee, go from the ball of the foot to the heel as your skate goes into the turn, and then immediately back to just behind the middle of the blade as you come out. Your shoulders and arms should check so that you come out of the turn with your free arm and shoulder in front of you.

Your free knee should straighten as you check out of the turn, with your free foot now slightly outside of the circle. This helps to keep the free hip slightly closed, and therefore checked.

Maintain this checked position until you reach the long axis, where you will repeat the forward inside and back outside threes again until you reach the end of the arena.

On a regulation-sized ice surface, I usually have the skater perform three forward and three backward turns on each side of the rink, but if the skater is very small they may need to skate extra lobes. The main thing is to 'skate the length of the arena', which means if there's room for another lobe, skate it. If there isn't, there's no need to squeeze in a tiny lobe that won't impress anybody.

At the completion of the first side, skate across the end of the rink, and then skate a right forward inside edge on a semi-circle to bring you around to place your foot on the short axis to start the left forward inside/right back outside threes.

For the second side of this move, use the same technique as the first side, but on the other foot.

PROBLEM AREAS:

- Skating diagonally to the top of the lobe on the forward inside threes, instead of placing the skating foot on the short axis and skating 'up and around' to the turn.
- Not rotating the shoulders enough on the forward inside threes, thereby 'blocking' the foot from turning easily.

Not checking the hips well enough after the back three turn, causing the skater to 'fight' to maintain a steady edge without wobbling.

Pattern 4

FORWARD AND BACKWARD POWER CHANGE OF EDGE PULLS

Focus: Power

Forward and Backward Power Change of Edge Pulls

The skater will perform consecutive power change of edge pulls – FIO to FOI – for the full length of the rink followed by backward change of edge pulls – BOI to BIO – for the second full length of the rink. The skater will change feet at the center of the rink. The end sequence and the introductory steps are optional. This move may start on either foot.

Focus: Power

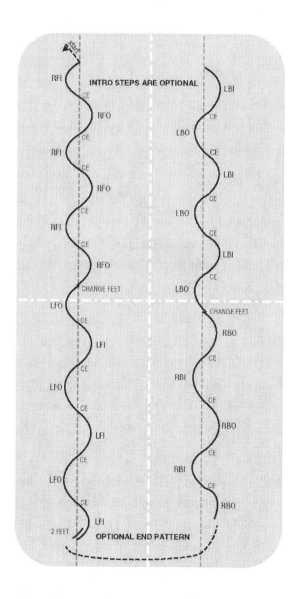

COMMENT

Power pulls involve consecutive changes of edge, a strong down and up movement on the skating knee, and a coordinated body movement, so it's important to master these movements because you will need to perform them again, combined with turns, at the higher levels. Just wiggling your hips is not going to achieve the desired effect.

I see far too many skaters trying to perform this move on a completely straight skating knee. *Even if you're making the right movement with your hips and shoulders, you have no chance to 'pull' the edge if you're already up on the knee.* There must be a rhythmic down and up movement on the skating knee, and your skating leg should feel like it's worked hard at the end of each set of pulls.

Forwards or backwards, you need to get on an edge with some knee bend, and then press up on the knee against the curve of the edge. Then, as you re-bend your knee, change edge and then press up on the knee again on the new edge. Pressing up on the skating knee against the curving edge is what is going to help us maintain, or gain, flow when we skate these power pulls.

Power Pulls are a very good example of 'where your hips go, your skate goes'. Your hips should go with the direction of your edge as your shoulders make an opposing checking movement. It's a very slight 'twisting', or counter-rotating, movement of the shoulders against the hips, but it doesn't need to be done excessively. You should find that, by making this movement as your edges go to the left and right, your shoulders will stay parallel to the end of the arena, whether you're going forwards or backwards. You should also try not to swing your arms wildly backwards and forwards. You do need to move your arms to have a coordinated movement, but the range of arm movement doesn't need to be too far forward or back.

Try to keep your core steady and under good control, because the movement of going down and up on the skating knee, and the switching of your arms, can easily throw you off balance. Hold in those tummy muscles!

Both forwards and backwards, you should feel that you switch your arms as you *rise* on the knee, not when you bend. This will make the movement feel coordinated. Keep your back nice and straight, your stomach held in a little, and your shoulders relaxed down. This should help you to stay right over your skate.

RECOMMENDED INTRODUCTORY STEPS:

Left, right, left, right, left, across the end of the rink, followed by a crossover or slide chasse on a RFI edge. This edge will bring you around to start the power pull movement heading down ice. Once you get on this edge, get your free leg nicely extended in front of you.

THE MOVE

On the forward power pulls, start on your right foot and keep your free leg nicely extended in front of you, over the tracing, with the free foot slightly turned out, and toe pointed. If you turn out too much, it can twist the free hip open too much, and cause your hips to be in an awkward position. Try to stretch the toe of the free foot forward as you rise up on the skating knee to have the feeling that your free leg is leading the way, with the skating foot following it, but don't lift the free leg too high because it may cause you to lean back and fall over.

Keep the tops of your thighs fairly close together, so that your free leg doesn't swing loosely from side to side, and try not to 'break' at the waist as you bend and rise. This can happen all too easily. When you get halfway down the rink (the red hockey line) change onto your left foot and continue doing power pulls until you get, at least, into the red circle at the end of the rink.

It's optional how you skate across the end of the rink to get to the back power pulls, but I would recommend skating forwards until it's time to turn to backwards. Then, skate a right forward inside Mohawk, followed immediately by a right back outside edge to start the back power pulls, but no back crossovers before them! They will take you too far down the rink, leaving little room for the first power pulls.

On the backward power pulls, I recommend holding the free foot about a foot behind the heel of your skating foot, with your free knee bent a little, but held firmly in that position. Try to rely on moving along the ice by pressing up from a bent skating knee each time you change to a new edge. You should feel like you're rising up and down directly over your skate, and balancing near the ball of the foot. This should help your skate to run well. Keep your back straight, shoulders down, and your stomach held in a little.

When you reach the red hockey line halfway down the rink, change feet and continue skating equally strong back power pulls on the other foot until you get inside the red circle at the end of the rink.

PROBLEM AREAS:

- Not keeping your core held well enough, causing a looseness that results in loss of balance.
- Skating knee too stiff, not allowing for the necessary 'down and up' movement.
- Swinging the arms too far forward and backward.
- Rocking forward onto the toe pick on the backward power pulls.

TRICK OF THE TRADE:

If at first you find it hard to balance on one foot while trying to achieve the necessary movement, i.e. the 'rise and fall' knee action and the feeling of a slight 'twisting' movement of the hips against the shoulders, try skating your power pulls first on two feet, rather like a slalom skier. They keep their bodies facing down the hill as their skis go to the left and right in much the same way you need to face down ice, with your shoulders parallel to the wall at the end of the rink. This should give you the chance to get used to the necessary coordinated movement.

EXERCISE:

Try skating these power pulls with your hands held behind your back. You'll find that you have to rely more on your hips and knees, and a firmly held core.

Pattern 5

BACKWARD CIRCLE 8

Focus: Edge Quality

Backward Circle Eight

The skater will push from a standing start onto a backward outside edge and complete one backward outside figure eight. Upon returning to center at the completion of the second circle, the skater will perform a backward inside figure eight by pushing onto a backward inside edge, thereby repeating the previously skated circle. The circles should be equal in size with each circle approximately three times the skater's height. The skater may mark the center. This move may start on either foot.

   Focus: Edge quality and continuous flow

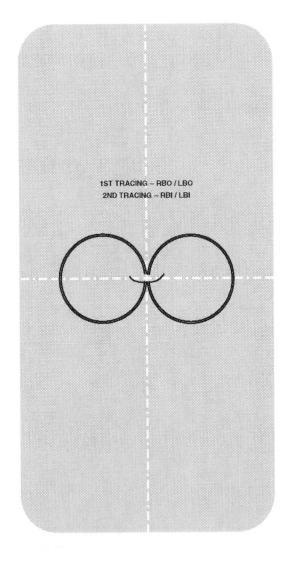

1ST TRACING – RBO / LBO
2ND TRACING – RBI / LBI

COMMENT

The red or blue hockey lines are usually used for the long axis of this move, and directly dissect both circles.

An important consideration is the size of the circles. They should be similar in size, and the diameter of the circle should be approximately three times the skater's height.

Although this move can be started on either foot, I am describing it starting on the right foot. I will also describe it using the red line as a long axis.

Even though the new moves have not long been in existence, it has become apparent that this move presents a few problems, not the least of which is achieving enough flow from a standing start. (Thank you, Tessa, for mastering this basic school figure, and for showing how well it can be skated). I'm also going to advise using 'half-movements'. This a method used in figure skating whereby we take advantage of using one half of the body to help keep us steady, while the other half moves, instead of moving the arms,shoulders and free leg at the same time.

As no introductory steps are permitted, it's essential that you get a good swizzle push to start the first circle because you have to get your body moving from a standstill. If you fail to generate enough speed from your push, you'll have difficulty making it around the circle, and may not even make it back to the center (the place where the two circles join together). Even if you make it back to the center you'll find that, without adequate flow, you'll probably have a wobbly edge. The pushes on the remaining circles should be easier because the body is already in motion.

This is a very methodical move, so I recommend that you divide each circle into four quarters. As we go through the move, I'll tell you what action I want you to take during each quarter.

RECOMMENDED INTRODUCTORY STEPS:

There are no introductory steps. This move is started from a standstill, and may be started on either foot.

THE MOVE

To start this move, stand over the red line and place your feet on each side of it, about shoulder-width apart, blades parallel. At this point your weight should be equally on both feet with your knees straight. Your hips, shoulders and arms should be parallel to the side of the rink, with your body facing down the red line.

Now we come to that all-important push.

Shift your weight over your left foot onto a well-bent knee, balancing on the blade near the ball of the foot (we are *not* going to use the toe pick to push), and just rest the toe pick of the right foot on the ice to steady yourself. At the same time you shift your weight, rotate your arms, shoulders, and hips so that your right arm is in front of you on the red line, and your left arm is back, in line with your left shoulder. Your arms should now be in an approximate 'L' shape.

With your weight entirely over your left foot, pick up your right foot and bring it to your left foot, toe-to-toe (pigeon toe). If your shoulders and hips are rotated the right amount, you shouldn't have any difficulty turning in your right foot to place it on the short axis to start the circle.

Ideally, you need to balance for a split second on your left foot, and keep your right foot just off the ice in this pigeon toe position. That way, you'll have all your weight on your pushing foot, and be able to get the most efficient swizzle push against the ice.

Immediately following this, a few things need to happen simultaneously. You need to get a strong swizzle push with your left foot; transfer your weight onto your right foot; get immediately over your skating hip; come up on your skating knee; draw your right arm and shoulder back on the circle, your left arm in front, and look inside the circle to the quarter mark. This movement of the arms actually helps create a good push. As soon as you're over your right foot, pick up your pushing foot and hold it over the tracing in front of your skating foot.

This first quarter is the foundation of the rest of the circle. If you get this right, a lot of the hard work is already done. This first position is an excellent preparation for the intermediate level back outside bracket, where your upper body will also be facing into the circle, with the skating arm and shoulder leading the way into, and out of, the turn. So, here we have a good example of the importance of learning the basic positions. They will help you when you come to skate the more difficult moves that incorporate these positions.

Now, you *could* skate the whole circle in the first position, proving that it's not the rotation of the body that makes the circle, but rather your body alignment over your skate and hip, and being on an edge that lets you make, and complete, the circle. But you will, of course, be changing position to complete the circle.

This is all you need to do on this first quarter. Just stay in alignment over your skate, gliding on the ball of the foot, and don't move your arms or let your shoulders and hips rotate. In fact, don't do anything! Just breathe. Let the edge do the work, as my coach would say.

During the second quarter, all you need to do is move your free foot back behind your skating foot by bending your free knee, so that your free toe is now held by the heel of your skating foot. That's the only movement needed at this stage. What could be simpler? Your shoulders, arms, and hips should still be held in that original position, and at the end of the second quarter you should be looking down the red line, back toward the center.

On the third quarter we need to rotate the body *over the skating hip* to be in the right position to finish this circle, and start the next. Having faced into the circle, you'll now be facing *out*.

To change position, lower your arms to pass them a little closer to your body, and rotate your shoulders so that your free arm and shoulder are now behind you on the circle, and your skating arm is just outside the circle. Turn your head at the same time you rotate your shoulders so that you can now look back toward your free arm I the direction you're traveling. You should complete this change of position by the time you've finished the third quarter.

For the last quarter, try to keep your edge steady by keeping your hips still until you get about a skate's length from the long axis. At this point, switch your arms (free arm in front of you, skating arm to your side), bend your skating knee, and turn your skating foot to get a good swizzle push onto the new circle. Place your left foot on the short axis to start the second circle, and repeat the same procedures you skated on the first circle, but now on the other foot.

As you approach the center at the end of the second circle, you need to prepare for the first of the back inside edge circles. This will be skated over the back outside edge circle you've just completed.

Just as on the previous push, switch your arms (free arm in front of you, skating arm to your side), bend your skating knee, and turn your skating foot to get a good swizzle push. In one movement, swizzle push with your left foot, place your right foot on the short axis on an inside edge, and transfer your weight to get your body in alignment over your right (skating) hip. Come up on your knee after you push, and adopt the basic first position of a back inside edge, i.e. free arm and leg in front over the tracing, skating arm held to the side (making an 'L' shape of the arms), head looking back at the center over your free arm. This position should be held for the first quarter of the circle.

On this back inside edge, the arms and shoulders are not held in the same position as they would be if you were preparing for a back inside three turn, where your upper body would be facing out of the circle. Your shoulders need to be more 'square' to the tracing at the start of this circle, so that you can easily rotate them into the second position where you will be facing into the circle.

At the quarter mark, start passing your free foot close by your skating foot and extend your free leg behind you over the tracing, keeping your arms in that first position. Here, we're using that 'half-movement', where you'll keep your upper body still as you move your free foot. Keep looking inside the circle all the way around.

During the third quarter, keep your free leg still and start switching your arms and shoulders so that your free arm and shoulder are now held back on the circle, and you skating arm is just inside the circle. From here to the end of the circle (fourth quarter), hold that position until you are about a skate's length from the center, and then, in one movement, turn the heel of your skating foot to swizzle push, switch your arms, and draw in your free foot close to your skating foot (pigeon toe). Bend your skating knee strongly, and get a good thrust from the inside edge of the blade, setting your arms back into the first position for the new circle (free arm in front over the free leg, and your skating arm held out to the side). Repeat the same movements for this circle as you did for the previous one. Finish the move by stepping forward when you reach the center.

PROBLEM AREAS:

- Making a scratchy push from the toe pick, and not from the ball of the foot.
- Not keeping aligned over the skating hip as you change from the first position to the second, ending up 'off' the hip.
- Feeling too 'twisted' when you start the back inside edges, because the arms and shoulders are rotated too much to the outside of the circle.

Pattern 6

FIVE-STEP MOHAWK SEQUENCE

Primary Focus: Edge Quality
Secondary Focus: Extension

Five-Step Mohawk Sequence

The skater will perform alternating forward inside mohawks, skated in consecutive half circles. Each series consists of a five-step sequence. The skater will skate one length of the ice with four or five lobes. Introductory steps are optional.

Focus: Edge quality

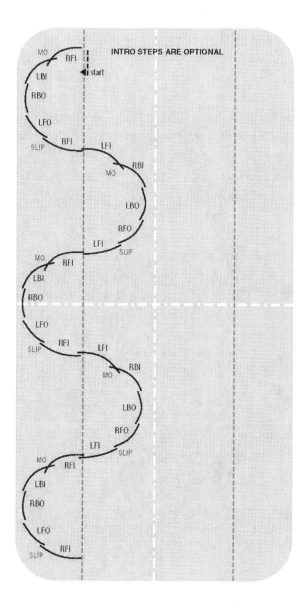

COMMENT

I consider this to be one of the easiest moves in the book, provided that the skater has a feeling for skating on a circle, and can extend their free leg. It doesn't need power. It doesn't even require much knee bend. It just needs good judgment, placement, posture, and the feeling of how to stretch your body lines.

There are three things that all five edges have in common. Firstly, they all have the same curvature. Secondly, they are all skated for the same length of time. And thirdly, they all need a nicely extended free leg.

You are required to skate four or five lobes the length of the arena. The size of the lobes will depend on the speed of the skater, but you should try to skate decent sized lobes and keep a nice even flow throughout. You will find that you can keep up this flow by pushing onto three of the five edges (first, third, and fourth).

Using the red 'dots' as a long axis (where the lobes start and finish) is alright for a small skater, but you might want to consider using an imaginary long axis about six feet further into the center from the barriers if you need more room. If you are too close to the barriers, your edges will be quite short, and you won't have time to get a nice leg extension (the secondary focus of this move).

Additionally, if the ice surface is smaller than regulation size (200x85), I would definitely recommend skating on a long axis further away from the barriers, and not use the red dots.

Throughout this move the free toe should be pointed and slightly turned out. Turning out the foot too much can cause the free hip to open too much.

Try to make this a very graceful move by keeping your body aligned over your skate, and not letting your free leg position tilt your upper body forward, especially on the back edges. You should have the feeling that your head and skating hip are directly over your skating foot at all times.

RECOMMENDED INTRODUCTORY STEPS:

Three power strokes; Left, right, left, then into the first edge of the move.

THE MOVE

Start each lobe with your skating foot on the short axis. This means that your toe should be pointing toward the side barriers as you place it on the ice. If you take a shortcut by stepping diagonally, your five edges won't make the required semi-circle shape.

Skate into the Mohawk with your skating arm and shoulder leading, so that you can check them back as you turn. After you turn onto the back inside edge and extend the free leg, draw the free leg and arm in to the body at the same time, allowing your shoulders to rotate, so that you can then extend your new free leg and free arm back on the third edge (back outside). If you are in the right position on this edge, with free hip and shoulder open (your body facing out of the circle), you can step forward onto the fourth edge without any further turning of the body – much like when you step forward into a waltz jump or axel. From here, it's an easy transition onto the final slide chasse, with free leg extended nicely in front of you. On this slide chasse edge it feels natural to switch the arms so that your skating arm is in front of you over the circle, but I usually have the skater leave their arms in the same position on the last two edges so that they are ready to lead into the Mohawk on the other foot with their skating arm leading.

Try using an equal timing on all the edges by counting 1, and 2, and 3, and 4, and 5. This timing should enable you to extend your free leg on all the edges - which, after all, is the second focus the judges are looking for.

PROBLEM AREAS:

- Starting the lobes diagonally.
- Not finishing the semi-circular lobe enough to be able start the next lobe on the short axis.
- Free leg extension causing the upper body to tilt (counterbalance) the other way.
- Stepping too wide between the steps. (Don't step any wider than your own hips).

Juvenile Moves in the Field Test

1. Stroking: Forward power circle Starting from a standing position, the skater will perform forward crossovers progressively increasing in foot speed and acceleration throughout the entire move, from a slow, but gradually accelerating pace to fully accelerated crossovers. As the skater accelerates, the circle circumference increases. Power circles are performed in both counterclockwise and clockwise directions. It is recommended that no more than 15 crossovers be utilized in completing each portion of this move. This move may start in either direction. Focus: Power

2. Stroking: Backward power circle Starting from a standing position, the skater will perform backward crossovers progressively increasing in foot speed and acceleration throughout the entire move, from a slow, but gradually accelerating pace, to fully accelerated crossovers. As the skater accelerates, the circle circumference increases. Power circles are performed in both counter clockwise and clockwise directions. It is recommended that no more than 15 crossovers be utilized in completing each portion of this move. This move may start in either direction. Focus: Power

3. Eight-step mohawk sequence The skater will perform two eight-step mohawk sequences counter clockwise. The step order is: Forward crossover into a LFO mohawk, followed by LBI, RBO, LBI cross forward and RFI. The skater should maintain a march cadence (one beat per step). Between the circles is a two-beat left foot transition. The sequence is then repeated twice in the opposite direction. Introductory steps are optional. This move may start on either foot. Focus: Quickness and power

4. Forward and backward free skate cross strokes The skater will perform free skate cross strokes the length of the ice surface. Forward cross strokes will be skated for one length of the rink and backward cross strokes skated for the second length of the rink. Introductory steps and end patterns are optional. This move may start on either foot. Focus: Power

5. Backward power three-turns The skater will perform three to five backward power three-turns per circle in a figure eight pattern. One complete figure eight is required. A one or two-foot glide may be utilized when changing circles. Introductory steps are optional. This move may start in either direction. Focus: Power

6. Forward double three-turns The skater will perform consecutive forward double three-turns on half circles, with alternating of feet. Four to six half circles will be skated depending on the length of the rink and strength of the skater. The sequence begins with FO double three-turns covering the first length of the rink. The FI double three-turns will cover the second length of the rink. Introductory steps and end patterns are optional. Focus: Edge quality Revised 7/1/2010

COMMENT

On this test, the first five moves are mostly about power and quality stroking. The remaining move (Forward Double Three Turns) is more about control, edge quality, and placement.

Pattern 1

STROKING: FORWARD POWER CIRCLE

Focus: Power

Stroking: Forward Power Circle

Starting from a standing position, the skater will perform forward crossovers progressively increasing in foot speed and acceleration throughout the entire move, from a slow, but gradually accelerating pace to fully accelerated crossovers. As the skater accelerates, the circle circumference increases. Power circles are performed in both counterclockwise and clockwise direction. It is recommended that no more than 15 crossovers be utilized in completing each portion of this move. This move may start in either direction.

Focus: Power

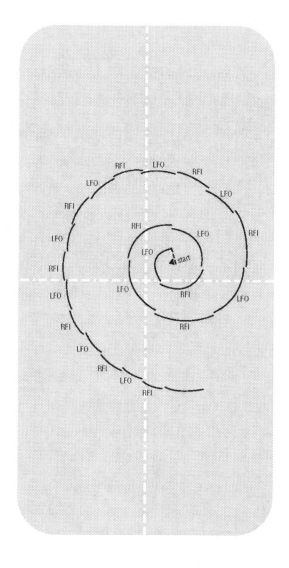

COMMENT

This is a relatively simple move. It requires power, and tests the skater's ability to be able to increase the tempo of the crossovers, while gaining speed and expanding the circle size. It also finds out whether a skater can keep their upper body still, and maintain control, while their legs are moving strongly on the crossovers.

On both the forward and backward accelerating crossovers, make sure your upper body position is set before the first crossover, so that there is no disruptive body movement right from when you start the first one. This move is pure 'leg work', as is most basic stroking.

You *can* start this move in either direction, but most skaters start with the counter-clockwise direction, so that's the way I'll describe it.

I recommend starting this move standing on the red line about three feet from the blue dot (center of the rink), but before we go any further, let me make it easy for you to skate in a position that works well, looks right, and is *comfortable*.

I see so many skaters looking awkward and uncomfortable because they've been told to place their right arm in front of them (for counter-clockwise crossovers), and their left arm pressed back (often further than their shoulder), which makes for some very weird angles. There's no reason a skater should have to look 'forced' when it comes to holding certain body positions. There's a very easy way of achieving the right position, and you don't have to be a rocket scientist to understand it.

The trick is, to think not only of rotating your arms and shoulders to get into the right position, but of your whole upper body. This will make it much easier to put your arms in the right place.

To attain this position, stand on the red line with your feet together, hips and shoulders square, arms extended out to your side. Now, from the waist upwards, rotate your whole upper body in one piece (rib cage, shoulders, and arms) so that your chest is facing into the circle with your shoulders at about a forty-five degree angle to the tracing. This should enable you to hold your right arm on the circle in front of you, and your left arm and shoulder back, just inside the circle. This will also enable you to keep a nice line through the arms and shoulders. This is very much a case of your arms being an extension of your shoulder position.

It's important that you're in a comfortable position at the start, because you're going to be holding this same position throughout the entire move.

RECOMMENDED INTRODUCTORY STEPS:

There are no introductory steps. This move is started from a standstill, and may be started in either direction.

THE MOVE

On this move, every edge is a power stroke, so you should be gaining speed with every push.

Start by holding each of the first six edges (three pushes and crossovers) for about two seconds. Count 'one, two' on each one, and then gradually increase the tempo from the fourth crossover so that by the time you reach the ninth or tenth crossover you are up to maximum tempo. The judges don't want to see just two speeds – slow and fast – they want to see that you have the ability to gradually increase the tempo of your crossovers. On those first six two-count edges there is no excuse for not having a really nicely extended free leg, but it's understandable that as you speed up the tempo of the crossovers, your free leg won't stretch out quite so much. On the faster crossovers, try to feel that your pushes are more 'explosive', and that as soon you push out, you immediately cross over. (Thank you for your help with that, Kaitlyn)

If you increase your speed by stroking the crossovers correctly, you should gain enough speed to be outside the hockey circle in the middle of the rink by the time you've finished the third crossover (assuming this is where this move is skated). Because speed should be increasing, as well as tempo, each edge should be taking you further out from the starting point, so that you never skate over the previous tracings. It's a bit like a rocket ship going into orbit. You must be prepared to use a lot of energy on this move. (Thank you, Kenna, for showing how a skater can gain flow by stroking powerfully on every edge).

I usually recommend a total of twelve crossovers, because that should be enough for a skater to complete this powerful move. The minimum number is ten, and the maximum number, fifteen.

There is another very important point to consider on this move. As you increase the tempo of the crossovers, make sure you keep pushing from the *edges* of the blades, and not turn the stroking into 'running'. The judges don't want to see your blades coming off the ice behind you from the toe-picks.

REMEMBER: Good stroking should result in the straightening of the pushing knee as you complete the thrust against the ice.

When you have completed the crossovers, finish with a burst of energy into a nice stretched position. Don't slow down the tempo and then go for a beautiful, ethereal end-pose. This move is definitely more 'Sabre Dance' than 'Swan Lake'!

For the clockwise forward crossovers, apply all the same comments I made on the counter clockwise crossovers, but in reverse.

I would also like to remind skaters of a comment I made on the Forward Figure Eight Crossovers at the Preliminary level, which applies again on this move. On these clockwise forward crossovers, try not to cross over with your free foot turned out, which seems to be the tendency with a lot of skaters. Cross over with your blade at least parallel to the one that's on the ice, or have it slightly turned in to help you continue skating on a circle, and not go off at a tangent.

PROBLEM AREAS:

- Not enough increase of tempo.
- Stroking turning into 'running'.
- Inability to hold the arms and shoulders in a steady position as the tempo of the crossovers increases.
- Circle staying small and not expanding
- Pushing off the heel, and not rolling the blade up to the front as it leaves the ice.

TRICK OF THE TRADE:

Now, I don't want this to cause skaters to have nightmares, but there is a very useful psychological tool that some 100 meter and 200 meter track and field sprinters incorporate to motivate them to go faster. It's based on the "fight or flight response" that prepares the body to "fight" or "flee" from perceived attack, harm or threat to our survival.

When you need to accelerate the crossovers on this move, try to imagine that something horrible is chasing after you. With the thought that, maybe, a snarling tiger is planning on having you for lunch, you may well find yourself speeding up your crossovers very effectively.

Pattern 2

STROKING: BACKWARD POWER CIRCLE

Focus: Power

Stroking: Backward Power Circle

Starting from a standing position, the skater will perform backward crossovers progressively increasing in foot speed and acceleration throughout the entire move, from a slow, but gradually accelerating pace, to fully accelerated crossovers. As the skater accelerates, the circle circumference increases. Power circles are performed in both counterclockwise and clockwise directions. It is recommended that no more than 15 crossovers be utilized in completing each portion of this move. This move may start in either direction.

Focus: Power

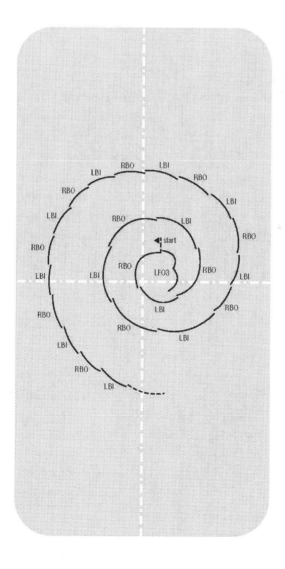

RECOMMENDED INTRODUCTORY STEPS:

From a standstill, turn a forward outside three turn and reach into the circle to start the crossovers.

This move may be started in either direction.

For the accelerating back crossovers, the same comments apply regarding increase of tempo, expansion of circle size, etc.

I will describe this move skating in a counter-clockwise direction.

THE MOVE

Just as on the Forward Power Circle, *every edge* is a power stroke, so, as you start this move, keep good control of the three turn, because you will need to get a good push from it as you reach into the circle with your right foot. Don't just step onto this back outside edge. As you reach in to the circle, it's important that you lean in and shift your weight over your right hip, on a well-bent knee.

Now let's talk about your body position. This one's very simple. Just rotate your upper body to the point where your arms and shoulders are on the circle, and your chest is facing inwards. This upper body position should enable you to look back to your right arm in the direction you're skating.

Most people can only turn their head as far as their shoulder, so you'll have no trouble seeing where you're going if your upper body is rotated adequately. If your shoulders are too square to the edges, you'll find yourself looking out of the corner of your eye to see where you're going.

On these backward power crossovers, try to get equal power from both legs. As you reach in with one foot, you should feel that you're pushing out of the circle with the other one. The feeling is almost as if you're 'splitting' your legs apart, creating distance. This is an 'equal and opposite reaction' moment that really helps to generate power.

Have you ever watched top level pair skaters building up speed around the end of the rink on their way to an important element? They do this by reaching well into the circle and using every ounce of their energy, but you will also see many skaters - even at International level - who don't get equal power from both legs because they just step into the circle and only get power on their crossover. This causes them to look a little 'lame'.

To continue with the move, use the same method that you used on the Forward Power Crossovers. Hold the first three pushes and crossovers (six edges) for about two seconds, but still try to gain speed on them to expand the circumference of the circle. Then begin gradually speeding up the tempo of your crossovers so that you're up to maximum tempo by the time you've reached the ninth or tenth crossover. Just as on the forward crossovers, you should be getting out of the red hockey circle by the time you've finished the third crossover.

To finish this move, you can either stay backwards and end in a nice landing position, or step forward and hit a nice stretch position.

For the clockwise backward crossovers, apply all the comments I made on the counter-clockwise crossovers, but in reverse.

PROBLEM AREAS:

- Not holding the first six edges long enough.
- Not keeping the upper body held consistently in position.
- Not reaching into the circle enough before crossing over.

Pattern 3

EIGHT STEP MOHAWK SEQUENCE

Focus: Quickness, Power

Eight-Step Mohawk Sequence

The skater will perform two eight-step mohawk sequences counterclockwise. The step order is: Forward crossover into a LFO mohawk, followed by LBI, RBO, LBI cross forward and RFI. The skater should maintain a march cadence (one beat per stop). Between the circles is a two-beat left foot transition. The sequence is then repeated twice in the opposite direction. Introductory steps are optional. This move may start on either foot.

Focus: Quickness and power

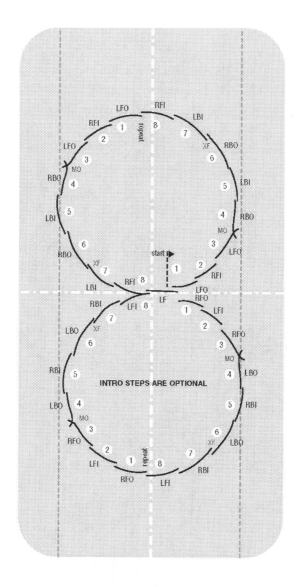

COMMENT

This move needs to be skated with some 'life' and a nice fast march tempo, but that doesn't mean you have to race through it. In march tempo, the beats are evenly spaced apart, so if you're nicely balanced over your skate you should be able to skate on each edge for the same amount of time. You can, and should, push and extend on seven of the eight edges. Even when you keep up a crisp march tempo, there is time to do this, and that brings me to an interesting point.

During a recent lesson, I criticized a student of mine for skating this move on very straight, stiff knees. Her answer was enlightening. "I thought I was supposed to look like I'm marching, so that's why I'm skating that way." She made a very good point, and I was glad she brought it up because there may be other skaters who think the same way. After I'd taken the smile off my face, I explained to her that the 'March' part only refers to the tempo and liveliness of the move, and not to the manner in which you skate it. Meaning that you shouldn't turn into wooden soldiers when performing this move. (Thank you, Amber, for pointing that out, and making the necessary adjustment to skate it really well).

If you should be practicing this move around Christmas time, try singing 'Jingle Bells' as you skate it. It has just the right lively rhythm, and counts nicely in 'eights'.

The size of the circles will be determined by the size and strength of the skater. More powerful skaters will need to expand their circles in order to fit in the two sets of eight steps on each circle, but smaller skaters may need to scale down the size of their circles. By trial and error you'll find out how big your circles should be, and how fast you will need to skate.

This may sound silly, but try to keep your feet underneath you throughout the move. This is a move where it's very easy to wide-step, especially on the back edges, so even though you should stroke and extend on most of these steps, put those feet down right underneath you and you'll be instantly on balance over your skate.

This move may start in either direction, but I'll describe it starting on the counter-clockwise circle.

RECOMMENDED INTRODUCTORY STEPS:

Left, right, left, right along the red line to the center.

THE MOVE

There are no corners on a circle, so try to start off with the feeling of skating on a steady curve. If you cut in on the first push and crossover you may end up going into your Mohawk on a straight line, or even an inside edge, and an inside edge into the Mohawk will take you out of the circle, making it difficult to finish the first eight steps on the midline.

Usually, when we skate crossovers, we lead with the outside arm and shoulder, but this is not advisable at the beginning of this move because the third edge is the entry into the Mohawk. What I would advise is that you lead only slightly with your right arm and shoulder on the first edge, and then start bringing your left arm and shoulder through smoothly during the crossover, so that they're leading by the time you stroke onto the left forward outside edge for the Mohawk.

As you'll be skating on a circle with fairly good speed, you should feel a natural lean over the circle on every edge. It won't be very much, but this lean remains constant no matter what edge you're on. It's a bit like if you were skating around a giant cone, and were leaning in slightly to follow its conical shape. This should give you a better feeling of being over your skating hip, and on an outside edge, going into the Mohawk. (Thank you, Kaitlyn, for bringing to my attention how easy it is to break out of the circle on the Mohawk, and for the way you made the necessary improvement to keep on a circle).

For the Mohawk, push onto the forward outside edge, lead with your skating arm, shoulder, and hip, and then come up a little on your skating knee to enable you to draw in your free foot so that it's close to your skating foot. Make sure that you turn onto a soft knee, and that your right foot is well turned out before you turn, so that the blade takes the ice 'running', and the turn isn't jumped or skidded.

As long as you turn from outside edge to outside edge, it's a Mohawk, and, although there are no hard and fast rules about the placement of the free foot (to turn an open or closed Mohawk), it does need to be tidy, so make sure your free foot is drawn in fairly close before you turn.

I've seen several skaters perform the Mohawk the way it's skated in the Fourteen Step ice dance. That is, an open Mohawk, where the heel of the turned-out free foot is placed by the instep of the skating foot to form a 'T' position before the turn. Then, as you turn onto the right back outside edge, your new free foot is held momentarily in that 'T' position to help the check of the free hip, and then immediately moved to be parallel to the skating foot in order to step onto the following back inside edge.

There's nothing wrong with skating the Mohawk this way, but I find it can look a bit 'mechanical'. I prefer to bring the heel of the free foot near to the heel of the skating foot, and then check the free leg back slightly after the turn, remembering to bring the free foot close again so that there is no wide step onto the next edge. A little more 'freestyled' than 'danced'.

On both edges of the Mohawk you should feel like your upper body is well over your skating hip, and that you have a strong, straight back.

As you turn, make a slight check of your left arm, shoulder, and hip, before releasing that check to let the body gradually rotate into the circle as you skate the remaining edges in preparation to step forward.

One of the 'common errors' on this move is wide stepping, and this would only happen on the last four of the eight steps when you're going backwards, unless you wide stepped into the mohawk. The most likely place to wide step is from step five to step six (left back inside to right back outside) because our old friend/enemy, 'muscle memory', may be prompting you to reach into the circle with the inside foot just like you do when you skate back crossovers. Try to put your right foot down close to your left, and get a little push to maintain flow. After that, cross over onto a left back inside edge, and step forward onto a right forward inside edge to finish the sequence.

When you step forward on the eighth step, don't hold it and stretch out your free leg. Keep it one count just like the previous edges because you need to continue straight on with the repeat of those eight steps. You're actually going to skate sixteen consecutive one-beat steps on the first circle, followed by an extra two-count left forward outside edge to complete the circle back to the center. Keep your weight on this edge as you bring your feet together, because this is the foot you're going to push with to start the second circle. As you bring your feet together on this final edge, switch your arms so that your left arm is slightly leading, and then start your second circle, repeating the same procedures as on the first, but on the other foot.

PROBLEM AREAS:

- Skating an inside edge into, or out of, the Mohawk. This is sometimes caused by cutting into the circle on the first two edges, and then diving outwards into the Mohawk.
- Even if you're in the right position before the Mohawk, you could still turn onto an inside edge after the turn if you don't check your free hip and shoulder. So if your hips continue to rotate after the turn, they could steer you blade onto an inside edge. ('Where your hips go, your skate will usually follow', as I stated earlier in this book).
- Skating too big on the first half of the circle, which can make it difficult to get back to the center.
- Not maintaining a crisp march tempo throughout the move.
- Not extending the free leg wherever possible.
- Wide stepping.

Pattern 4

FORWARD AND BACKWARD FREE
SKATING CROSS STROKES

Focus: Power

Forward and Backward Free Skate Cross Strokes

The skater will perform free skate cross strokes and length of the ice surface. Forward cross strokes will be skated for one length of the rink and backward cross strokes skated for the second length of the rink. Introductory steps and end patterns are optional. This move may start on either foot.

Focus: Power

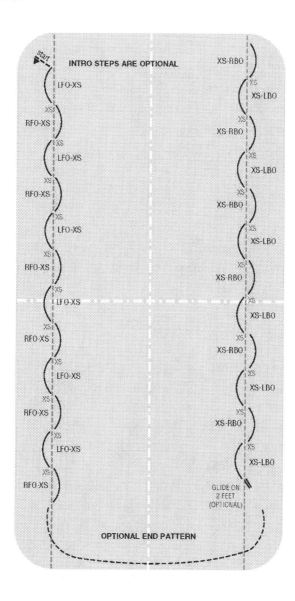

141

COMMENT

On paper, this move doesn't look too complicated, having only two different edges down each side of the rink, but there are still quite a few points I'd like to make.

They are called cross strokes because the new foot crosses the tracing where the old foot would be going, and the 'stroke' part comes from the fact that we're not just stepping onto the new edge, but getting a powerful stroke onto it.

This is very much a power move, so cross strokes need to be skated boldly on a well-bent skating knee. They are always skated on outside edges, and it's much easier to get a good stroke against the ice when you're on a strong edge. Generally, you will be skating from bent knee to bent knee without any rise and fall, as though the roof of the building is just above your head. If you're really 'into' the ice you should hear a 'rip' sound from the pushing foot as you stroke onto the new edge.

RECOMMENDED INTRODUCTORY STEPS:

Left, right, left, right, across the end of the rink, then a strong left outside edge to bring you around to the long axis to start the first cross stroke.

THE MOVE

As it shows on the diagram, you are not required to skate full semicircular lobes on each edge. I recommend that each edge should start by placing your foot at about 45 to 60 degrees to the long axis you are skating down (see diagram). That way, your blade will automatically hit an outside edge if you are over your new skating hip, and, always cross-stroke onto a *bent* knee.

If you place your foot down at ninety degrees to the long axis, the move will not flow easily down the rink. So, although you should be on strong outside edges, this move is not about edge quality, it's all about skating strongly from one outside edge to the other.

Let's talk about the body movement on these cross strokes.

It's not essential to do this, but I like to see a skater making a slight counter-rotational movement of the upper body against the movement of the free leg. This means that, just after your free leg starts moving to cross stroke, you should feel that you're rotating your opposite shoulder and arm forward to counteract this movement, and also feel your weight changing from the old skating hip to the new one. This should result in a coordinated movement of 'opposite shoulder and hip'. Be careful, though, not to let your hip come around too much. It should only come around enough for the foot to cross the tracing. And, if you co-ordinate this movement of your hips and shoulders correctly as you skate down the ice, you should find that your shoulders remain parallel to the end of the rink. Remember, too, that it's not necessary to move your arms too far forward and back. You should feel that they're just an extension of your shoulder position.

Changing your weight from hip to hip is very important because you're changing direction on each cross stroke, and, therefore, the natural lean of the body has to change to go with the edge. If you're not over your new skating hip at the beginning of the edge, you may find yourself stepping on a flat, or even an inside edge, before the blade rocks over to an outside edge.

If you keep your body over the long axis as you cross stroke each side of it, you'll find that you'll be over skating hip at the start of each edge, with the correct natural lean. This means that your body is not directly over the edge, but inside each tracing on a natural lean. (Thank you again, Keeyana, for bringing that to my attention, and helping me to find a better way of explaining it).

In Ice Dancing, these cross strokes are called cross-rolls. I've already talked about the 'cross' part, but the 'roll' part comes from the fact that, when viewed from in front or behind, the skater has a natural 'rolling' movement as they change lean from skating hip to skating hip.

Treat the stroke from the back foot the same as you would for a forward crossover or progressive. The only difference is that, instead of continuing on the same circle onto an inside edge, you are changing direction onto an outside edge, but the stroking action should feel the same.

Once you finish the forward cross strokes, I would recommend skating forwards across the end of the rink until you get to the axis you'll use for the back cross strokes. When you reach it, turn a right forward inside Mohawk, immediately followed by a right back outside edge to start the back cross strokes.

On these back cross strokes, try not to swing your free leg back before it crosses the tracing, because this could make you pitch forward. It needs to come around your skating leg, to allow you to make the movement of 'cross, push, extend'. The free leg extension should be in front, not behind.

Because we should be skating the back outside edge before the cross stroke on a well bent skating knee, the free knee has to start bending as it passes the skating leg before it crosses the tracing, and you also need to take care not to step down on the toe pick. You shouldn't be stepping down as though you were walking backwards (putting your toe down first). You have to start flexing the free foot before you step down, so that your blade immediately takes the ice near the ball of the foot (the ideal balance point on a back edge).

At the same time your free leg is coming around to cross stroke, rotate your opposite shoulder and arm back a little so that, once again, you should find your shoulders mostly parallel to the end of the rink.

I see a lot of skaters pull their bodies around in an effort to try to make their edges curve, essentially trying to steer the edge by pulling their free shoulder back too far. This is a common fault. There needs to be a certain amount of upper body movement, but it shouldn't be excessive. You should be able to make you edges curve nicely by being over your skating hip, on a well-bent knee, with a nice natural lean.

PROBLEM AREA:

- On the back cross strokes, skaters tend to 'pull' their bodies around too much, especially with their shoulders, as though they are trying to 'steer' themselves. Try not to rely on upper body movement to curve your edges.
- Not pushing correctly from the outside edge of the blade on the forward cross strokes.

- Placing the foot on a flat, or even inside edge, on the forward cross strokes.
- Rising up on the knee after the push on the back cross strokes instead of staying 'into the ice'.

EXERCISE:

Try skating forward and back cross strokes with your arms folded in front of you. It's harder, because you no longer have your arms to help you, but it will teach you how you have to control your core and hips to make the cross strokes work.

TRICKS OF THE TRADE:

1) To get the feeling of being on an outside edge on each cross stroke, skate across the red or blue hockey lines, or the red line at the end of the rink - making them the long axis - and keep your body over the line as your feet go each side of it to cross stroke. This should put you on an immediate natural lean over an outside edge.

2) To get the right feeling of how you should use your skating knee and foot to push against the ice when you skate back cross strokes, go back and take advantage of the 'backward change of edge power pulls' to help you with this simple exercise:

Skating a power pull before the cross stroke should give you a better feeling of how you push *against* the ice.

Start by pulling onto an inside edge, then pull onto an outside edge, cross stroke and push. Then swing your free leg back behind you, change edge to an inside edge, and repeat on the other foot (pull, pull, push). Keep switching your arms, whether you're doing a power pull or a cross stroke.

The power pull should put you onto a solid outside edge on a bent knee, from which you can feel a good push from the outside edge of your blade.

Pattern 5

BACKWARD POWER THREE TURNS

Focus: Power

Backward Power Three-Turns

The skater will perform three to five backward power three-times per circle in a figure eight pattern. One complete figure eight is required. A one or two-foot glide may be utilized when changing circles. Introductory steps are optional. This move may start in either direction.

Focus: Power

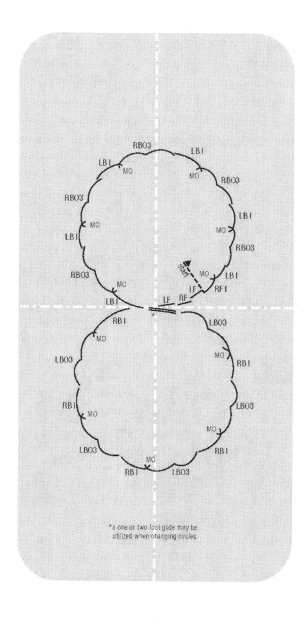

*a one or two foot glide may be utilized when changing circles.

147

COMMENT

Now we get down to a move that's got some meat in the sandwich! The back three-turn-mohawks in this move are used in freestyle programs, as a preparation for salchow and loop jumps, and are also a useful warm up move.

There are two reasons why I would advise starting with your 'weak' circle first.

1) If you impress by skating powerful three turns your 'good way' of rotating, and then show that you have trouble pushing onto the threes that rotate the other way, you will end up looking weak, leaving a bad impression at the end of the move.

2) You will probably feel less disoriented if you start with your 'bad' circle first, because you won't have become accustomed to rotating your 'good' way first, and then find it *more* difficult to reverse your rotation for the second circle.

Try not to treat these threes as you would the Pre-Juvenile back outside threes. On *those* threes you needed to check your shoulder and hip rotation on the exit of the turn in order to stay on a controlled edge back to the long axis. These threes are followed immediately by a Mohawk, so there needs to be continuity from the three turn to the Mohawk. This means the body should be turning at an even rate throughout the circle. (Thank you, Sofia, for helping me find the right words to explain how the body has a continuous, steady rotation on this move).

I like to see five back three turns per circle because that gives the skater the opportunity to create a good-sized circle and look powerful. The other good thing about using five turns is that the third turn will be on the midline of the rink, so you have an easy point of reference as you skate. Place your five turns as if they're numbers on a clock. With twelve 'o' clock being the center of the figure eight, the evenly spaced turns will be at ten, eight, six, four, and two 'o' clock.

RECOMMENDED INTRODUCTORY STEPS:

This move is usually started with the counter-clockwise circle, but you may start in either direction.

If you start with the counter-clockwise circle, skate three powerful strokes along the red line (left, right, left), and then, at the midline of the rink, push into the right forward inside Mohawk to start the move.

If you start with the clockwise circle, skate four strokes and then a left forward inside Mohawk to start.

THE MOVE

As you turn the Mohawk before the first back three, you should be starting a rotation of the body that should be continuous.

Three things need to happen simultaneously when you are skating these three's. You need to get a good swizzle push immediately after the Mohawk, bend your skating knee, and start rotating your arms and shoulders. Don't set your arms as though you're going to do a loop jump, and then switch them. Your hips should 'catch up' with your shoulders by the time you perform the first turn, so that from there onwards you should feel your body rotating 'in one piece', with your shoulders and hips fairly parallel to each other. Try to avoid merely stepping onto a back outside edge, and then 'whipping' the shoulders around to turn.

When you push, your pushing foot will 'swizzle' out of the circle, but try to bring it back to be extended in front of the skating foot by the time you turn the three. This shouldn't be difficult because the body is starting to rotate, and the free leg almost automatically ends up in front.

If you push onto a well-bent skating knee, you'll find that you only need to rise on the knee to turn because your body is already turning. Roll from the ball to the heel for the turn, and then back to just behind the middle of the blade as you exit.

As you exit the turn, try to keep your free leg extended in front of your skating leg to make sure that it doesn't swing around into the circle, or be held too high. Extending doesn't mean lifting. If the rotation of the turn causes your free leg to swing around after the turn, your free foot may not be 'underneath' you when you go to turn the mohawk, which puts it in the wrong place for you to push properly onto the three turn. Let the body continue to rotate after the three turn, so that you're prepared to turn to backwards on the Mohawk. Turn the Mohawk onto a slightly bent knee, make a slight check of your free hip, and then *immediately* bend to push onto the next three turn. This is the 'power' part of the move.

Once you get going, your feet and knees are going to do nearly all the work. In fact, once you start rotating, your upper body is, essentially, unemployed. Your arms can be held quite still (unless you choose to add arm movements, such as raising one or both arms up as you turn) and your body should just remain in alignment over your skating foot, rotating at an almost even rate.

You need to keep an even timing on each of the three edges (the back and forward edge of the three turn, and the back edge of the Mohawk), so your timing should be: 1 (push), 2 (rise and turn), 3 (Mohawk).

An often overlooked aspect of this move is that you should actually be gaining speed (flow) as you progress around the circle. This doesn't mean you should try to speed up the rotation of the body, but rather gain flow across the ice by making strong pushes into the turns.

After you've turned the final Mohawk on the first circle, hold a nice back outside edge on the other foot with good free leg extension until you get back to the center, and then bring your feet together to push onto the first power back three on your other foot for the second circle. From here, apply the same principles that you used on the first circle.

PROBLEM AREAS:

- Free leg lifting too high after the turn. This can cause you to tip back. Also, try not to let your free leg swing around as you exit the turn.
- Leaving the pushing foot on the ice too long after pushing (trailing), giving the impression that you need to steady yourself on two feet.
- Making a 'double push' onto the back threes because you're not ready to transfer you weight immediately onto the turning foot.

- Not getting enough push!
- Difficulty keeping in alignment over the skating hip when rotating the un-natural way.
- Lacking ability to maintain a circle shape. I have seen skaters deviating so far away from their circles that we've almost had to send out a search party for them.

TRICK OF THE TRADE:

Try this useful exercise.

On a circle, skate a repetitive 'pumping' movement, getting used to pushing out (swizzling) with the outside foot, at the same time bending the skating knee (inside foot). You can't push out properly if you don't bend you skating knee as you're pushing. As you do this, make sure you keep aligned over your inside hip and foot. Repeat in the other direction.

Pattern 6

FORWARD DOUBLE 3-TURNS

Focus: Edge Quality

Forward Double Three-Turns

The skater will perform consecutive forward double three-turns on half circles, with alternating of feet. Four to six half circles will be skated depending on the length of the rink and the strength of the skater. The sequence begins with forward outside double three-turns covering the first length of the rink. The forward inside double three-turns will cover the second length of the rink. Introductory steps and end patterns are optinal.

Focus: Edge quality

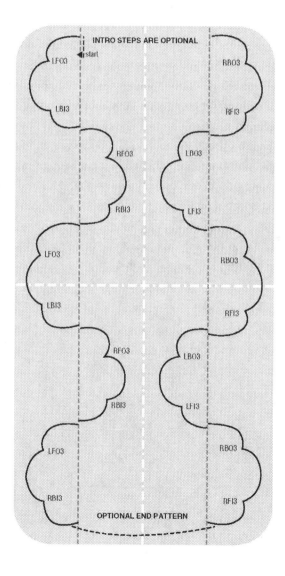

153

COMMENT

You are required to skate four to six lobes down the length of the arena.

We now come to another move that has it's foundations in basic figure skating. It requires edge quality, control, and correct placement of the threes. It also tests a skater's ability to skate two consecutive three turns on the same lobe.

At every stage of this move, you need to feel a perfect alignment of your body over your skate. Whether you're going forward or backward, on outside or inside edges, you should feel that you're right over your skating hip, and foot. Problems arise when the skater comes 'off' their skating hip as they change position between the threes. Whatever movements you make, you must rotate your body over your skating hip.

A fairly common fault on this move is the 'Sub curve', which occurs when the body starts rocking around and changing lean, mostly after the first turn. This causes the blade to change edge and pull out of the circle.

On the turns, use the rocker of the blade the same way as on previous three turns, and try to keep your edges flowing nicely throughout the move. If you skate too slowly, you run the risk of wobbling on unsteady edges.

In figure skating, double threes are skated on a figure eight pattern with the threes being placed at the third, and two thirds, mark on each circle. In Moves in the Field, you only have a semi-circle on which to complete these double threes, but there is enough time to prepare for, and check, each turn.

You may want to discuss with your coach the matter of free leg positions on this move. In the P.S.A. 'Moves in the Field Manual' it states 'Extra credit for a controlled extended free leg'. I have nothing but the greatest respect for this manual – and, indeed, refer to it frequently – but my teaching on this move calls for an extended free leg only before, and after, the back inside three turn, and after the back outside three turn. I'll explain why as we go along. And, I have to add that in all the tests I've watched, I haven't seen coaches asking their skaters to extend their free leg throughout this particular move. I certainly wouldn't ask my skaters to perform the forward three turns with an extended free leg, but it *is* a matter of choice.

RECOMMENDED INTRODUCTORY STEPS:

Four strokes across the end of the rink. Left, right, left, right, then start on the long axis with the left forward outside double three.

THE MOVE

As is the case with the Pre-Juvenile forward outside threes, it's optional whether you start with your skating arm or free arm leading when you start the lobe, but, whatever method you employ, I would draw the free foot in close behind the skating foot after the push, with the toe pointed and turned out.

Turn when you are a third of the way around the lobe, and check your free arm and shoulder so that your left arm is in front, and your right arm back. Now, we're going to take advantage of those 'half-movements', whereby you move one half of your body while the other half keeps you steady.

Keeping your free foot held in the same position, start moving your left arm back and your right arm in front, rotating your shoulders around so that your chest is now facing out of the circle. Now, with your upper body held still, bring your free leg forward, extended in front of you, rise a little on your skating knee, and turn to forward. Be very careful not to pull your edge or tilt your body inwards to turn the back inside three. Rely on enough upper body rotation to turn. You don't want to suddenly dip down to pull your skate through the turn.

As your foot turns, make a strong checking movement of your arms and shoulders so that your left arm and shoulder is now in front, and your right arm and shoulder behind. From here to the long axis, keep your hips very still, and switch your arms and shoulders so that your right arm and shoulder are now in front, ready to strike onto the right forward outside double three. If you're using the method where you start with the free arm and shoulder already in front, then there's no need to switch the arms and shoulders after the back inside three.

Keep in mind that when you turn the first three turn you are still heading toward the top of the lobe, so there should be the feeling of going 'up and around' the top of the lobe between the turns, and not straight down the rink.

For the right forward outside double three, repeat the same procedures, but on the other foot.

You should have no problem reaching the end of the arena using four to six lobes. Most skaters do it in five or six, but if you need more than six, you're not skating with enough flow.

Make sure you finish your last lobe back to the long axis before skating across the end of the rink to start the forward inside double threes.

You should prepare for these threes the same as you would for the forward inside three on the Pre-Juvenile test, but keep in mind that there is less time from the push to the turn.

Immediately after you've pushed onto the lobe, move your right arm and shoulder in front of you, and you left arm and shoulder back, simultaneously drawing in your free foot close to the skating foot, toe pointed and turned out. Your upper body should now be facing into the circle. Rotate your arms and shoulders a little more to make the turn, and then check them as you come out of the turn so that you're still facing into the circle.

As soon as you've checked the turn you need to start rotating your body over the skating hip to prepare for the back turn, but there are two different ways of positioning the free leg for it. You can either (a) move your free leg in front of your skating leg, slightly crossed over as you rotate your free arm and shoulder back, as most skaters do on their Pre-Juvenile back outside three turns, or (b) you can use the method I prefer, whereby your free leg is going to end up in front of your skating leg after the turn, but it's going to stay behind before the turn. I would recommend using this method, as follows:

After the forward turn, start preparing for the back three by lowering your arms, passing them near to the body. This will allow you to rotate your shoulders so that you now have your left arm and shoulder behind you, and your right arm just outside the circle. Remember, the important thing, here, is not to rotate your hips. By only rotating your upper body, while keeping everything below your waist totally still, you can create a 'twist' feeling at your waist, with your free shoulder further back than your free hip. Meanwhile, your free foot should still be held close behind your skating foot because you're not going to move it until you turn the back three.

When you're two thirds of the way around the lobe, release the twist, letting your foot turn to forward, check your shoulders and hips, and straighten your free leg so that your free foot is held slightly across the tracing. Your free leg should straighten at precisely the same that you turn the three. I think you'll find this is a very solid way of checking this turn. The free knee is bent before the turn, and straight after.

As I explained much earlier in this book, your foot will turn 180 degrees, your hips will turn about 90 degrees (just enough for your foot to turn to forward), and your shoulders will hardly need to turn at all because they're pre-rotated before the turn.

From here, all you need to do is finish the lobe and use the same method for the other foot.

PROBLEM AREAS:

- Difficulty maintaining a steady curving edge after the forward turn as the body rotates to prepare for the back turn.
- Difficulty maintaining a steady curve back to the long axis after the back turn.
- Not placing the skating foot on the short axis to set a true semi-circular lobe.
- Toe pushing when starting the forward inside three turn lobes.
- Skating without adequate flow. This move actually works better with a little speed.
- Pulling your edge to turn the back inside three turn, instead of relying on upper body rotation.

TRICK OF THE TRADE:

You can help yourself place the turns correctly by using a count. As you start the lobe, count one, two, three, four, turning on 'four'. Then count again from the forward turn to the back turn, one, two, three, four, turning again on 'four'. Of course, the speed of the count will depend on how fast you're skating, but, by trial and error, you'll find the right tempo. This counting method should space your three turns evenly on the lobe.

Intermediate Moves in the Field Test

1. Backward double three-turns The skater will perform consecutive backward double three-turns on half circles with alternating feet. Four to six half circles will be skated depending on the length of the rink and strength of the skater. The sequence begins with BO double three-turns covering the first length of the rink. The BI double three-turns will cover the second length of the rink. Introductory steps and end patterns are optional. Focus: Edge quality and extension

2. Spiral Sequence The skater will begin with a LFO spiral that should be held until the long axis of the rink. The skater then brings the free leg down into a RFI open mohawk and steps wide with a two-foot power push transition to a backward R over L crossover. The skater will then push into a LBO spiral to be held until the long axis of the rink. Skater must step immediately into a RFI spiral. The free leg will drop into a RFI mohawk and lift again into a LBI spiral, also to be held until the long axis. Optional steps to repeat pattern in opposite direction starting with RFO spiral. Note: all spirals should be sustained with an extended free leg to demonstrate the skater's form and flexibility. Introductory steps are optional. This move may start on either foot. Focus: Extension and edge quality

3. Brackets in the field sequence The skater will perform two sets of turns on half circles (RFO-LBI) down approximately half the length of the rink. Continuing down the remaining length of the rink the skater then will perform two sets of turns (LFO-RBI) with an optional step to transition to the LFO edge. Once completed, the entire sequence is repeated, performing two sets of turns (LFI-RBO) down approximately half the length of the rink. The skater then performs two sets of turns (RFI-LBO) down the remaining length of the rink with an optional step to transition to the RFI edge. Introductory steps are optional. This move may start in either foot; the FO/BI brackets will precede the FI/BO brackets. Focus: Edge quality

4. Forward twizzles Forward outside twizzles: The skater will begin from a standing start with a LFO roll, forward cross stroke to a RFO twizzle which ends on RBI after 1 & 1/2 revolutions. The skater will then step LFO to complete the set. Three twizzle sets are to be repeated across the width or down the length of the rink and they should be repeated on the opposite foot in the same manner. Forward inside twizzles: For the second part of the move, the skater will begin from a standing start with a LFI roll to a RFI twizzle which ends on RBO after 1 & 1/2 revolutions. The skater will then step LFI to complete the set. Three twizzle sets are to be repeated across the width or down the length of the rink and they should be repeated on the opposite foot in the same manner. This move may start in either direction. Focus: Turn execution and continuous flow

5. Inside slide chassé pattern The skater will perform four alternating patterns of inside slide chassés preceded by backward power three-turns. The pattern should cover the entire length of the rink. Introductory steps are optional. Focus: Edge quality and extension
Revised 7/1/2010

COMMENT

Unlike the Juvenile moves, most of the moves on this test don't require a lot of power - except on parts of the spiral pattern and slide chasse pattern – or 'quickness' of foot movement. They are much more about edge quality, control, and good body positions. And, I want to stress that on two of the moves – the twizzles and brackets – you'll find that it's essential to have your body in perfect alignment over your skate.

Pattern 1

BACKWARD DOUBLE THREE TURNS

Primary Focus: Edge Quality
Secondary Focus: Extension

Backward Double Three-Turns

The skater will perform consecutive backward double three-turns on half circles with alternating foot. Four to six half circles will be depending on the length of the rink and strength of the skater. The sequence begins with backward outside double three-turns covering the first length of the rink. The backward inside double three-turns will cover the second length of the rink. Introductory steps and end patterns are optional.

Focus: Edge quality and extension.

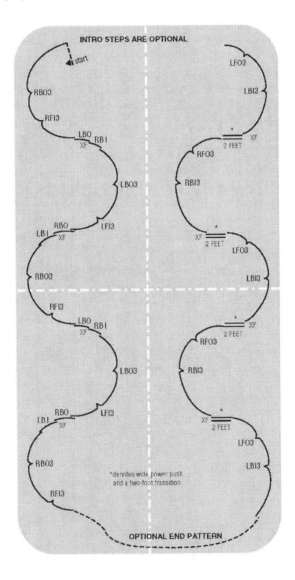

COMMENT

Clearly, edge quality is a major factor on this move, and is the primary focus. Just as on the forward double threes, the judges will expect the turns to be on a continuous arc around the top of the lobe, but the placement of the threes on this move is a little different to the placement of the Juvenile double threes. The back turn should be on the top of the lobe (halfway mark), and the forward turn at the two-thirds mark.

The secondary focus is extension, and the only two places I recommend you show this extension are before and after the first turn, and after the second turn.

RECOMMENDED INTRODUCTORY STEPS:

Three strokes across the end of the arena (left, right, left), followed by a right forward inside Mohawk. Alternatively, you could add a push and crossover after the Mohawk, but you shouldn't need that many edges to attain the right speed.

THE MOVE

Think of this as a 'long edge' move. On the first side, skate it this way: Long push, long crossover, then a good swizzle push onto the back three. Don't just step onto this turn. By getting a good push you'll keep your edges flowing nicely, and be able to skate nice large lobes.

Skate the back outside three the same as you would on the Pre-Juvenile test. That way, you should get a nice swizzle push onto the three, and you can bring your free leg back in front of your skating leg to be extended nicely through the turn.

As you turn, you will need to check your arms and shoulders momentarily, before releasing them to rotate your upper body in preparation for the forward inside three at the two-thirds mark. This comes up fairly quickly, but you shouldn't be rotating continuously because this may cause the threes to be too close together. There is enough time to rotate, check, rotate, check.

To make the forward turn, I recommend that you first move your free foot back behind the heel of your skating foot, and then immediately start rotating your arms and shoulders for the turn. As soon as you've checked the forward turn, switch your arms and shoulders so that your free arm and shoulder are back, and extend your free leg. You can then bring your feet together to push and cross over for the start of the left back outside three turn lobe.

Go through the same procedures for the new lobe, but on the other foot, and repeat the lobes the length of the arena. You should be skating four to six lobes, depending on the size of the arena, and the strength of the skater.

When you've completed the first side, I recommend skating forwards across the end of the arena to start the back inside double threes on the second half of this move.

As you're required to skate a crossover into these turns, I would precede the first left back inside three by skating a right forward inside Mohawk, followed by a right back outside edge. You will then be able to cross over to skate the left back inside three.

It will be important to judge how far back from the long axis you need to be to skate into the mohawk. If you leave it too late, you'll probably be late turning the back three.

On the crossover into the three, start rotating your arms and shoulders, stroke down on your skating knee, and extend your free leg so that it's just outside the circle. Then, to turn the three on the top of the lobe, rise on the skating knee, draw your free foot in close behind your skating foot, and go from ball to heel into the turn, and back to just behind the middle of the blade coming out. Make a slight check of your free hip and shoulder, and then immediately let your shoulders rotate again for the forward turn at the two-thirds mark, keeping your free foot held close until after the turn. If you turn these threes too close together, they may end up looking like a back inside twizzle instead of a double three.

As soon as you've checked the forward turn, extend your free leg back with your free hip and shoulder open, toe pointed and turned out.

When you reach the end of the lobe, skate a wide step onto a right back inside edge on a well-bent knee – this is the two foot transition – and then push from that wide step onto a left back outside edge. From here, make a right back inside crossover, rotating your arms and shoulders to make the right back inside three. Use the same method of rising on the skating knee and drawing in the free foot to the skating heel, as you did on the other foot, to turn on the top of the lobe, and then turn the forward outside three at the two-thirds mark. Extend your free leg again, just as you did on the previous lobe, and then skate a wide step onto a left back inside edge.

From this wide step, get a good push onto a right back outside edge, and then cross over onto a left back inside edge to repeat the double threes again, the length of the arena.

Generally, try to feel 'into' the ice on the pushes and crossovers, and then rise for the turns.

PROBLEM AREAS:

- 'Whipping' the back threes around, causing the forward turn to be early.
- Turning the back three onto a straight edge (there's that oxymoron again), instead of continuing on a circle.
- Not shifting the weight adequately onto the wide step on the second side, thereby missing the push from it.
- Turns being too close together, especially on the second side (back inside to forward outside). This is usually caused by the skater rotating their body too quickly after the back inside three.

Pattern 2

SPIRAL SEQUENCE

Focus: Extension, Edge Quality

Spiral Sequence

The skater will begin with a LFO spiral that should be held until the long axis of the rink. The skater then brings the free log down into a RFI open mohawk and stops wide with a two-foot power push transition to a backward right over left crossover. The skater will then push into a LBO spiral to be held until the long axis of the rink. Skater must step immediately into a RFI spiral. The free log will drop into a RFI mohawk and lift again into a LBI spiral, also to be held until the long axis. Optional steps to repeat pattern in opposite direction starting with RFO spiral. Note: All spirals should be sustained with an extended free log to demonstrate the skater's form and flexibility. Introductory steps are optional. This move may start on either foot.

Focus: Extension and edge quality

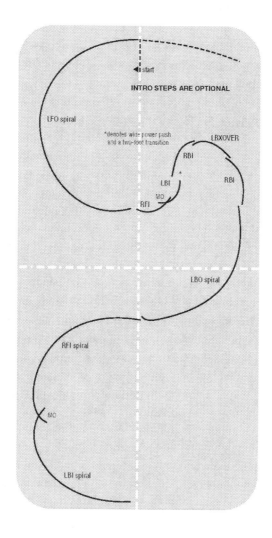

This move may start in either direction.

COMMENT

The first half of this move is relatively easy. Seven introductory steps to get up speed, a forward outside spiral, Mohawk, wide step, and push, crossover. Nothing very difficult about that, but the second half of this move has its difficulties, not the least of which is maintaining enough flow on the section incorporating the back outside spiral, forward inside spiral, and back inside spiral. You cannot afford to miss any of the power strokes, especially the very important swizzle push before the back outside spiral, otherwise the spirals will just not cover enough ice to make the correct pattern. And, as with the old Novice spiral move, it's essential that you get a good push from the back outside spiral onto the forward inside spiral.

RECOMMENDED INTRODUCTORY STEPS:

You *could* start by skating basic 'left, rights' across the end of the arena (no more than seven) until you reach the midline, where you would start the first spiral, but I can suggest a much more effective way of going into this move.

Standing on the midline about a quarter of the way down the rink from where the first spiral will start, stroke right, left, right in a diagonal direction toward the corner, and then two crossovers on a curve that will take you straight onto the LFO spiral on the midline of the rink. The beauty of this is that the crossovers are on the same curve as the large semi-circle on which you will skate the LFO spiral.

This start uses seven steps, but you are actually getting eight power strokes because you should be getting a good push onto the first spiral. After that, you must take every opportunity to push throughout this move.

Experiment with your starting steps, and, by trial and error, you'll find out what works best for you.

THE MOVE

The first spiral (forward outside) is the longest of the four spirals in this move, so get onto a solid outside edge and be patient. Stretch your body lines, and hold up your free leg as high as you can by using your quad muscle. If you try to raise your free leg by pulling up your free foot, you may only raise the lower part of your leg, and end up with a bent free knee. From this spiral to the back outside spiral you have five chances to get a good push, and you'd better not miss one of them, otherwise you may not have enough speed to carry you through the second half of this move.

You can get power from every edge leading up to the back outside spiral. When you get to the midline you can get a good push into the Mohawk, then onto, and off, the wide step.

On this Mohawk, you can use an arm movement that will actually help you gain momentum onto the wide step. For example, as you turn the right inside Mohawk, let your right arm come across you by bending your elbow, and then, as you push onto the wide step, sweep your right arm out to your side at the same time. This actually helps give you momentum.

After this, you only have one back push and crossover before the back spiral, so get good power on these. When you get to the back spiral edge, bend and get a strong swizzle push immediately before you raise your free leg, otherwise you will lose valuable speed. Make sure that you don't just fling your free leg back into the spiral position without any push beforehand.

On this back spiral, keep your weight solidly over the skating hip, with your shoulders and hips fairly square to the tracing. I see a lot of skaters letting their free shoulder rotate back too far, which can cause the body to rotate, and the edge to curve too strongly. This makes it difficult to reach the midline of the rink in the right direction to set up the step forward for the forward inside spiral (see diagram). The edge of your back outside spiral may also curve too strongly if you lean into the circle too much.

It's essential to skate a power stroke from the back outside spiral to the forward inside spiral. To do this, keep your weight on your skating side as you come out of the back spiral position, and open your free hip and shoulder a little in preparation to step forward. Then, bring your free foot close to your skating foot, turned out. At this point, you should still be up on your skating knee. Pre-bend both knees and ankles, and feel the blade of your skating foot rock over to the inside edge to grip the ice as you push. If you rotate your hips and shoulders too much when you come out of the back spiral, it may cause you to turn a back three turn, which is incorrect.

At first, when you step forward, place your skating foot on an inside edge, but with the toe aiming out to the side of the rink to ensure that you don't take a diagonal 'short-cut'.

If you don't get a good push onto this forward inside spiral, it will seem like an eternity before you reach the end of the first half of this move.

On this forward inside spiral I recommend having the skating arm and shoulder leading, so that when you turn the Mohawk to the back inside spiral you'll be able to check back that arm and shoulder, with your new skating arm and shoulder in front of you. I also recommend that you arch your back well over your skating hip (on the forward inside spiral) so that you're almost leaning out of the circle.

The Mohawk is turned at the side of the rink, which means it's the halfway point of the large semi-circular arc that is made by these two spirals. After you turn, hold the back inside spiral position until you reach the midline of the rink. This spiral is hard enough, but it's even worse if your speed has died down to a crawl. Obviously, it's much easier to balance when you have speed.

A lot of skaters have difficulty holding their position on the back inside spiral because they let their arms and shoulders rotate, and also because they lean inwards, which causes the edge to curve too strongly and not end up on the midline of the rink. If you arch your back a little, it will help you keep your upper body over your skating hip, and this may help to prevent you from falling inwards.

It's no coincidence that in freestyle programs you'll see forward outside and inside spirals, and back outside spirals, but you'll almost never see back inside spirals skated in a competition for one simple reason. They're ugly. They don't feel good, and most of the time they don't look good. So, do your best to hold a nice position, and try to make it to the midline.

On all spirals the free foot should always be turned out, with the toe pointed. Both knees should be completely straight.

There will be many different ways of transitioning from the first half of this move to repeat the pattern in the opposite direction, but here are two options you can try.

After you finish the back inside spiral near the midline, bring your feet together and skate a back outside edge on the other foot (like a jump landing position with a nicely extended free leg) on the same circle. This will bring you away from the end barrier, and give you room to skate clockwise back crossovers on a large circle that will take you back to the midline. Then, standing on a left back outside edge, step outward – but make it a stroke - onto the forward outside spiral that starts the second half of this move.

Alternatively, if you feel better facing forwards when you start the first spiral, skate the same back crossovers, but step inwards to a left forward inside edge, and then take two strokes (right, left) before pushing onto the right forward outside spiral on the midline.

The advice for the second part of this move is exactly the same as for the first part, but, obviously, starting on the other foot.

PROBLEM AREAS:

- Not maintaining enough speed from after the first spiral.
- Not finishing the lobe of the back outside spiral, causing a diagonal step forward in the wrong direction.
- Turning the body too much as you step forward after the back outside spiral. This can cause the forward edge to curve in the wrong direction.
- Not getting a good push on the step forward into the forward inside spiral.
- Not being able to hold a good position on the back inside spiral.
- Free leg not held high enough, and often with a bent free knee.

TRICK OF THE TRADE

To fully understand the step forward from the back outside spiral to the forward inside spiral, forget about the spirals for a moment, and just practice skating from one circle to another. On the first circle, skate on a back outside edge with your free hip and shoulder open, so that you find yourself facing out of the circle. This is, in fact, the second position of a back outside eight, and puts you in the perfect position to step forward onto the forward inside spiral. You should now find it easy to step forward - without turning your body - onto a new circle with your skating hip, shoulder and arm leading. This what will be happening between the two spirals.

Pattern 3

BRACKETS IN THE FIELD SEQUENCE

Focus: Edge Quality

Brackers in the Field Sequence

The skater will perform two sets of turns on half circles (RFO-LBI) down approximately half the length of the rink. Continuing down the remaining length of the rink the skater then will perform two sets of turns (LFO-RBI) with an optional step to transition to the LFO edge. Once completed, the entire sequence is repeated, performing two sets of turns (LFI-RBO) down approximately half the length of the rink. The skater then performs two sets of turns (RFI-LBO) down the remaining length of the rink with an optional step to transition to the RFI edge. Introductory steps are optional. This move may start in either foot; the FO/BI brackets will preced the FI/BO brackets.

Focus: Edge quality.

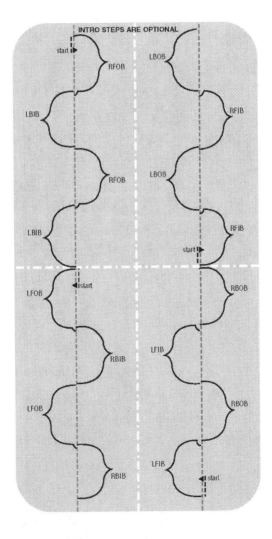

COMMENT

The basic bracket is one of my pet subjects. Brackets are the easiest of all one-foot turns if the body is positioned correctly before the turn. Considering that it's a relatively simple turn, you'll notice that I have a lot to say about it, but I think you'll find the following information very useful.

Most diagrams in the rule book are accurate and representative of how the judges expect the pattern to be laid out on the ice, but because the diagram for this move has to show two sets of brackets on each side of the rink, the first set had to be drawn so that it ends halfway down the rink, otherwise there would be no room to fit in the second set.

A skater *could* quite easily skate four lobes using only half the length of the rink, but in the PSA 'Moves in the Field' manual it states, 'Extra credit when skated with greater speed and control', so, in my book (no pun intended) if you only use half the rink, you won't be able to skate good sized lobes with decent flow. It depends on the size of the rink, of course, but you're almost certainly going to need more than half the length of a regulation-sized rink for each set. In all the tests I've witnessed, skaters usually need about two-thirds of the length of the rink to perform each set of brackets on good-sized lobes, so don't feel that you *must* complete each set using only half the length of the rink. It's just that, on the diagram, they can't show the lobes going two thirds of the way down the rink because they would have had to draw overlapping lobes, and that would look very confusing.

When you're first learning to skate brackets they may feel a little awkward, therefore you won't want to skate into them with very much speed. But, as soon as you get used to them, start skating them a little faster across the ice because judges don't want you to skate them as slowly as they were skated in tests and competitions in the 'old' days. Back then, skaters had to turn perfectly clean turns and trace the circles so that the edges were superimposed, or at least very close together. In order to do this, they had to skate more slowly and deliberately, but now these brackets must be skated with more flow.

Before I describe the move itself, here are some general points I would like to make about all brackets.

- A bracket is, in effect, an inverted three-turn. To put it in simple terms, whereas three-turns turn (point) into the circle, brackets turn (point) out of the circle. (see diagram)

- At first, some skaters find it confusing knowing which way to rotate in preparation for a bracket, but, in simple terms again, on forward brackets you should find your upper body facing *out* of the circle before the turn, and on back brackets your upper body should be facing *into* the circle before the turn. This means that you will be *counter-rotating* your upper body in preparation for the turn.

- This is a move where the old saying 'less is more' is very good advice. Too much body movement during the turns will cause you to lose balance, scrape the turns, and interfere with the continuity of the edge.

- Because you need to maintain the circle shape, it's important that you don't let any change of position interfere with the natural lean of the body. Although the lean is minimal, it must remain constant for you to continue on a circle.

- Keep in mind that you'll probably be standing up nice and straight when you start each edge, but all that goes to waste if you break your body line just before, or during, the turn.

- You should have the feeling that your free hip is slightly lower than your skating hip as you turn any of the brackets. This can be done by 'bracing up' the skating side of your body. I, personally, feel as though I'm bracing myself up under the rib cage on my skating side, but *not* by lifting up my shoulder.

- When it comes to turning brackets, you have a great advantage if you are, as I put it, 'rotationally flexible'. This means that you are able to rotate your shoulders further than your hips without too much effort, and can, therefore, pre-rotate your upper body to the right degree. If your torso is not that flexible, you'll have to rely on your arms a little more to help you rotate into, and out of, the bracket.

- On all brackets, making a slight rise on the skating knee will help you to use the rocker of the blade into, and out of, the turn, but the use of the skating knee must be subtle, so just bend slightly before the turn so that you have something on which to rise. Generally, throughout the rest of the lobe, you need to be up on the knee.

There are a variety of different ways of using the free foot on bracket turns, but I'll describe the method I prefer as we get to each bracket.

On Forward Outside and Back Inside brackets, the free hip is slightly open before the turn, and closed afterward. On Forward Inside and Back Outside brackets, it's the opposite. The free hip is slightly closed before the turn, and open afterward.

On Forward brackets your leading arm moves across your chest before you turn. On back brackets your trailing arm moves across your chest before you turn.

Another important thing to consider is the avoidance of 'flat-topped' circles. These can occur when a skater goes onto a 'flat' edge (there's that oxymoron again) when they reach the top of the lobe and travel, maybe, five or six feet in a straight line before they turn, and then continue on a straight line after the turn before getting back onto a circle. The pity is, that they may have started a very nicely shaped lobe, but waited too long to turn.

There is another problem you must try to avoid. Even though you may place your foot correctly on the short axis in order to start the lobe, make sure you don't make the error of setting off in a straight line, and then have to suddenly turn a corner in order to get to the top of the lobe. I repeat again, think about the circle first, then the turn.

Basically, think of a four stage preparation for all brackets.

1) Set your lobe, getting your body aligned over your skating hip.
2) Move your free foot into place and keep it still, unless you're going to use a free leg movement or 'scissoring' action for the turn.
3) Prepare the counter rotation as you approach the turn, feeling a slight 'twist' at the waist.
4) Rise a little on the skating knee to use the rocker of the blade to turn. On forward brackets, rock from behind the middle of the blade to the front to go into the turn, and then back to the ball as you exit. On back brackets, rock from the ball to the heel to go

into the turn, and then back to just behind the middle of the blade as you exit.

On all brackets, you should rotate your shoulders to be near parallel to the tracing, and your hips to about forty-five degrees to the tracing. Then, when your foot turns, the shoulders hardly rotate at all (0 degrees),staying in the same place, the hips turn approximately 90 degrees, but not as far as the foot, and the foot turns a full 180 degrees. This is my 0-90-180 theory.

Before I describe the move, I must mention one more thing.

Try not to be 'hippy' on these brackets, and that isn't a social comment. By being 'hippy', I mean that skaters can have too much hip movement as they turn, and push their hips out of alignment, instead of only making a small checking movement. It can also cause the blade to scrape the turn.

RECOMMENDED INTRODUCTORY STEPS:

Two strokes to the long axis. This should be enough for you to achieve nice flow throughout the lobe.

THE MOVE

FORWARD OUTSIDE/BACK INSIDE BRACKET

The following advice applies whether you're starting on the left foot or right, but I'm going to describe the move starting on the right forward outside bracket. You are required to skate two forward, and two backward brackets on each set.

To start this move, I usually recommend skating two strokes to get to the long axis, and then *go back to basics*. Don't even think of the bracket. You have a quarter of a circle to prepare for it, so, first place your arms, shoulders, and hips in the same position you would for the outside edge on the Pre-Preliminary test, or the Forward Circle Eight on the Preliminary test, and then set a nice lobe on a solid outside edge.

After you push onto the edge, draw your free foot in behind the heel of your skating foot with the free toe pointed and turned out. Hold your free foot in this position until you reach the turn. This is how I like to see the free foot positioned, but there *is* something to be said for bringing the free foot in front of the skating foot after the push to 'lead the way', so to speak. The curve of the edge will often feel steadier when the free foot is leading. Whichever method you use, you will still have to bring your free foot back behind your skating foot before the turn. At this stage of the lobe you should be up on your skating knee.

As you approach the top of the lobe, simultaneously counter rotate your shoulders a little more - but *not* your hips - move your right (skating) arm slightly across your chest, outside the circle, and bend your skating knee a little. Your shoulders will now be pre-rotated in the direction that your skate will turn, but try to keep your hips still so that the curve of the edge is not disturbed, or pulled. Remember, where your hips go, your foot generally follows.

If your shoulders are in the right position before the turn, you should find them parallel to the barrier on the other side of the rink, and, if you check the turn correctly, your upper body will still be facing out of the circle directly after the turn.

To make the turn, rise up on your skating knee, rocking your blade up to the front (but not as far as the toe pick), and then back to the ball as you exit the turn. At the same time, check your arms and shoulders so that your free arm is now in front of you on the circle, and your skating arm is checked back a little, outside the circle. Your free leg should straighten at the time you turn, and extend in front of you over the circle, with the free foot neither turned out or in (neutral). You can also leave your free foot behind the skating foot after the turn, but just make sure you check your hips well.

To skate the rest of the lobe back to the long axis, I would, again, go back to basics. Treat the remainder of this edge the same as you would for the second part of the back inside edge on the Juvenile Back Circle Eight. Pass your free foot close by your skating foot and extend your free leg back over the tracing. Alternatively, you could just move your free foot back and hold it close behind your skating foot until you reach the long axis. As your free foot is passing your skating foot, start rotating your arms and shoulders so that you end up with your free arm and shoulder behind you on the circle.

Just before you reach the long axis, draw your free foot close to your skating foot and release your free arm a little, in preparation for the swizzle push onto the new lobe. You'll be pushing onto a left back inside edge, just as you did for the back inside three turn on the Pre-Juvenile move, but that's where the similarity ends. On *that* back inside edge, your shoulders needed to be rotated so that your upper body was facing out of the circle, pre-rotated for the three turn, but, because you're going to be rotating your upper body *into* the circle for the back inside bracket you don't need your shoulders in that same position. In fact, I recommend starting the back inside edge with the shoulders fairly square to the tracing, the free arm in front of you, over the tracing, and your skating arm held out to the side so that your arms are in an 'L' shape. The hips are also square to the tracing at this stage.

Immediately after the swizzle push, move your free foot back so that the toe is held by the heel of your skating foot, pointed and slightly turned out. Your free knee should also be slightly open, and you should be turning your head to look inside the circle so that you can see where to place your turn.

Now we need to prepare for the turn. Start by lowering your arms to allow you to rotate your shoulders so that they are parallel to the long axis before the turn, with your free arm and shoulder back on the tracing, and your skating arm a little inside the circle. You should now be ready to turn.

Just before the top of the lobe, move your left (skating) arm a little more across your chest, so that you'll be able to check both arms when you turn.

To make the turn, rise a little on your skating knee and rock the blade from the ball to the heel as you go into the turn, and then immediately back to just behind the middle of the blade as you come out.

Check your arms and shoulders so that you now have your free arm leading in front of you on the circle, and your skating arm held back.

Make sure you stay over you skating hip (and therefore over the circle) in order to maintain the natural lean, and continuation of the circle. Otherwise, it's all too easy to shoot off in a straight line after the turn if you come off your hip.

During the turn, I like to keep the free foot held close to the skating heel, but after the turn the free foot and knee are no longer slightly turned out, but neutral, because we don't want the free hip to be open. Once you have checked the turn, extend your free leg nicely in front of you over the tracing until you get back to the long axis. Then, draw in your free foot in preparation to repeat another forward and backward turn.

It's been my experience that some skaters feel they have no time to get into position for this back inside bracket, and rush their movements so much that they end up turning early. Don't panic. There's time to make each movement if you do them in order. These changes of position may seem a little 'mechanical', so try to link your movements so that they are performed smoothly.

Of the four brackets, the back inside bracket usually presents the most problems when it comes to keeping good alignment over the skating hip. It's all too easy to break your body alignment as you rotate your upper body in preparation for the turn, usually by tilting inwards, so be very aware of staying solidly over your skating hip as you move your arms and shoulders. Nothing must interfere with the steady curve of the edge.

When you've completed the second back turn, and finished the edge back to the long axis, skate back down the rink to perform the left forward outside/right back inside brackets, but make sure you leave enough room for the four lobes, which occupy about two-thirds of the length of the arena. Then, go through the same procedures as before, but this time starting on the left foot.

I can't stress enough the need to use the rocker of the blade to make turns, especially on forward and backward outside brackets and counters. These are the turns you're most likely to 'catch' your edge on, which can result in a quick fall, often right on your hip bone! So, once again, on forward turns, rock forward, and then back to the ball, and on backward turns rock back to the heel, and then back to just behind the middle of the blade.

FORWARD INSIDE/BACK OUTSIDE BRACKET

The forward inside bracket is probably the easiest of the four brackets. The position before the turn is not hard to master, and checking the turn shouldn't be too much of a struggle. I'm going to describe this part of the move starting on the left forward inside bracket.

Just as on the forward outside brackets, skate two introduction steps to the long axis, and then stroke onto a basic left forward inside edge with the free arm leading on the circle, and the skating arm held out to the side. Remember, don't even think 'bracket', yet.

Now we need to decide on how to use the free foot, because there are different ways. Other coaches may have even more variations, but there are two different methods from which I choose, depending on what best suits each skater. Whichever method you use, you will still be adopting the same arm and shoulder positions before the turn.

The first method involves no movement of the free foot during the turn.

After you push onto the forward inside edge, draw your free foot in close behind your skating foot, with the toe pointed, but not turned out. Then, as you approach the top of the lobe, counter-rotate your upper body a little more so that your free shoulder is leading, and your free (right) arm is slightly across your chest. Your free knee will be in neutral position (neither turned in or out).

Just before the turn, you should find your shoulders parallel to the barrier on the other side of the rink, and because they are rotated further than your hips, you should also feel that slight 'twist' at the waist.

To turn, rise a little on your skating knee, rock the blade from just behind the middle to the front as your skate goes into the turn, and then immediately back to the ball as it comes out, making a strong checking movement of your arms and shoulders. The rocking motion of the blade is necessary to make a clean turn, and it happens fairly quickly.

The second method involves a free leg movement that synchronizes with the turn. I prefer this method because, when performed correctly, it actually makes it easier to check the free hip and shoulder back after the turn.

After you push onto the forward inside edge, bring your free leg through to be extended in front of you, over the tracing. Prepare your arms and shoulders in the same position previously mentioned, but, as you turn, bend your free knee to pull your free foot back behind the heel of your skating foot, with the toe turned out, and the free hip and shoulder checked back. Keep looking in the same direction as you turn, which shouldn't be a problem if your free arm and shoulder are checked back correctly.

When skating the original school figures, the free foot would be extended in front of the skating foot before the turn, because the skater needed to pull the free foot back in a 'scissoring' movement to make the turn deeper in order to gain more points. Pulling the free foot back pushes the skating foot deeper into the turn. On Moves in the Field, judges aren't looking for 'deep' brackets, just well-controlled ones.

Now, for the final bracket. You should have no problems performing the back outside bracket if your upper body is in the correct position, and you'll find it a lot easier if you set the position of your arms and shoulders right at the start of the edge. Therefore, try this four-stage preparation.

(1) At the same time you push, rotate your upper body so that your right shoulder is drawn back, and your arms are on the circle. Your shoulders are now in the right position to make the turn, but don't undo all your good work by letting them go back to a square position before the turn.

This position should be familiar. It's exactly the same as the first position on the Pre-Juvenile Back Circle Eight. You should feel that you are right over your skating hip, and 'bracing up' the skating side of your body. Your free hip should feel slightly lower than your skating hip, and you should be balancing near the ball of the foot, up on the knee.

(2) Without moving anything else, move your free foot back to the heel of your skating foot, with the toe pointed, neither turned in or out.

(3) As you are approaching the top of the lobe, move your free arm a little inside the circle to finish the preparation.

(4) When you're ready to turn, rise a little on the knee, rock the blade from the ball to the heel, and turn to forward, going back to just behind the middle of the blade as you come out of the turn. Check

your arms and shoulders so that your right (skating) arm and shoulder are leading on the circle.

Your free foot should still be held in place, but it will now be slightly open, as will your free hip and knee.

Now, all you have to do is leave your arms and shoulders in that same position, and extend your free leg in front of you over the tracing until you get back to the long axis. I think this looks nice, but, alternatively, you can leave your free foot held behind the skating foot until you get back to the long axis.

With your arms in that same position you can now repeat the left forward inside and right back outside brackets once more.

If you have a spare minute, take a close look at your bracket on the ice. On a cleanly turned bracket the tracings should 'criss-cross' at the point of the turn. We used to call these 'bunny-eared' brackets because the crossed edges on the turn resemble the ears of a rabbit. The tracings should cross each other as the blade rocks over from one edge to the other as it turns.

PROBLEM AREAS:

- Scraped turns caused by the skater not using the rocker of the blade.
- Lobes looking too 'square', caused by the skater setting off in a straight line.
- Inability to check the turns and hold a steady edge back to the long axis.
- Toe pushing, especially onto the forward inside edges.
- Falls caused by 'catching an edge' (especially on the forward outside and back outside brackets) because the skater failed to lift to the front of the blade on forward turns, and to the back of the blade on back turns.
- Skated too slowly.

Pattern 4

FORWARD TWIZZLES

Focus: Turn Execution, Continuous Flow

Forward Twizzles

Forward outside twizzles: The skater will begin from a standing start with a LFO roll, forward cross stroke to a RFO twizzle which ends on RBI after ½ revolutions. The skater will then stop LFO to complete the set. Three twizzle sets are to be repeated across the width or down the length of the rink, and they should be repeated on the opposite foot in the same manner.

Forward inside twizzles: For the second part of the move, the skater will begin from a standing start with a LFI roll to a RFI twizzle which ends on RBO after ½ revolutions. The skater will then stop LFI to complete the set. Three twizzle sets are to be repeated across the width or down the length of the rink, and they should be repeated on the opposite foot in the same manner. This move may start in either direction.

Focus: Turn execution and continuous flow.

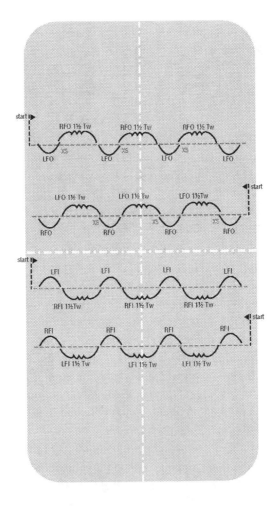

186

This move may start in either direction.

COMMENT

There are three twizzles to be skated in each set. They can either be skated across the width, or down the length of the rink. In every test I've seen, skaters use the blue or red hockey lines to skate across the width of the rink, which means that the second twizzle should be, approximately, on the midline.

If you look at the tracing left on the ice, you'll see that a twizzle is, in effect, a series of tiny three turns, and on this move both the outside and inside twizzles consist of three of these turns.

Since the inclusion of this new move, it's become obvious that skaters find the forward inside twizzles a lot more natural, and easier to skate well, than the forward outside twizzles. This is partly because the free foot closes easily to the inside of the skating foot on inside twizzles, whereas on outside twizzles it has to be pulled in to be close to the outside of the skating foot.

It's a common error for a skater to rock onto their toe-picks after they turn to backwards on forward outside twizzles, much more so than on forward inside twizzles. I'm firmly of the belief that muscle memory is partly to blame for this, because a twizzle is a rotating movement, and when we go into a basic scratch spin from a forward outside three turn, we are accustomed to grabbing the ice with the bottom toe pick as soon as we turn to backwards. It works for a spin, but it's not what you want on a twizzle.

On previous moves I've explained about the way we need to use the full rocker of the blade to make clean turns, but because the blade is going to be turning so much faster on a twizzle, there is no time to do this. Therefore, you'll find it's best to go into the twizzle just behind the middle of the blade, and then rock slightly forward, back, forward through the three quick turns the blade makes, without actually using the full length of the blade.

This rocking should only be felt in the foot, and not by rocking the body forwards and backwards.

And now some comments about the head.

For many skaters, it's human nature to want to look down to see what's going on. Try to resist this temptation, and look straight ahead as you go into your twizzle, with your head held nicely, and your eyes level. Ballet dancers realize the importance of holding the head in alignment with the body. And try not to turn your head before you twizzle. It should rotate *with* your body.

Finally, take the opportunity to re-group - physically and mentally - on the rolls, especially the rolls on the inside twizzles after stepping forward.

RECOMMENDED INTRODUCTORY STEPS:

There are no introductory steps for these twizzles. They start from a standstill on the long axis, and commence with a roll.

THE MOVE

FORWARD OUTSIDE TWIZZLES

The outside twizzle move can get quite 'swingy' if you don't control your arms and free leg, and it's all too easy to toe-push on the cross stroke. Personally, I don't think a cross stroke is a good idea on this move, but that's how it must be skated, so make sure you push from the outside edge of the blade, and not the toe pick. Many skaters I've seen actually turn *out* their pushing foot (incorrect) and end up pushing from the inside edge of the blade.

Take things in order. This move starts with a forward outside roll, and then a cross stroke into a forward outside twizzle.

After you push onto the roll, hold your free leg back at first, and then only bring it through in time to cross stroke on the long axis. Normally, a cross stroke is considered to be a power stroke, but on this move power is not the object. And, normally, on cross strokes I usually advise an opposite hip and shoulder movement. That is, when the free leg comes around to cross, the opposite arm and shoulder rotate forward at the same time, making a counteracting movement. However, this is a different situation, so the method I use is as follows:

As the free leg comes around to cross stroke, let the free arm and shoulder come around, too, so that they are now in front of you. Then as you push from the outside edge of the back foot, you can let your arms and shoulders start rotating back the other way for the twizzle. It's almost like 'winding up' one way, to release back the other way. Not that you need to do this very strongly for a twizzle.

When you place your foot on the short axis, be careful not to make the lobes too big, otherwise you'll have a long wait back to the axis after the twizzle. Also, be careful not to lean into the circle too much. Just like on a basic scratch spin, the body must be perpendicular to the ice when twizzling.

Keep in mind that you don't have to twizzle the moment you step onto the edge, so take advantage of the fact that you have just enough time to find your balance after you push onto the lobe. (This advice also applies for the Inside Twizzles). The twizzle turns around the top of the lobe, so you have time to make a decent cross stroke – and even extend your free leg afterwards – before bringing your free foot in for the twizzle. You shouldn't feel like you're throwing yourself into it.

Working on the principle of a basic scratch spin, whereby the arms and free leg are held out to begin with, and then pull in to increase the rate of rotation, try letting your body start to rotate a little as you start the edge, and then draw in your free foot and arms close to the body to speed up the rotation. The good news is that you are not expected to twizzle right at the beginning of the edge, so you have time to use the method described.

There are no rules on what the skater must do with their arms, hands, and free leg on these twizzles, but, clearly, a body rotates more efficiently, and looks better on a twizzle, if the hands and free foot are brought in close to it. I like to see the fingers and thumb touching the thighs, the elbows a little away from the body, and the free foot held close to the ankle of the skating foot, but there are many other ways of holding the arms, and some of them can be quite stylish. Theoretically, though, a skater rotates faster when the hands and free foot are brought in close to the body.

In my opinion, if the free foot is held too high the skater's legs can look 'stork-like', but I believe that in Synchronized Skating this is the 'norm', so if you're involved in that sport, don't worry if you hold your free foot a little higher. You don't have to change how you hold it if it doesn't cause a problem. The last thing I want is for an army of Synchronized Skating coaches to come down on me like a ton of bricks!

One thing you don't want is to have your free foot circling around the skating foot, far away from the vertical axis that runs through the body. If your free foot is 'loose' it could throw you off balance.

Skate into the twizzle just behind the middle of the blade, and draw your arms and free leg close to your body, as previously described, to start the rotation. Because of the speed of rotation, you need to be checking out of the twizzle as you're turning the last turn, so try to think this way: turn, turn, check - or 1, 2, 3, checking out on 3, with your free shoulder, arm, and hip checked back, and your free foot turned out. With your body in this position, you should have no trouble stepping forward on the long axis, with your blade on the short axis. You have to time the checkout in much the same way as you do when landing a jump. If you time it too late, your hips and shoulders will rotate around too far after the twizzle, and you'll find yourself with your back to the long axis. In this position you'll find it very difficult to step forward correctly, and will probably put your foot down going back in the direction you've been skating.

Step forward on the long axis in the same position that you used for the first outside roll, and then repeat twice more, finishing with a final roll.

After you've completed this set of twizzles, wait for the judges' signal before repeating on the opposite foot.

FORWARD INSIDE TWIZZLES

For most people who rotate counter clockwise in their spins and jumps, the left forward inside twizzle is sometimes a bit of a problem because it just feels unnatural, and it's almost like having to learn to skate all over again. But, the good news is that you don't have to twizzle the moment you step onto the edge. You have time to feel your alignment over your skate, and then twizzle around the top of the lobe.

Start this move by skating a forward inside roll with the skating arm and shoulder leading. You could start with the free arm leading, and then switch your arms as the free leg comes through, but on the inside rolls that follow the twizzles I advise skaters to already have their skating arm leading when they step forward.

After you push onto the roll, bring your free leg through so that it's extended in front of you. At the long axis, draw your free foot back to your skating foot, and then skate the following movements in this order: Start with your free arm in front of you, and then push onto the twizzle edge. Next, start the rotation with your arms and shoulders as described on the outside edge twizzles, and then draw your free foot in to your skating foot so that it's held close *by the time you're twizzling*. You'll probably have no problem holding it close when rotating your 'good' way, but you may not feel well-enough balanced to draw it in when you twizzle your un-natural way.

The method I described earlier, of starting the rotation with the arms and fee leg out, and then pulling in for the twizzle, seems to feel easier on the inside twizzles. You can get a nice push, extending your free leg while you start the rotation, and then pull the free foot in close to your ankle and draw in your arms to rotate quickly.

As your upper body rotates, your hips will 'catch up' with your shoulders by the time you're twizzling, so that your hips and shoulders are parallel to each other. Your body should now feel like it's rotating in one piece.

Once again, you need to feel that 'forward-back-forward' movement on the blade, and not get onto that bottom toe pick.

You'll be turning one and a half revolutions, ending up on a back outside edge, so you need to know when to check out. I recommend checking out with the arms and shoulders fairly square to the tracing, so that your body doesn't over-rotate. Your free leg should be held back with nice extension (like a jump landing position), a little outside the tracing.

If your body over-rotates after the twizzle, it may cause you to turn a back three turn as you step forward onto the next forward roll. This is incorrect. Hold your position until just before the long axis, and then open your free shoulder and arm back a little so that you can step forward with your new foot on the short axis. Even if you don't feel totally in control when you step forward, you have time to re-group on that inside roll before you step onto the next twizzle.

PROBLEM AREAS:

- Failing to maintain correct alignment through the body.
- Leaning too much into the circle, causing the skater to fall off the edge.
- Over-rotating the exit of the forward outside twizzles, causing the skater to turn their back on the long axis.
- Stepping forward well before the long axis.
- Starting the twizzle as soon as you start the edge, instead of letting the edge run, and then twizzling around the top of the lobe.

Pattern 5

INSIDE SLIDE CHASSE PATTERN

Primary Focus: Edge Quality
Secondary Focus: Extension

Inside Slide Chasse Pattern

The skater will perform four alternating patterns of inside slide chasses preceded by backward power three-turns. The pattern should cover the entire length of the rink. Introductory steps are optional.

Focus: Edge quality and extension.

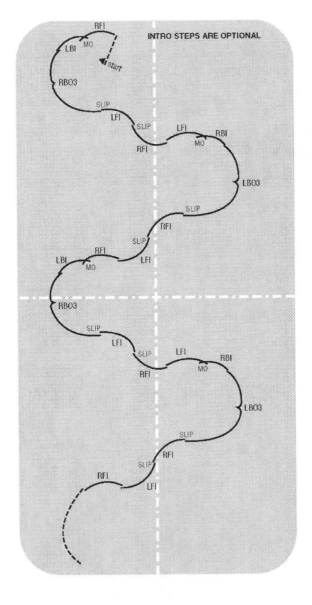

COMMENT

This move is 95% about the slide chasses, and 5% about the Mohawks and back three turns between them. You won't have slide chasses on any other move, so the judges want to see you get them right on this one. They already know you can turn forward inside Mohawks and back outside threes. The sliding action on solid inside edges, and the 'rip' sound, are two of the most important aspects of this move, so be prepared to skate this move with strength.

I can't stress how important it is to make good use of the skating knee on this move. It can either make it, or break it. You need to 'sink' into the skating knee on the slide chasses, because this will increase the pressure of the blade on the ice, and create the 'rip' sound the judges are looking for. You'll also find that skating the slide chasses on strong edges actually makes this move easier – certainly more secure - and almost guarantees the 'rip'.

Without leaning back, skate a little bit further back on the blade than normal on these slide chasses (with more weight on the heel than the ball). This presses the blade into the ice, which also helps to get that 'rip'. This, too, should also make you feel more secure.

RECOMMENDED INTRODUCTION STEPS:

Left, right, left, across the end of the arena, then push into a RFI Mohawk. Add another right stroke at the beginning if you can't gain enough speed.

THE MOVE

This move is often skated far too carefully, so skate into it with a little more 'gusto', as if it were part of a freestyle program. Push into the mohawk, and the back three turn, just like you did on the back power threes in the Juvenile test, because, apart from maintaining your speed from the use of the knees on the actual slide chasses, these are your only power strokes.

The move starts with a right forward inside Mohawk, followed by a right back outside three turn that should be on the top of the lobe.

Most of the time we check a Mohawk turn, but as this particular Mohawk is followed shortly afterwards by a back outside three turn, I advise you not to check too much. Instead, as you turn the Mohawk, let your arms and shoulders continue rotating so that they'll be prepared for the back three turn, but do not let your hips rotate.

Through the three turn, hold your free leg nicely extended in front of you, over the tracing. By making these movements, you should find yourself in much the same position you were for the basic back outside three turn on the Pre-Juvenile move.

You *can* check the Mohawk, but as the back turn happens shortly afterwards, you're going to have to start rotating your arms and shoulders immediately to prepare for it, so why not just let the upper body rotate at a smooth rate through the Mohawk to the turn?

You should be performing this back three turn at greater speed than you would the back turn on the Pre-Juvenile move, so make sure you're solidly over your skating hip and foot. Push onto a well-bent knee, and then only rise a little to allow you to use the rocker of the blade to turn. Remember, balance near the ball of the foot before the turn, quickly lift back to the heel as you turn, and then go immediately back to just behind the middle of the blade as you exit.

You need to be well in control of this back three, because at greater speed you'll feel more force as you exit the turn, and the first slide chasse follows immediately afterwards. I've noticed many skaters find it hard to make that first slide, so that's why it's best to increase your knee bend after you come out of the turn, and then be able to rise slightly to 'un-weight' your foot to enable it to slide easily.

The good news is that, after you turn the three turn, you have to wait until the edge comes around enough to be heading in the right direction, slightly diagonally across the ice, before you start the first slide. Slide chasses are on inside edges, but if you change feet too soon after the back three to start the first slide, your new blade may go onto an outside edge before it rocks over to an inside edge. Use this time to increase your knee bend, and switch your arms from the checked position after the three turn (passing them fairly close to the body), so that your skating arm is now over your extended free leg. This will enable you to feel coordinated as you switch your arms on each of the following two slides. There is an alternative way of turning the back outside three, and that is not to check your arms and shoulders, but to let them rotate with the turn so that you come out with your skating arm already in front of you. This latter method works just as well, but needs good hip control, otherwise the body can over-rotate.

Now we come to the slide chasses.

A slide chasse should be a very easy thing to perform, but it's not a matter of 'pick up and extend'. It's all about sliding your foot forward past your other foot before it leaves the ice, and then extending your free leg further in front of you. (Toe pointed and slightly turned out, of course).

Slide chasses are quite different to anything you've done before, unless you've already used them in a footwork sequence. Since you started skating you've been told, basically, that you must 'push back to go forward', so there is the temptation to push back, or even sideways, instead of sliding forward when performing these chasses. So, try not to push back. There is no 'power' in a slide chasse, except that which comes from the use of the skating knee.

The foot that's going to slide is the foot on which you're skating. Therefore, to avoid the mistake of simply picking up that foot and extending your free leg, you need to keep your weight on it longer. It should still be on the ice as it slides past the new foot on which you're going to skate. Then, the weight transfers completely onto the new foot as your free leg extends in front of you over the tracing.

Very simply, the order of movement is: rise a little, step slightly wide onto an inside edge, slide and sink into the new knee, and bring your opposite arm over the extended free leg.

It's important not to rise too much, because you need to be sinking into the new knee as soon as you change feet. There should still be weight on the skating foot, but, rising up on the skating knee enables you to transition onto the next edge in much the same way a skier 'un-weights' their ski when they are changing direction, *but only rise a little*. Just enough to 'un-weight'. You still need to feel 'into the ice', otherwise you'll look, and feel, too stilted.

I've explained before that you can gain speed – or at least maintain what speed you have – by the use of your skating knee, so on these slide chasses you can help maintain your speed by pressing up on the knee against the inside edge just before you slide. It's a little bit like the feeling you get when you press up against the inside edge on forward power pulls, but you're not going to come up on the knee anywhere near as much.

On each slide chasse hold your skating arm over your free leg, but don't let your other arm pull back behind you. It will only have further to travel to get back in front of you on the following slide. So, by placing your arms in an 'L' shape, your free arm will be to your side, and you'll be able to switch your arms on each slide without too much movement. Be careful, also, not to let the shoulders turn too much.

This may seem contradictory to my advice on previous moves, but don't lean into the inside edge. Rather, keep your upper body well over your skating hip, which is *almost* like leaning outside the edge. It may seem odd, but it works well on slide chasses.

If you're on a well-bent knee at the end of the second slide chasse, you'll be able to stroke (push back) strongly into the following left forward inside Mohawk. DON'T treat this edge as a slide chasse. You'll miss a valuable power stroke.

You need this Mohawk to set up the lobe on which you'll be turning the left back outside three, so make sure you push onto a good inside edge, and then go through the same procedures as on the first Mohawk and three turn. That is, letting your arms and shoulders rotate around in preparation for the three turn, and then switching them after you've checked the turn to start the next set of slide chasses.

If you push into the Mohawk on a straight line you might end up too far across the rink, and turn your three turn well before the top of the lobe because your edge hasn't curved around enough.

After the back three turn, use the same technique for performing the slide chasses as before, except that you'll be starting on the other foot.

Once you've completed this set of slides, skate into a right forward inside Mohawk to repeat the two sequences, making a total of four.

After the last left back outside three turn and two slide chasses (RFI & LFI), skate a right forward inside edge to complete the move.

PROBLEM AREAS:

- Not using the Mohawk to help set up the lobe for the three turn.
- Making the three turn early, causing the exit edge to head in the wrong direction.
- Not bending the skating knee enough to produce the 'rip' sound.
- Losing control after the three turn, causing the first slide chasse to be stepped.
- Breaking at the waist on the slide chasses.

TRICK OF THE TRADE:

If you're having trouble getting the right feeling for the slides, here's a little trick of the trade that may work.

You've probably seen children playing at being wooden soldiers, marching on the spot, extending their leg in front of them with the opposite arm moving forward at the same time. I incorporate this in a three stage exercise to try to give the skater the right feeling for slide chasses.

First, on the flat of the blade and with straight knees, skate in a straight line down the ice, making that marching movement, 'slipping' the foot forward to leave the ice. Second, continue the 'slipping' movement, but start making your blades go onto inside edges, still with fairly straight knees. Third, start bending the skating knee while maintaining the 'slipping' movement on inside edges. This should gradually give you the coordinated feeling and rhythmic movement you need.

FIVE DOWN, THREE TO GO!

You've now been through the first five levels of Moves in the Field, so, congratulations! You're well on your way up the ladder, and not too far from the top.

I hope I've been able to help you understand and master the first twenty-seven moves of this necessary discipline, and that you've found my advice both informative and logical. I also hope that the skills you've learned have helped you to skate confidently, and will continue to serve you well on the remaining moves.

By now, you should have developed more strength and better control, and this should stand you in good stead for the final three levels of moves. Naturally, the moves become more difficult and present new challenges, but you'll be able to draw on many of the techniques you learned at the lower levels to help you master them. There will, however, be elements you haven't come across before, such as forward and backward loops, rockers, counters, toe steps and Choctaws, to mention just a few. These new elements should be looked upon as a new and exciting challenge, and I'm sure you'll meet that challenge with success. Now, it becomes even more important that you improve the quality of your skating.

Novice Moves in the Field Test

1. Inside three-turns/rocker choctaws The move should be skated across four semi-circles down the long axis of the rink. The first two lobes consist of FI and BI three-turns and the second half of the move will consist of rocker/choctaw sequences. Four to five 'sets' of each turn per lobe are recommended. The skater will begin with RFI3-LBI3 sets repeated four to five times (depending on rink size). After the last LBI3 the skater should step RFI and begin the second lobe with a LFI3-RBI3 set and repeat in the same manner. To transition to the rocker/choctaw sequences, the skater should perform LFI mohawk and change edge to RBO crossing in front. The third lobe begins with a LBI rocker/LFI closed choctaw set repeated four to five times (depending on rink size). After the last choctaw and cross front, the skater should step RFI and perform a RFI mohawk and change edge to LBO cross forward. The fourth lobe consists of RBI rocker/RFI closed choctaw sets repeated four to five times. Introductory steps are optional. This move may start in either direction. Focus: Power and quickness

2. Forward and backward outside counters The skater will perform forward outside counters followed by two backward free skating cross strokes to a backward outside counter. Each backward counter is then followed by two forward free skating cross strokes to a forward outside counter. The skater has the option of starting the first length with either the right or left forward counter. The second length will be performed with forward and backward outside counters on the opposite foot. The introductory steps and complete loop are optional. Focus: Edge quality and power

3. Forward and backward inside counters The skater will perform forward inside counters followed by two backward inside rolls to a backward inside counter. Each backward inside counter is then followed by two forward inside rolls to a forward inside counter. The skater has the option of starting the first length with either the right or left forward counter. The second length will be performed with forward and backward inside counters on the opposite foot. The introductory steps and the end patterns are optional. Focus: Edge quality and power

4. Forward loops The move may be skated across the width or down the length of the rink and begins from a standing start. The skater will begin with a LFO swing roll to prepare for the first RFO loop. The skater then pushes into a LFO loop when returning to the axis. This is repeated twice. After the last LFO loop the skater should perform a RFI chassé to prepare for a LFI loop. This loop is followed by a push into a RFI loop. These loops are also repeated twice to complete the move. This move may start on either foot. Focus: Edge quality and continuous flow

5. Backward rocker choctaw sequence The skater will perform a backward inside rocker-choctaw followed by a deep backward outside edge. This sequence is performed in six to eight consecutive half circles on alternating feet. The introductory steps are optional. This move may start on either foot. Focus: Edge quality, extension and power

6. Backward twizzles Backward outside twizzles: The skater will begin with a LFO three-turn changing edge into a LBO double twizzle with a two-foot push to assist the twizzle rotation. The skater then steps forward into a RFO three-turn, changing edge into a RBO double twizzle, completing a 'twizzle set'. Each 'twizzle set' is performed three times down the length of the rink. BI Twizzles: The second part of the move begins with a RFI mohawk whose exit edge is the entry for a LBI double twizzle. The skater then steps on a RFI edge into a LFI mohawk whose exit edge is the entry for a RBI double twizzle, completing a 'twizzle set'. Each set is performed three times down the length of the rink. This move may start in either direction. Introductory steps and end pattern are optional. Revised 7/1/2010

COMMENT

In my opinion, the progression from Intermediate Moves to Novice is the biggest barrier to break through. Although the number of moves in the Novice test has been reduced from seven to six, it still represents quite a challenge. When you have mastered, and passed, this test, you are well on the way to becoming a good skater.

Pattern 1

BACKWARD AND FORWARD INSIDE THREE TURNS/ROCKER-CHOCTAW SEQUENCE

FOCUS: POWER, QUICKNESS

Inside Three-turns/Rocker Choctaws

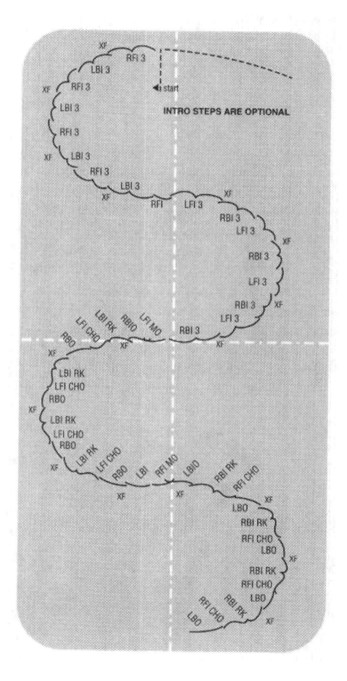

This move may start in either direction

RECOMMENDED INTRODUCTORY STEPS:

Three power strokes (left, right, left) across the end of the rink, toward the midline, should be enough to attain the right speed to start this move.

COMMENT

A higher standard of skating is expected now that you're at Novice level, so it's going to be really important to keep up good flow throughout this move, especially through the first two lobes of forward inside/back inside three turns, because it's not so easy maintaining that flow through the remaining rocker/Choctaw lobes. Therefore, use your introduction steps to achieve the necessary speed, and then try to carry it through the relatively easy forward inside/back inside threes on the first half of this move. If you can do that, you'll have some flow into the more difficult rocker/choctaw section. And, even if you lose a little of that speed on the first half, you should still be able to maintain enough flow to make the move presentable.

Every time I watch this move performed, the skater starts with the right forward inside three, but as you're allowed to start this move in either direction you may well want to experiment starting on the other foot, with a left forward inside three. It may not make much difference, but the fact is that most skaters are much more comfortable rotating counter-clockwise, so they skate the first lobe easily with good flow, but are then a bit more cautious on the clockwise rotating threes. This means that they lose flow, and go into the rocker-Choctaw section slower than they should.

If you should turn things around, and skate the right forward inside/left back inside threes on the second lobe, then you have a good chance to gain flow as you do them. This will enable you to start the rocker/Choctaw section with ample flow, and the final rocker/Choctaws (left back inside) should help you finish strongly. Having said this, I must admit that I've never yet seen a skater start with a left forward inside three.

You are allowed either four or five sets of forward inside/back inside threes, and four or five sets of rocker/Choctaws, but, as one the focuses is 'quickness', it will be more impressive if you use five sets, turned a little more quickly, than four slower - possibly more deliberate - sets. Of course, if you have very good flow across the ice, you'll only need four sets. Because you'll be skating into the beginning of this move with a fair amount of speed, you'll need to set out the pattern carefully so that you don't end up too far down the rink after the first two lobes. Too much speed on the introductory steps could cause you to make these lobes too big, and you'll probably need to start right up at the end of the ice surface in order to skate the correct pattern.

One final word of caution on this move. You obviously need to skate strongly, but try to skate quietly. It's usually very quiet at a test session, and it's easy for the blades to make a lot of noise. On the opening forward and backward three turns the judges will hear if your turns are scraped, or if your toe pick rips into the ice as you stroke under when you cross in front, or, worse still, if you 'slap' your foot down onto the ice when you cross in front. You need to 'place' you new foot on the ice. The *good* thing about a test session being quiet is that the judges will hear the necessary 'rip' sound more easily, on moves that involve power pulls, slide chases, etc.

THE MOVE

I'll describe this move starting with the RFI three turn, which means you will be rotating counter-clockwise.

After the three introduction strokes, start the move on the midline by stroking into a RFI three turn, with the free leg extended back over the tracing. As you push, start the rotation of the arms and shoulders, and then rise on the knee to turn, leaving the free leg over the tracing. Don't try to check these turns, but rather let the body rotate at an even rate throughout the turns, albeit in a controlled fashion. As soon as you turn to backwards, bring your free foot down to cross in front for a LBI three turn, stroking down on the knee a little. This will enable you to rise for the back turn. On the forward threes, lift to the front of the blade, and then back to the ball, and on the back threes, lift to the heel, and then back to just behind the middle of the blade.

When you cross in front for the back turn, try to get an under stroke from the outside edge of the right foot. This will help maintain your speed, but you'll find that the stroke into the forward three is usually the stronger, and easier, one.

Draw the free foot close to the skating foot as you're making the back turn, so that your blades are parallel. This makes it tidier, and also makes sure you'll be ready to stroke onto the next forward inside three, instantly balanced over the new skating foot. Because there is a continuous rotating movement, you will now be able to turn out your pushing foot as your hips rotate, and not toe-push into the forward turn.

Once you get going, you should get into a nice rhythym, timing the rise on the knee with the steady rotation of the body, so that your foot turns easily and quietly. You should push just enough to maintain an even flow. You also need to feel that you have perfect posture (not hard on these turns), and that your body is turning 'in one piece'. As you'll be skating a reasonably large arc, there is no lean of the body, so you should keep your shoulders parallel to the ice.

After the last back three, push onto a RFI edge, and then a LFI edge to start the LFI - RBI turns.

You'll now be rotating clockwise on these turns, so you have to immediately get oriented into letting your body turn the other way. Use the same technique on these turns as on the first lobe, and slightly check the last RBI three turn so that you can be in control as you push into a LFI Mohawk to transition onto the rocker/Choctaw lobes. Try to get a power push into this Mohawk to help you keep up flow. As soon as you check the Mohawk, immediately bring the left foot in front to cross in front onto a LBI rocker. As your left foot moves to cross in front, the RBI edge of the Mohawk should rock over onto an outside edge so that you can get an under stroke from the outside edge of the blade to keep up the flow of the move.

The second half of this move incorporates a 'twisting action' of the body on the rocker-Choctaws, whereby the shoulders check against the rotation of the hips and feet, much like you feel when you turn consecutive brackets on one foot. Using this twisting action effectively will help you create the rotation for the rocker turn, and help you turn back again on the Choctaw.

When you cross in front to turn the LBI rocker, move your free arm in front of you on the circle, and your skating back a little, but not too far. It's easy to rotate the arms and shoulders too much for this turn, and it's not necessary. Rise up on the knee and lift to the heel to turn, immediately checking the arms and shoulders against the hips. Additionally, as you turn, draw your free foot in close to the heel of the skating foot in a 'T' position (free instep to skating heel), but leave the free foot turned out. You will now be able to turn the Choctaw to backwards with the free leg extending forward in readiness for the next cross in front. If the feet are in a 'T' position, the free foot is out of the way of the skating foot as that foot leaves the ice.

The 'Quickness' required in this move refers to the speed the feet turn, and not to the speed of the skater across the ice. That 'twisting action' I mentioned earlier will help you achieve this.

Once again, it depends on the speed you're traveling, but if you use five rocker/Choctaws you'll have to turn them nice and quickly, which should make a good impression, but if your speed across the ice is good, four may suffice very nicely. Whether you use four or five sets of turns, after you turn the last Choctaw you need to cross in front on a back inside edge, and then step forward, near the midline, on a RFI edge to start the rocker/Choctaws on the opposite foot. You'll notice that you probably have your right arm in front of you when you check that last Choctaw, so when you cross in front you need to rotate your right arm and shoulder back so that you lead with it into the RFI Mohawk that starts the remaining rocker/Choctaws.

Use the same method on the second set of rocker/Choctaws as you used on the first, placing the free arm on the circle in front of you as you cross in front for the back inside rocker.

You need to have enough flow to make it to the midline after four or five sets of turns, so try to get some power on that under stroke, and keep your turns from being scratchy. The blade needs to flow without interference.

PETER DALBY

Remember that these rockers turn from back inside to forward inside, and the Choctaw turns onto a back outside edge. These edges won't be very steep, but make sure that they are correct.

PROBLEM AREAS:

- Getting on the toe pick on the back inside threes.
- Making the first two lobes too big, causing the skater to be well past the red line (halfway down the rink).
- Losing flow on the rocker/Choctaws, resulting in the last lobe finishing well before the midline of the rink.

Pattern 2

FORWARD AND BACKWARD OUTSIDE COUNTERS

PRIMARY FOCUS: EDGE QUALITY

SECONDARY FOCUS: POWER

Forward & Backward Outside Counters

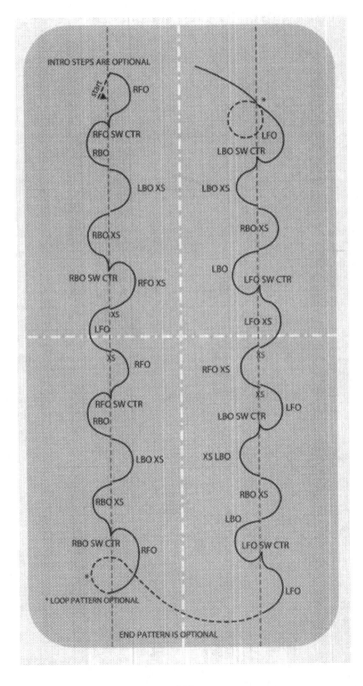

This move may be started on either foot, but I'll describe it as starting with the RFO counter.

RECOMMENDED INTRODUCTORY STEPS:

Left, right, left, right, across the end of the rink, then a left outside edge to bring you around to the long axis. You can then cross stroke onto the edge for the RFO counter.

COMMENT

- One dictionary definition of the word 'Counter' is: 'In a contrary direction or manner'. Basically, it means 'opposite', or 'opposing'.
- On *all* counters, the counter rotation needed for these turns is made with the upper body, against, and opposite to, the hips, and against the curvature of the edge. A counter is actually a 'forced' turn, inasmuch as you will not be rotating naturally with the circle, as in a three turn, but against it. The hips need to go with the edge and help it curve, while the upper body, especially the shoulders, rotate in the opposite direction to prepare for the turn.
- If you can remember how you prepared your body position for the brackets on the intermediate test, then you'll know how to be in the right position for the counters.
- Counters and cross strokes require a coordinated movement of the upper and lower body. There's a lot of 'opposite' movement going on, so you'll find that you won't be able to counter-rotate correctly before the turn if your arms and shoulders are already counter-rotated at the beginning of the edge.
- If you counter-rotate correctly, you should find your shoulders almost parallel to the end of the rink just before the turn, with your chest facing down the long axis. You should also find it easy to see the long axis to place your turn correctly.
- VERY IMPORTANT. On outside counters, try not use your free leg too forcefully before the turn, because this can pull

your edge too far (thank you, Lauren, for helping me make this important point, and thank you, Lily, for realizing that you don't need to make an extra 'kick' of the free leg if your shoulders are counter-rotated strongly enough). It's all very well being taught to skate strong edges, but if your edge is too strong approaching the counter, and retrogresses (making an 'S' pattern on the ice), you're probably going to change edge before the turn. Your counter then becomes a change-edge three turn. Rely more on the counter rotation of the upper body to help you turn. Have a look at your tracing on the ice, because the evidence is there. Just before your counter, the tracing should be no more than ninety degrees to the long axis. The curve of the edge you set from the cross stroke should remain constant right up to the turn.

- Talking of edge quality, lobes don't have to be large to show edge quality, but they do need depth of edge, and consistency of curvature.

- Try to keep the opening lobes the same size as the lobes you'll be repeating down the ice. After gaining speed on the introduction strokes, it's all too easy to make the lobe into the first turn much too big, and then have to squeeze in the remaining lobes. The same advice will apply on the Junior level Rockers.

- As a guideline, if you can place your first back turn before, or no further than, the red line (halfway down the rink), then you should be able to fit in the last back turn before you get to the end of the rink. The same advice applies to the inside counters.

- 'Looping around' at the end of each set of turns doesn't mean making a small loop like the loops in Pattern 4. It means letting the exit edge of the last back turn continue around until it crosses itself, as the diagram shows. To do this, hold your checked position after the last back turn and wait until the edge comes around to cross itself. It states in the rulebook that 'Looping around' gives extra credit.

THE MOVE

You'll need to skate this move with good flow, because you'll be expected to cover almost the full length of the ice surface. Therefore, start close to the end of the rink to make sure that you don't run out of room when you come to the last back turn.

After you've skated the introduction strokes (left, right, left, right), skate a strong left outside edge to come around to the long axis. When you reach it, skate a cross stroke onto the right forward outside edge, get over your skating hip, and lead with your free arm and shoulder, but not too strongly. Now we come to the necessary counter-rotational movement to prepare for the turn. The free leg is brought forward, not too wide of the tracing, and at the same time the free arm and shoulder rotate back, and the skating arm moves in front. When you extend your free leg before the forward outside counters, be careful not to let it 'pull' the edge too steep, causing it to retrogress, or 'S'. If you do, you run the risk of the edge changing to an inside edge as you bring your free foot back for the turn. Therefore, it's essential to keep your blade on an outside edge right up until you turn, otherwise you'll be skating a change-edge three turn, which is not a counter. Counter turns must be outside edge to outside edge, or inside edge to inside edge.

Try to time it so that you achieve the counter rotated position just before you turn, and don't have to hold the position too long.

In the days of figure skating, a 'scissoring' movement of the free foot was used to push the skating foot deeper into the turn, but this is not necessary, or expected, on these counters. Just as on the Intermediate brackets, judges are not looking for deep turns. Just well-controlled ones, placed on the long axis on correct edges. However, a synchronized movement of the free foot does help, and should feel 'natural'.

To make the turn, I would recommend bringing the free foot back slightly behind your skating foot, by bending your free knee, and then immediately extend it forward in front of the skating foot as you exit the turn. Pulling your free foot back should 'push' your skating foot into the turn. Apart from demonstrating a nice synchronized free foot movement, this free foot position after the turn will help check your hips, so that your free hip is closed.

After you turn to backwards, you should have your free arm and shoulder in front of you, and your skating arm and shoulder checked back.

The other essential is to use the rocker of the blade correctly. Skate just behind the middle of the blade as you're approaching the turn, and then lift to the front of the blade as your foot goes into the turn. Immediately go back to the ball of the foot as you exit the turn. I have seen too many skaters take an unnecessary fall because they stayed back on their blades and 'caught' their outside edge.

After you turn, hold your free leg in an extended position, but release, and switch, your arms so that your free arm and shoulder go back, and your skating arm and shoulder come forward. Now, you'll be able to skate a natural opposite hip and shoulder movement when your free leg comes back to cross stroke, which is exactly the same movement I recommended on the back cross strokes in the Juvenile test.

Be patient while you're on this edge, and wait until it comes back to the long axis. The cross strokes start on the long axis, so if you cross stroke too early you'll shift your long axis to one side. One of the things the judges are looking for is that you start all edges on the long axis, and place your turns there, too.

Skate two cross strokes, which will now put you on the edge for the right back outside counter. You should be starting this edge with your skating arm and shoulder in front of you, and your free arm and shoulder back a little. Keep over your skating hip, and move your free leg back behind you, near the tracing, and then counter-rotate your upper body so that you press your skating arm and shoulder back, and your free arm across your chest. You should now find your shoulders parallel to the end of the rink just before the turn. Draw your free foot in close to your skating foot, and lift from the ball of the foot to the heel to turn to forwards, and then back to just behind the middle of the blade while checking the turn so that your skating arm and shoulder is leading, and the free arm is held back. Immediately after you turn, stretch your free leg back again to be extended behind you.

Counter turns are greatly helped by a strong counter-rotation of the upper body, and it should help a lot if you press back your skating arm before the back outside turn, and then release that 'twist' feeling you have at your waist in order to turn.

Use the same method of holding the free leg extended while you release and switch your arms, as you did after checking the forward turn, so that you're ready to skate two forward cross strokes with an opposite shoulder and hip movement to repeat the forward and back turns once more.

As you stroke the second cross stroke, you're now going to repeat the forward and backward turns, so that there are two forward and two backward turns on each side of the rink. Use the same method to prepare for the turns as you did at the beginning.

After the last back turn, hold the checked position and wait until the edge loops around to cross itself so that you're now facing across the rink. Skate across the end of the rink to the long axis that you'll be using for the left forward and backward counters, and skate onto a left forward outside edge for the counter. Just as on the right forward outside counter, start the edge with your free arm and shoulder leading, so that you can counter-rotate to make the turn. From here to the end of the rink, repeat the same movements you made on the right turns, but this time on the left foot. Forward turn, followed by two cross strokes, backward turn followed by two cross strokes, and then repeat so that you perform two forward and backward turns on each side of the rink on opposite feet. Once again, judges are supposed to give extra credit if you loop around after the last back turn.

PROBLEM AREAS:

- By far, the most common fault is a distinct change of edge before the forward outside counter, caused by a rocking over of the body as the free foot is brought back for the turn. This now becomes a change edge-forward inside three turn.
- Not keeping the start of each edge, and the turns, on the long axis. This can be caused by cross stroking too early, and by skating the first lobes too big.

- First lobes skated too big, causing the skater to 'shrink' the final lobes in order to fit in the last back turn. Losing flow through the move will also cause the lobes to decrease in size.
- 'Catching' your edge (mostly on the outside counters) by not using the rocker of the blade properly. Getting a bruised hip from a fall caused by catching your edge will quickly make you learn your lesson.
- Pulling the free leg too much before the turns, causing the edge to retrogress into the circle.

Pattern 3

FORWARD AND BACKWARD
INSIDE COUNTERS

FOCUS: EDGE QUALITY

SECONDARY FOCUS: POWER

Forward & Backward Inside Counters

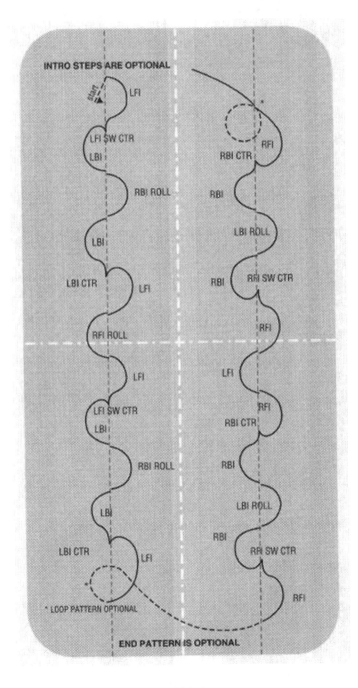

INTRO STEPS ARE OPTIONAL

LFI

LFI SW CTR

LBI

RBI ROLL

LBI

LBI CTR

LFI

RFI ROLL

LFI

LFI SW CTR

LBI

RBI ROLL

LBI

LBI CTR

LFI

* LOOP PATTERN OPTIONAL

RFI

RBI CTR

RBI

LBI ROLL

RBI

RFI SW CTR

RFI

LFI

RFI

RBI CTR

RBI

LBI ROLL

RBI

RFI SW CTR

RFI

END PATTERN IS OPTIONAL

220

This move may be started on either foot

I'll describe it with the left foot turns on the first side of the rink.

RECOMMENDED INTRODUCTORY STEPS:

Left, right, left across the end of the rink, and then a right inside roll starting on the long axis to bring you back to the long axis to start the move with the left forward inside counter.

COMMENT

I've always found that inside counters are more 'friendly' and natural than outside counters, and I think they're easier to control because the free foot is *inside* the circle at the turns, and is less likely to be loose or 'swingy'.

There needs to be edge quality on the rolls. It's easier to do this on the forward rolls, but many skaters skate straight down the rink on the back rolls because they don't aim the heel out enough, away from the long axis. If you can do this, it will help you set a nice edge at the beginning of the second roll, and this will give you the necessary curvature into the back turn.

THE MOVE

The lobes need not be too big, but they should be skated on strong, solid edges.

After you've skated the right inside roll to bring you around to the long axis, push onto a left forward inside edge for the first turn as if you were skating a basic forward inside edge. That is, with the skating hip and free arm leading, and the free leg extended back. Now, make the very basic movement of switching your arms at the same time you bring your free leg through to be leading over the tracing. This should be the same movement you made on the forward inside edges on the second move in the Pre-Preliminary test, keeping your edge curving beautifully around toward the long axis where you'll place the turn.

Switching your arms when your free leg comes forward makes for a nice coordinated movement, but as we need to prepare for the counter, don't switch them very far. (Let your free arm go back only as far as the side of your body). Once you've done this, start switching your arms again, rotating your free arm and shoulder so that they are now leading, just as they would be for a forward inside bracket.

This may seem like a lot of movement for one lobe, but there is time to change your arm positions smoothly, and it does allow you to create a nice 'wind-up' of counter rotation leading up to the turn. The alternative is to leave your free arm and shoulder leading from the beginning of the lobe to the turn, and then just check them back as you turn.

As you're approaching the turn, you should be able to glance down the long axis to see where to place it, and when you reach that point your shoulders should be parallel to the end of the rink.

It's important to synchronize a free foot movement with the turn, but you only need to move the lower leg, keeping the knees fairly close together. Bend your free knee to pull your free foot back just behind your skating foot as you go into the turn, rocking to the front of the blade, and straighten your free knee and extend your free leg over the tracing as you come out of the turn, going to the ball of the foot. This should create a quick 'scissoring' movement through the turn.

After the turn, you should have your free arm and shoulder checked back, and your skating arm and shoulder in front of you, both arms on the circle. Hold this position and wait until you come back to the long axis, where you'll skate two back inside edges, each one starting on the long axis. The second one (left back inside) will be the edge for the first back inside counter, but first a word about the back inside rolls.

These edges should be considered power strokes, to keep the move flowing, but try not to make a long swizzle-push onto them. They need a sharp, powerful push, not leaving the pushing foot on the ice too long. As soon as you've pushed, move your free foot behind so that the toe is close to the heel of the skating foot, and simultaneously move your free arm in front of you, with your skating arm back a little. You also need to turn your toe in a little - or your heel out - when you step down on the edge to make sure the blade's on an inside edge. It's not uncommon for skaters to put their foot down on an outside edge that changes to inside.

When you push onto the next roll, switch your arms so that your free arm is in front, and your free foot is held by the heel of your skating foot (opposite position of the previous edge). You're now setting the edge for the left back inside counter.

To prepare for this turn, keep well over your skating hip and wait until the top of the lobe before you rotate your free arm and shoulder back, at the same time bringing your skating arm in front of you. Many skaters counter-rotate too quickly and too soon before this turn, causing their foot to turn early. You must also be careful not to open your free hip as you counter-rotate your upper body because it could cause a change of edge before the turn. (Remember my axiom - 'Where your hips go, your skate will usually follow'). Just keep your hips fairly square as you counter-rotate your shoulders against them. Make sure, also, that the movement of rotating back your free arm and shoulder doesn't cause you to lean out of the circle. This could also cause a change of edge before the turn. If you were going into a back inside bracket, you wouldn't (I hope) dream of leaning out of the circle before the turn. You would stay over the circle, so this is how you should feel before a back inside counter, even though you're going to change direction immediately after the turn.

Now let's think about what you're going to do with your free leg. Not too much, is my best advice. I recommend extending it back a little before the turn, and keeping it low (too high causes your free hip to lift and tilt the body), and then drawing it in close to the skating heel for the turn. Lift from the ball to the heel into the turn, and quickly back to just behind the middle of the blade coming out. Check your free arm and shoulder in front, and bend you skating knee so that you can immediately extend your free leg across the tracing behind you, outside of the new circle. Your skating arm should be checked back a little behind your skating shoulder.

As on the forward turn, you should be able to glance down the long axis to place your turn correctly.

As your edge comes back to the long axis, switch your arms and bring your feet together in readiness to push onto a right forward inside roll. Skate this like a basic forward inside edge, switching the arms as the free leg comes through to extend in front. From here, you're now going to repeat the left forward inside counter, followed by the same two back inside rolls to the left back inside counter.

After you check the last back turn, hold the checked position, and let the edge loop around before bringing your free leg through to extend in front, switching your arms as you do so.

To skate the forward counters on the other foot, skate across the end of the rink to the long axis you'll use, and stroke straight onto a right forward inside edge for the first turn. No roll is needed before you skate this first turn. Then go through the same movements as on the first side, but reverse all the instructions to make the turns on the other foot.

PROBLEM AREAS:

- Changing lean going into the turns, making them change-edge three turns.
- Shifting the long axis by not waiting to finish the lobe.
- Stepping too straight onto the back inside rolls.
- Pulling or kicking the free leg before the back turns, causing the skater to tilt.

Pattern 4

FORWARD LOOPS

FOCUS: EDGE QUALITY, CONTINUOUS FLOW

Forward Loops

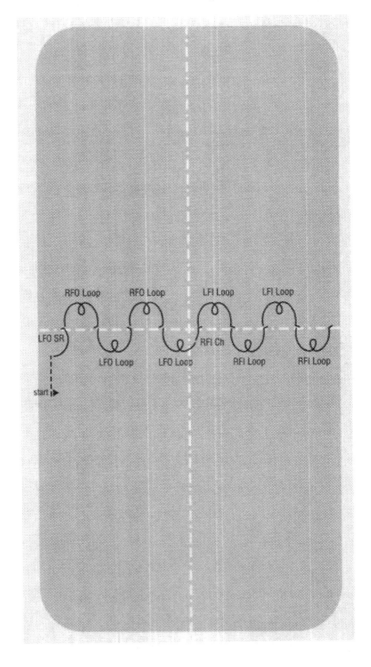

This move may be started on either foot

RECOMMENDED INTRODUCTORY STEPS:

There are no introductory steps. The lobes start on the long axis, preceded by an outside swing roll.

COMMENT

Now we come to a move that seems to strike fear into the hearts of some skaters. Loops! But try not to worry. They're really quite harmless. You will, however, need good balance, a correct starting position, and also patience, because you'll need to wait until you're well into the loop before you try to get out of it. In very simple terms, you have to be able to hold a steady, balanced position to the top of the loop, and then control the way you bring your free leg forward, switching your arms and shoulders to counteract that movement.

Technically, a loop can be defined as 'a single edge that crosses itself'. In order to do this, the circumference of the circle has to decrease (tighten up) to the point where the edge will cross itself. Therefore, I must differ from the rule book and make this bold statement. A loop is *not* a turn. Not in the strict sense of the word. The blade doesn't turn from forwards to backwards, or vice versa. Now, admittedly, you could argue that on a Mohawk or Choctaw the blade still doesn't make a turn, and yet it's called a turn because our body turns from forwards to backwards, or vice versa. On a loop, however, neither the body nor the blade makes a turn. That is, not in relation to the edge. They just keep going forward or backward. The body does, however, rotate 360 degrees in relation to the ice surface, because it follows the edge around as it curves into the circle in order to cross itself, and then follows it out again.

In the days of school figures, the loop was placed on the long axis, halfway around the circle. This gave the skater ample time to prepare to enter the loop, but the forward loops in Moves in the Field are positioned at the top of a semi-circle (lobe), so it's essential that you start off with your arms and shoulders in the right position, because there's very little time to adjust your body position once you start the lobe.

As I mentioned earlier in this book, it's important to move what's necessary, and keep the rest still, and loops are a great example of that wonderful saying 'less is more'. You really need to let the edge do most of the work, and be patient, especially around the top of the loop where you have to keep your hips and core very still. (Thank you, Juliet, for learning to be patient, and letting the edge do the work around the top of the loop).

At first, think of the loop in two halves. Around to the top, and then out.

On both outside and inside loops, a well held free leg can be a very useful balancing aid. Take advantage of this. However, the movement of the free leg is quite different on outside and inside loops. On these outside loops, your free leg is going to remain straight, and then be brought level with the skating foot at the top of the loop before extending forward over the tracing. On the inside loops, your free leg is going to be held straight at first, but then bent so that it can be brought inside the loop beside the skating foot. It will then be held still, until the blade has gone around the top of the loop before it is brought forward.

Be careful not to move your free leg too quickly, especially on the inside loops, because it can cause your loop to 'spin' around. And try not to rotate your body any more in the loop. Just keep still, and 'ride' the edge as it does its work.

It stands to reason that the blade should slow down a little to go around the top of the loop due to the tightness of the edge, and then speed up again as you press up on the skating knee to come out.

Another, quite important, aspect of skating these forward loops is your balance point on the blade. You should feel you're gliding on the middle, or just behind the middle, of the blade when you start the lobe, and then press very slightly forward to the ball of the foot around the top of the loop so that there is less blade on the ice. As you exit the loop, go back to the middle, or just behind the middle, to finish the lobe.

THE MOVE

The move can be performed down the length of the rink, or across the ice surface on the blue or red lines. It commences with an outside roll, followed by four alternating forward outside loops, and four alternating forward inside loops.

I've never seen any skater perform these loops down the length of the rink, so I'll describe them being skated across the red or blue lines, starting with the right forward outside loop. This is preceded by a outside roll on the left foot.

Basically, to skate loops consistently, you need to start in the right position and hold it until you reach the top of the loop.

With regard to your body position, you should find that your upper body is facing into the circle going into these loops, and out of the circle coming out.

The size of the lobe, from the long axis to the top of the lobe, should be a bit less than the height of the skater. The loop itself should be about a skate's length wide, and one and a half skate lengths long, from the top of the loop to the cross of the loop.

You can start the outside edge roll that precedes the loops with either arm leading, but make sure that your left arm is in front at the end of it, ready to start the right forward outside loop. My feeling is that, as you're going to be switching your arms as you exit the loops, you may as well get into the rhythm of things by doing that on the starting roll, too, so start that edge with your free arm in front, and your skating arm back. Make sure your skating foot is on the short axis, and then push onto a lobe. Rise up a little as you bring your free leg forward, and switch you arms so that your free arm is now in front, and your skating arm back.

Start the right forward outside loop with your left arm and shoulder leading, and your right arm and shoulder back. Place your right foot on the short axis, but get on an outside edge right at the start of the lobe. A semi-circle doesn't start on a straight line, so if you go straight and then try to curve, you may throw you body out of alignment and end up off your skating hip.

After you push onto the edge, your free leg should be held back, and your skating knee bent a little. Keep well over your skating hip, and increase your knee bend when you are about a third of the way into the lobe. This will make the edge tighten up and curve into the circle to take you to the top of the loop. At the same time, go from just behind the middle of the blade to the ball, so that there is less blade on the ice. This makes it easier for the blade to go around the smaller circumference of the top of the loop. At this stage, you should still be maintaining your arm and shoulder position, with your left arm and shoulder leading in a clockwise direction during the loop. As you enter the loop your extended free leg needs to move slightly outside the circle, but be careful. On outside loops it's very easy to come off your hip when you move your free leg.

After you go around the top of the loop, move your free leg forward so that your free foot is over the tracing, and reverse your arms and shoulders. This movement should help check any over rotation of the edge out of the loop. At the same time you bring your free leg forward, rise up on the knee and hold your position until you reach the long axis. Your arms will now be in the correct position for the start of the next loop on the other foot.

To skate the left forward outside loop, repeat the method used on the right foot, but do everything the other way around. Right arm and shoulder leading; skating arm and shoulder back; increase the knee bend to enter the loop; hold the free leg until the top of the loop; rise up and bring the free foot in front over the tracing; reverse the arms and shoulders to check against the free leg.

You will now repeat the right and left loops once more, and then prepare to skate a chasse in order to skate the left forward inside loop.

A chasse is merely a change of weight from one foot to the other. In this case, it's used to make the transition from the last left forward outside loop to the left forward inside loop. It's the bridge between the two loops.

As you finish the left outside loop, keep your arms and shoulders in the checked position and bring your free foot beside your skating foot. Change your weight onto your right foot in order to push onto the lobe for the left forward inside loop. Perform the chasse just before the long axis so that you start the left forward inside edge *on* the long axis.

Start the lobe with your arms on the circle, skating arm leading and free arm back. You need to hold this position until just after the top of the loop, so don't let your arms and shoulders 'square off' as you enter it.

The free leg is held back and extended at the start of the edge, trailing the skating foot. A third of the way into the lobe, increase your knee bend and draw your free foot close to the heel of your skating foot, so that it will be inside the loop until it leads the way out. Expect your skate to slow down a little as it goes around the top of the loop. Your free foot will be held still, momentarily, until you pass the top of the loop, and then it leads the way out of the loop as you rise up on the knee.

Think of the free foot movement as 'drawing' a loop inside the loop itself, and even though your free knee is bent, keep the toe of your free foot pointed from the start of the lobe to the end. It just feels 'right' to lead the way out of the loop with a pointed toe.

After the free leg comes forward, over the tracing, switch your arms so that your free arm and shoulder are now leading, with your skating arm and shoulder held back. Try to 'ease up' on the knee to come out of the loop, and not snap up on the knee or make a jerky movement.

Keep your arms in the same position until you reach the long axis, and then push onto a right forward inside edge for the right forward inside loop. Repeat the method used for the left loop, but do everything the other way around. Right arm and shoulder leading; free arm and shoulder back; increase the knee bend to enter the loop; bring the free foot inside the loop and hold it until the top of the loop; press up on the knee and bring the free foot in front over the tracing after you exit the loop; reverse the arms and shoulders to check against the free leg.

Repeat one more left and right loop, and then finish with a nice stop.

As in many aspects of skating, the timing of your movements on these loops is all-important. As you gain experience, you'll develop a nice timing of setting the edge, bending your skating knee, and then rising up and using your free leg to bring you out of the loop. Loops are, however, one the more difficult moves to keep consistent.

TRICKS OF THE TRADE:

- Using the red or blue lines, skate consecutive outside edge lobes across the rink, without the loops, starting with your free arm and shoulder leading, and then reversing your arms and shoulders as the free leg moves in front.
- Do the same again, but on inside edge lobes with no loops, starting with your skating arm and shoulder leading, and then reversing them when your free leg comes through.
- To get used to being over your skating hip on an outside loop, glide onto the lobe on two feet, with your skating knee well bent, and your free leg held back straight and outside the circle, but still on a running edge. Your free leg now becomes like the training wheels on a bicycle. Your free arm and shoulder need to be leading, with your skating arm and shoulder back, so that your upper body is facing into the circle. When you get around to the top of the loop, rise up on the skating knee and bring your free leg through in front of you, off the ice. Reverse your arms and shoulders as soon as your free leg is in front.
- As an exercise, push onto a circle that decreases in size, like you were in a whirlpool going around and around until you almost get to the center. Stay in your first position and wait until your edge tightens up and then bend your skating knee to make a loop.

PROBLEM AREAS:

- Skating too fast into the loops.
- Swinging the free leg around too wide on the outside loops.
- Moving the free leg too soon, especially on the inside loops.
- Starting the loop too late on the lobe.

Pattern 5

BACKWARD ROCKER CHOCTAW MOVEMENT

PRIMARY FOCUS: EDGE QUALITY, EXTENSION

SECONDARY FOCUS: POWER

Backward Rocker Choctaw Sequence

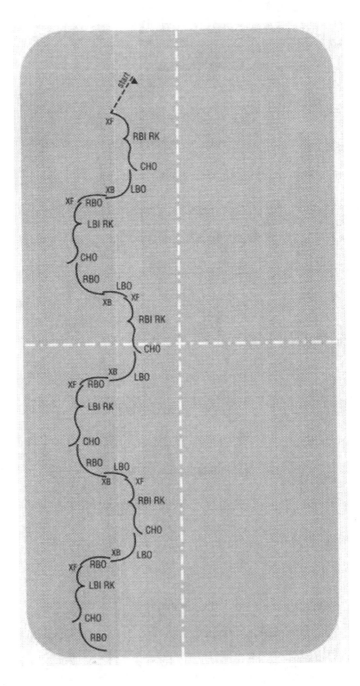

This move may start on either foot.

RECOMMENDED INTRODUCTORY STEPS:

I'll describe this move starting with the right back inside rocker.

Standing on the midline, and between the two circles at the end of the rink, I like to have the skater perform a left edge, followed by a right forward inside Mohawk, and two back crossovers, the last of which will bring the skater around far enough to be able to cross the right foot in front, on the long axis, to start the move with a right back inside rocker.

COMMENT

This is a move of long flowing edges, with no 'quickness' required. The skater is required to skate six to eight lobes down one side of the rink, but a good skater will only need six lobes to complete this move. This move can be very impressive if the skater has good flow, but having said that, be careful not to make the first couple of lobes too big – the result of building up a lot of speed on the introductory steps – because you could find yourself halfway down the rink after performing only two lobes, and then have to squeeze in the remaining lobes to perform a minimum of six. Try to make six to eight evenly sized lobes, with the same continuous flow throughout.

The other common problem is that some skaters slow down after two or three lobes, which causes the remaining lobes to shrink in size.

I recommend some very 'set' positions of the arms and shoulders on this move, which I'll list at the end of 'The Move'. These positions should make you feel comfortable, and not twisted or forced.

The only places to get any power to maintain speed are the cross behind, and the cross in front. You can, however, get a slight leverage off your skating foot as you turn the Choctaw to backward.

THE MOVE

Starting on the long axis, you're going to be skating a lobe that incorporates a back inside rocker, and a forward inside Choctaw.

Simultaneously, cross in front onto a right back inside edge, and bring your free arm in front of you on the tracing. I want to stress that you don't need to rotate your shoulders as strongly to prepare for a simple back inside rocker, as you would if you were winding up for the entry into a forward spin. Your free shoulder only needs to be slightly forward, and your skating arm and shoulder slightly back. You shouldn't need to have your free arm way across your chest.

Make sure that you bend your skating knee and extend your free leg when you stroke onto the edge for the rocker. You have time to do this because you need to wait until you're on the top of the lobe to make the rocker/Choctaw turns. You should also get a certain amount of power from the stroke of the back foot as you cross in front, rather as you would winding up for a spin, but not rotating the upper body anywhere near as much.

To turn the rocker, rise up on your skating knee and draw your free foot in close behind your skating foot into a 'T' position just as you turn, with the free foot turned out (free instep, or ball, to skating heel). As you turn the rocker, you should have the feeling that your free foot is right underneath you, in the perfect position on which to turn the Choctaw.

In addition to this, checking your arms and shoulders correctly against the rocker turn will ensure that they're in the right position to help you turn again to backward on the Choctaw.

To use the blade correctly, go from ball to heel as you turn the rocker, and then turn to the ball of the left foot after you turn the Choctaw.

Turning the Choctaw should be a matter of just 'swiveling' the feet in that 'T' position, and checking your arms and shoulders so that they are back in the same position as they were just before you turned the rocker, except that you'll now be on the other foot. Left arm in front (which is now the skating arm), and right (free) arm and shoulder checked back. And, very importantly, getting good alignment over your left (skating) hip.

If your free foot is behind the heel of the skating foot before the choctaw, it won't be in the way of the foot that's coming off the ice as you turn, and you'll be able to extend your new free leg in front of you, with the heel just outside the tracing. Make sure you check, and stay checked, out of the Choctaw, until you finish the lobe at the long axis.

Your free leg will be in front after you turn the Choctaw, but it's optional what you do with it for the remainder of the back outside edge. It's absolutely fine if you leave your free leg extended in front until it's time to bring it back to cross behind, but there is another option you can try. As this is the longest edge in the move - and remembering that one of the focuses is 'extension' - I would recommend that after you've first extended your free leg forward, you then extend it back, keeping the free knee straight, the toe pointed and slightly turned out. Be careful, though, not to let the backward swing (extension) of the free leg tip your body forward. You also need to stay on a solid back outside edge until you get back to the long axis.

At the end of this edge, bend a little, so that you can get a push from the skating knee as you cross behind - you should feel as though you're pressing upwards against the ice - and cross behind to a straight knee. By being up on the knee after you cross behind, you'll be able to re-bend that knee to stroke onto the next edge. Next, you need to do two things simultaneously.

When you cross behind on the long axis, change your weight over to your new skating hip and - this is the next important position - move your arms and shoulders to be completely square to the tracing, with neither side in front or behind. It's really important not to completely reverse the position of the arms and shoulders as you cross behind, because this can make you feel too 'twisted', and make it difficult to cross in front on the next edge. Just concern yourself with being over your new hip, and starting the new lobe. Then, bring the free arm in front when you cross in front for the back inside rocker on the other foot.

You're now going to repeat the same movements as the first lobe, but on the other foot, with a left back inside rocker, and a left forward inside Choctaw. After you've completed this lobe, keep repeating the lobes until you're near the end of the rink. As stated earlier, you're required to skate six to eight lobes, so by trial and error you'll find out how large to make them, and how much flow you need. If you get to the end of the rink in less than six lobes, then you are either skating extremely fast, or your edges are going straight down the rink without enough curvature. And if you haven't got near the end of the rink skating eight lobes, then you're skating far too slowly, or your lobes are too small.

In conclusion, the four set upper body positions I want you to clearly define are as follows:

1) Before the back inside rocker –

Free arm in front on the tracing, skating arm back, but not too far. This should make an angle of about 135 degrees between your arms. Shoulders slightly rotated.

2) Checked position after the rocker –

Skating arm in front of your chest, free arm checked back a little. Again, keeping an approximate angle of 135 degrees between your arms.

3) Checked position after the Choctaw –

Skating arm in front on the tracing, free arm checked back, again making that 135 degree angle. Shoulders rotated so that your skating shoulder is forward, and your free shoulder is back in line with your free arm.

4) Position after the cross behind –

Arms and shoulders completely square to the tracing, but the upper body in alignment over the new skating hip.

This is followed by a cross in front to skate the lobe on the other foot, where you will repeat the same positions.

PROBLEM AREAS:

- Stepping, and therefore not getting any power on the cross behind, and cross in front.
- Losing flow during the second half of the move.
- Scratchy turns.
- Turning the rocker/choctaw early.

Pattern 6

BACKWARD TWIZZLES

FOCUS: TURN EXECUTION, CONTINUOUS FLOW

Backward Twizzles

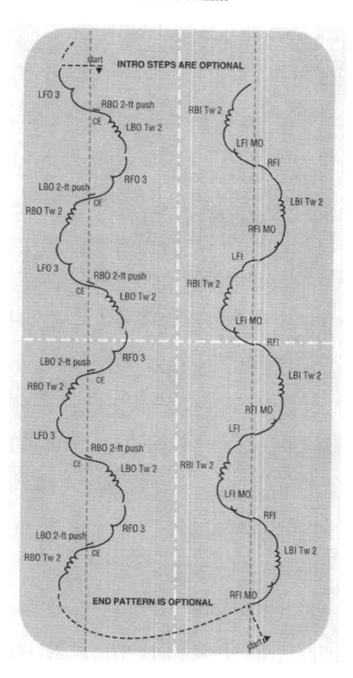

This move may start in either direction (meaning on either foot)

RECOMMENDED INTRODUCTORY STEPS:

I would recommend no more than two strokes before the three turn that starts the first side. That should be enough to achieve the required flow.

COMMENT

This move needs a certain amount of flow because you only have three sets of twizzles on each foot, and you'll be expected to get most of the way down the ice by the time you've finished the last one. You're required to skate three back outside twizzles on each foot down the first side of the arena, and three back inside twizzles on each foot down the second side of the arena.

Each twizzle is two revolutions, starting backward, and ending backward. The blade actually turns four very quick consecutive three turns, but you need to be thinking of checking out on the fourth turn – one, two, three, check out – or you may find yourself over-rotated after the twizzle. Keep in mind that it can only be called a twizzle if there is continuous rotation from when the body starts turning.

Obviously, with your body turning this fast, you need to be immediately aligned over your skating hip, with hips and shoulders level to the ice. You may find it helpful to focus on (spot) something just before you start your twizzle, to know that your head is 'one piece' with your body by the time you start twizzling. And you'll have a much better chance of rotating your twizzles quickly if you bring your hands and free foot in close to your body. You won't rotate very quickly if they are left wide and loose.

THE MOVE

BACK OUTSIDE TWIZZLES

I'll describe this move starting with the left back outside twizzle.

From about two thirds of the way across the end of the rink, skate two strokes to the long axis. When you reach it, skate a left forward outside three turn with your skating arm leading and free leg extended, almost as though you're going into a salchow jump. When the back inside edge of the three turn reaches the long axis bring your free foot beside your skating foot, on the ice, and allow your arms to rotate a little, counter-clockwise, to prepare for the push onto the left back outside twizzle. This movement of the arms is similar to that of a ballet dancer, as they wind up one way, in order to pirouette the other way (not that there needs to be a very strong wind-up).

From the three turn to the start of the twizzle, stay in perfect alignment over your left hip, even though you'll need to have some weight on your right foot to push properly.

To start the twizzle, rotate your arms and shoulders clockwise, and make a short swizzle push outwards, away from your skating foot. Your free foot should then be brought in close to your skating foot *by the time you start rotating*, and your arms and hands brought in close to your body, so that everything is near to the vertical axis around which you're rotating. Make sure that your hips 'catch up' with rotation of the upper body, so that during the twizzle your hips and shoulders are parallel to each other.

When you push onto the twizzle, be very careful not to let the swizzle push cause your pushing foot to end up behind you. This can cause severe alignment problems. It needs to take the shortest possible route to your skating foot without swinging around. Be careful, too, not to fling your arms around to start the rotation. Any movements you make with your arms and free leg mustn't interfere with your body alignment.

Fortunately, your blade doesn't start twizzling the very moment you start the edge. You actually have a split second longer(!), which should give you just enough time to get centered over your twizzling foot.

There are several different positions in which you can hold your arms and hands. I prefer to see the fingers and thumb touching the sides of the thighs, elbows held out a little, but you can also bring your hands in front of you, a little away from you chest, as if in the air position of a jump. The important thing is that everything is held totally still as you twizzle.

This is one of the many moves where the positions of the arms and free leg are left up to the discretion of the skater, so let your creative juices flow, and experiment with a variety of different positions.

You'll be rotating quickly on this twizzle, and it's crucial that you step out of it onto your new foot at the right time, so timing plays an important role. As I stated earlier, your twizzle is two revolutions, starting backwards, and ending backwards, and your blade is making four tiny consecutive turns. If your timing is late, your blade may turn an extra turn to forward before you can step forward, which is not correct. You start backward, and should end backward, so you must be checking out as your blade turns the fourth turn. Think, turn, turn, turn, out (1,2,3, out).

At the end of the twizzle, keep your back perfectly straight, and check out after two revolutions as if you were landing a jump – but stay up on the knee – with your free leg extended, arms and shoulders fairly square to the tracing.

Keeping on the lobe, immediately step forward onto a right forward outside three turn, free leg extended, and hold that position until you reach the long axis. When you reach it, bring your free foot beside your skating foot, on the ice, and let your arms rotate clockwise a little to make that wind up movement again, this time for the right back outside twizzle.

You're now going to repeat the same movements to skate the right foot twizzle, i.e. short, precise push; free foot and hands in close to the body; check out after two revolutions; immediately step forward onto a left forward outside three turn to return to the long axis.

Once you've completed these first two twizzles, repeat the same technique again on the remaining four, alternating on each foot.

The first side of this move should have a nice feeling of 'weaving' from one way to the other as it progresses down the ice.

When you come out of the last twizzle you don't have to skate another three turn, so you can step forward and skate nicely across the end of the rink to start the back inside twizzles.

BACK INSIDE TWIZZLES

When you reach the long axis for the back inside twizzles, skate a right forward inside Mohawk to begin the lobe. I have a simple, but very effective, method that works well on these twizzles, when it comes to checking out and stepping forward correctly and easily. It's all about where your hips and shoulders are facing, in relation to your skating foot, as you rotate during the twizzle.

As you turn to backwards, check the turn (with your free leg extended) so that your skating arm and shoulder are in front, and your free arm and shoulder checked back. Make sure you feel well-centered over your skating hip. You'll only be holding that checked position for a split second, during which time you should be looking over your skating arm momentarily, and not turning your head around to the way you'll be rotating. Keep you free leg low after the Mohawk, otherwise it can tilt your body forward, and be careful not let your 'muscle memory' bring your free leg around, 'salchow-style'. The free foot just needs to take the shortest possible route to be close to the skating foot for the twizzle, and not swing around.

To perform the twizzle, draw your hands and free foot in close while still keeping your skating hip and shoulder slightly in front, and your free hip and shoulder slightly back. If you can maintain that position - free side slightly back in relation to your skating foot - during the twizzle, you'll find it easy to check out because your free hip, shoulder and arm are already back. You just have to snap your arms out as you check. In this position you'll then be able to step forward on a right forward inside edge without having to turn your body at all. Your right side, that was checked back after the twizzle, now becomes the leading side on the forward inside edge. This should make it easy for you to finish the lobe back to the long axis.

You need to have very quick reflexes to know exactly when to check out of the twizzle. It's important to keep your free foot close to your skating foot, but the moment your blade turns that final turn, you must quickly extend your free leg back on the tracing, and check back your free hip, shoulder and arm.

Try not to be scratchy when performing your twizzles. It's easy for the judges to see if your blade isn't turning cleanly.

As I mentioned on the previous twizzle moves, the blade does make a series of tiny turns, but they happen so fast that there is no time to use the full rocker of the blade. Therefore, starting at the ball of the foot – because you're going backwards – use a short section of the blade to lift slightly back, forward, back, forward, during the four tiny turns the blade makes.

I've already mentioned that, after the twizzle, you should be stepping forward onto an *inside* edge to finish the lobe. The problem that sometimes arises is that many skaters don't start their lobe on the long axis. This makes the Mohawk late, which means the twizzle doesn't start until the top of the lobe, so by the time the skater checks out of the twizzle they've finished the lobe, and have no option but to step forward on an outside edge. This takes them past the long axis, and then the whole process of being late starts all over again on the new lobe, so try to avoid this problem by starting your Mohawk on the long axis.

Finally, be careful not to fall inwards as you exit the back inside twizzles. It's easily done.

When you finish the lobe back to the long axis, bring your feet together, and switch your arms so that you can now lead into the left forward inside Mohawk with your skating arm and shoulder leading. You're now going to use the same movements you made on the left back inside twizzle, but this time on the other foot. Briefly, check the Mohawk, keeping your skating side slightly in front, draw your hands and free foot in close to twizzle, check out with your free side back, and step forward on an inside edge with your skating arm and shoulder leading back to the long axis.

When you reach the long axis, switch your arms again, and repeat the same process for the four remaining twizzles.

PROBLEM AREAS:

- Turning a back three turn (on outside edge twizzles), and *then* starting to twizzle. The twizzle must start right from when the blade starts turning.
- Twizzles rotated too slowly.
- Failing to keep the body in alignment when rotating the 'unnatural' way.
- Lack of control when checking out of the back inside twizzles.
- Scratchiness on the back inside twizzles.
- Back inside twizzles ending too far around the lobe, causing the skater to step forward on an outside edge.

Junior Moves in the Field Test

1. Forward and backward outside rockers The skater will perform FO rockers followed by two backward cross strokes to a BO rocker. This BO rocker is followed by two FO cross strokes to a FO rocker. The skater has the option of starting the first length with either the right or left forward rockers. The second length will be performed with the FO BO rockers on the opposite foot. There should be two forward and two backward rockers. Note: This move may start in either direction. The introductory steps and end sequence of steps are optional. Focus: Edge quality and power

2. Forward and backward inside rockers The skater will perform forward inside rockers followed by backward inside rolls to a backward inside rocker. This backward inside rocker is followed by forward inside rolls to a forward inside rocker for the length of the rink. The skater has the option of starting the first length with either the right or left forward rockers. The second length will be performed with the forward and backward inside rockers on the opposite foot. There should be two forward and two backward rockers. The introductory steps and end sequence of steps are optional. Focus: Edge quality and power

3. Power pulls The skater will perform a sequence of three power pulls followed by two quick twisting rockers. This sequence is then repeated consecutively down the entire diagonal of the rink. It is then performed on the opposite diagonal of the rink on the other foot. There should be a total of three to four sequences per foot. The introductory and end steps are optional. This move may start on either foot. Focus: Power and quickness

4. Choctaw sequence The skater will perform a choctaw sequence that covers the entire diagonal length of the rink and which is then repeated on the second diagonal. This sequence is performed with two consecutive choctaws that are then performed in the opposite direction. Introductory steps are optional. This move may start in either direction. Focus: Edge quality and power

5. Backward loop pattern Backward outside loops: The skater begins from a standing start with a LFO3 into three BI rolls. The last BI roll is followed by a RBIO change of edge into a RBO loop. The skater then performs a change of edge to push LBI into three more BI rolls followed by a LBIO change of edge into a LBO loop. This sequence should be repeated twice down the length of the rink. Backward inside loops: For this side of the move the skater begins from a standing start with a RFI3 into three backward outside cross strokes. The third cross stroke is immediately connected to a LBOI change of edge into a LBI loop. The skater then performs a change of edge to push into three more BO cross strokes, beginning with RBO. The third cross stroke is immediately connected to a RBOI change of edge into a RBI loop. This sequence should be repeated twice down the length of the arena. Introductory steps are optional. This move may start in either direction Focus: Edge quality and continuous flow

6. Straight line step sequence The skater begins from a standing start with two open strokes R and L. The skater will perform a RFO rocker and cross forward to LBI rocker, which enters immediately into a LFI counter. Next is a RBO double twizzle, stepping forward into a LFO Chassé to LFO swing counter. The counter is immediately followed by a cross in front to RBI, followed by three clockwise toe steps and another cross in front RBI. The skater then steps forward onto LFI and changes lobe with a 1-1/2 revolution RFI twizzle followed immediately by an edge pull to change edge into a RBI double-three. Finally, the skater pushes into a LBI rocker followed by a LFI rocker, and then a RBI loop. Sequence is to be repeated starting on the other foot. This move may start in either direction. Focus: Edge quality and continuous flow Revised 7/1/2010

COMMENT

In my experience, the three moves that need the most work -and control - are the outside rockers, Choctaws, and back loops.

The hips are more easily controlled on inside rockers, and the power pulls usually don't present too much of a problem if the skater is right over their skate on the rocker turns, and uses the rocker of the blade correctly, and quickly. The straight line step sequence only has a couple of places where control problems arise.

Pattern 1

FORWARD AND BACKWARD OUTSIDE ROCKERS

PRIMARY FOCUS: EDGE QUALITY

SECONDARY FOCUS: POWER

Forward & Backward Outside Rockers

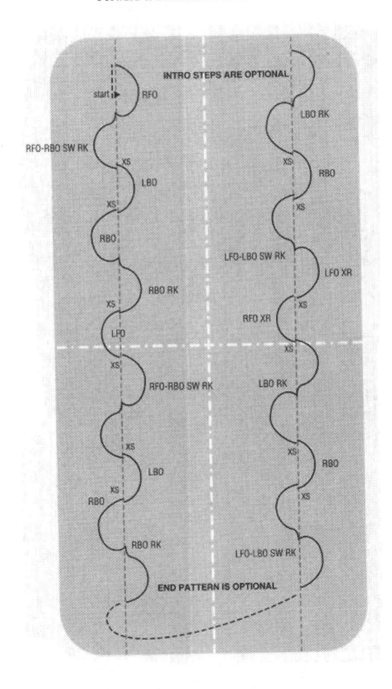

This move may be started on either foot

RECOMMENDED INTRODUCTORY STEPS:

(For starting with the right forward outside rocker)
Four strokes across the end of the rink (left, right, left, right), and
then a left forward outside edge to bring you around to the long axis.

COMMENT

Before all the rocker turns, rotate your shoulders further than
(against) your hips. Then, when you turn, you will be able to check
your shoulders against the turning foot, and there will be less hip
movement through the turn.

The lobes should be fairly equal in size, so your speed needs to be
even throughout. To achieve this, make sure you use the introduction
steps to start the move at a speed that you will be able to maintain from
start to finish, but be careful that your initial speed doesn't cause you
to skate a lobe that's way too big before the first rocker. If you do, you
may find yourself having to skate much smaller lobes further down the
rink, in order to fit in the last two turns.

As with the Novice counters, if you can turn your first back turn
before, or at the very latest, on the red line, then you should be able to
fit in the last back turn before you get to the end of the rink, and not
have to shrink the size of the final lobes.

THE MOVE

The first essentials are that you have a strong enough edge around
to the long axis (edge quality), and that you turn on the long axis
(correct placement). Therefore, you must have the feeling that you're
going across the long axis when you turn these rockers, and not straight
down the ice.

Cross stroke onto a right forward outside edge, with your free
arm and shoulder leading. You're upper body is now pre-rotated for
the turn. *Without rotating your hips*, bring your free leg through so that

it's in front of you on the circle. Your hips should be fairly square to the tracing, and you should feel a slight 'twist' at your waist. Your free knee can remain straight, and then bend immediately after you turn, or you can bend it in front of you before the turn (with the free foot slightly across the tracing), and then straighten it to turn, re-bending it immediately afterwards. Some skaters find the latter method gives them a nice rhythmic movement. Try both ways, and see which works best for you. After the turn, the free foot will be held back behind the skating foot, well turned out, and slightly inside the new circle.

If your hips are square to the tracing before the turn, you should be able to check you free hip back after the turn without too much difficulty, along with your free arm and shoulder.

To turn, simultaneously rise on the knee, lift to the front of the blade and then back to the ball, release the twist feeling you have at your waist, and check your free arm, shoulder and hip back. You should find your skating arm slightly across your chest.

The first control problem usually occurs after the turn, where some skaters finds it hard to hold that checked position without releasing it. If you can't hold it, and let your hips and shoulders start rotating the other way, you'll find it very difficult to curve your edge back to the long axis to finish the lobe.

The moment your foot turns the forward rocker, you should feel that you are checking your free hip back strongly, while keeping over your skating hip, as the lean changes strongly on the turn. Your free hip position should feel the same as when you turn to backwards on the Choctaw sequence, and when you check your free hip back like this, you should feel like you're squeezing the Gluteus Maximus muscles together.

Although the free foot and knee should be turned out after the turn, to compliment the open free hip, decrease the amount of 'turn out' by the time you cross stroke, otherwise you may actually retrogress on it. We want to keep moving down the ice surface. (Thank you, Rachel, for making me aware of that problem, and helping me fix it).

If you come out of your forward rocker with some knee bend, you'll be able to get the same power on the following two basic back cross strokes as you did in the juvenile moves test.

After you push onto the second cross stroke, you need to prepare for the backward rocker turn. Move your free foot back first, with the free toe held close to the skating heel, toe turned out. *Then* rotate your arms and shoulders, so that your free arm is pressed back, and your skating arm is in front of your chest. Towards the end of this rotation, increase your knee bend so that you can then rise through the turn, and then re-bend afterwards. Just before the turn, you should find your chest facing down the long axis, with your shoulders parallel to the end of the rink. This is a sure sign that you've rounded your edge adequately, and your upper body will stay facing the end of the rink as you go through the turn. During this preparation, leave you hips square to the tracing, so that you again feel that 'twist' at the waist.

To turn, rise on the knee, lifting from the ball to the heel, release the twist, and exit the turn going back to just behind the middle of the blade, with your free arm and shoulder leading strongly.

Through the turn, hold your free foot still, toe by the heel, until just after you check, then immediately extend your free leg back, a little outside the tracing. Your free leg position will help counter-balance the natural lean of the upper body.

Unless you come out of this first back rocker in a good position over your skating hip, and in reasonable control, it's hard to get power on the following forward cross stroke, but even if you wobble a bit, try to re-group so that you can get power on the second cross stroke, which will set up the second forward rocker.

You'll now repeat the forward and back rockers once more, making a total of four rockers (two forward, and two back).

Once you've completed the first side of this move, skate across the end of the rink to start the left foot rockers.

When you reach the long axis, stroke onto a solid outside edge, well over your skating hip, with your free arm and shoulder leading. Leaving your hips square to the tracing, bring your free foot through in front of you as you curve your edge around to the long axis, and then use the same free leg movement through the turn as you did on the other foot - straight, and then bend it after the turn, or bend it before and after the turn. As on the first side, you now have two cross strokes to the back outside rocker. After the second cross stroke, prepare for the turn the same way as on the first side, i.e. get on a solid edge, bring your free foot back by the skating heel with the toe slightly turned out, rotate your arms and shoulders so that your free arm is back, and your skating arm is in front of your chest. Lift to the heel and then back to just behind the middle of the blade through the turn, and check out strongly with your free arm and shoulder leading. Refer to the first side of this move for the smaller details.

All that remains is to skate two cross strokes, and repeat the forward and back rockers one more time.

TRICK OF THE TRADE:

For the back outside rockers - but not so much on the forward rockers - plan on rotating your upper body enough so that you're facing down the long axis just before the turn. Once your shoulders are parallel to the end of the rink, it's time to turn.

PROBLEM AREAS:

- Not being able to hold the checked position after the forward turn.
- Going into the turns too diagonally, with not enough curvature of the edge before the turn.
- Keeping a steady body position and edge after the back rocker.
- Not keeping alignment over the skating hip as the upper body rotates before the back rocker.

Pattern 2

FORWARD AND BACKWARD INSIDE ROCKERS

PRIMARY FOCUS: EDGE QUALITY

SECONDARY FOCUS: POWER

Forward & Backward Inside Rockers

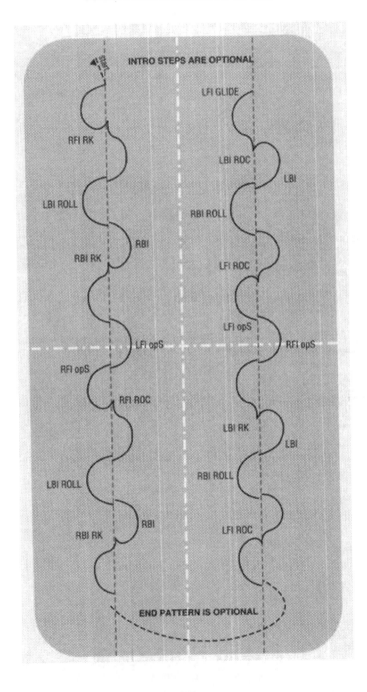

This move may be started on either foot, but I'll describe it starting with the left forward inside rocker.

RECOMMENDED INTRODUCTORY STEPS:

Across the end of the rink, left, right, left, and then a strong right forward inside edge to bring you around to the long axis to start the move.

COMMENT

Inside rockers are more 'user-friendly' than outside rockers, and I think this is because the free foot is mostly inside the circles, and doesn't have the chance to get loose, as it can do on the outside rockers.

When you stroke onto the inside edge for the forward turn, your free leg should extend back at the end of the stroke, but you then have a few options on how you move your free leg, and in what position you hold your free foot, before and after the turn.

Before the turn, you can hold your free foot close behind your skating foot - my preferred method - or you can bring your free leg through in front, as on a basic forward inside edge, but if you do that you'll still need to bring your free foot back behind your skating foot again before the turn.

After the turn, you can either keep your free foot held close behind your skating foot, or straighten your free knee and extend your free leg in front of you, with your free foot slightly outside the tracing. This free leg position helps keep the free hip closed (a very good example of where one part of the body can help control another part). I find both methods work well, but I slightly favor leaving the free foot behind, as long as you can check your hips well.

THE MOVE

After the introductory steps, including the right inside edge that brings you around to the long axis, stroke onto a solid left forward inside edge with your free arm leading. Simultaneously, bring your free foot close to the heel of your skating foot, with the toe pointed and slightly turned out, and rotate your arms and shoulders so that your skating shoulder is leading, and your skating arm is slightly across your chest. *Leave the hips square* so that, once again, you feel that 'twist' at the waist. Bring your edge around strongly to the long axis, and when you reach it, rise on the knee, lift to the front of the blade and turn to backwards, going immediately back to the ball of the foot. As you turn, check your skating arm, shoulder, and hip back strongly, and press your free arm across your chest.

If you use the alternative method of extending you free leg in front of you after the turn, check your free foot slightly across the tracing with the toe neutral, or slightly turned in, because we need to keep the free hip closed to enable us to hold that position back to the long axis. Although the free toe is slightly turned out before the turn, it's slightly turned in afterwards, so that, once again, the free foot position is dictated by the free hip position. The hips are just about square going into the turn, but the free hip is closed coming out of the turn. Before you reach the long axis, draw your free foot in close to your skating foot.

Hold that position, with good knee bend, and when you reach the long axis push onto a strong right back inside edge on a well-bent knee, and switch your arms so that your free arm is in front of you, and your free foot is held close behind your skating foot. This is the first back inside roll. When you reach the long axis, you're now going to push onto a left back inside edge (the second roll) to set up the back inside rocker.

Be careful, because it's all too easy to over-rotate the upper body as soon as you push onto this edge, and then have to hold an awkward, twisted, position until you reach the turn. Therefore, my advice is not to fully rotate the arms and shoulders at the beginning, but rather wait until you're nearer the turn to complete the pre-rotation. By doing this, you'll be able to create a nice rhythmic movement (rotate and bend, rise, turn, and re-bend) into, and out of, the turn. So, start the edge with the arms on the tracing, skating arm and shoulder back, looking where you're going, and then as you approach the turn, simultaneously press your free arm around to be in front of your chest, and increase the bend of the skating knee. You'll now be able to rise up on the knee to make the turn, going from ball to heel and back to just behind the middle of the blade, and have a rhythmic checking movement as you turn to forwards, re-bending your skating knee. After the turn, you should be leading with your skating arm and shoulder, and extending your free leg.

Just as on the back outside rockers, if your shoulders are parallel to end of the rink just before the back inside turn, and your chest is facing down the long axis, you'll know that you've rounded you edge adequately to set up the turn. Your foot will then do the turning, while your upper body will stay facing the end of the rink before and after the turn.

As you come back to the long axis, bring your feet together to push onto a right inside roll, and then skate a left inside roll to repeat the forward and backward inside rocker turns one more time. Make sure you start all the rolls on the long axis.

When you've completed the first side of this move, skate across the end of the rink to perform the inside rockers on the right foot. There will be no need for a roll before the first forward rocker, so skate onto a strong right forward inside edge with your skating arm and shoulder already leading, in preparation for the turn. From here, use the same technique as on the left foot, but now your turns will be on the right foot.

TRICK OF THE TRADE:

When it comes to knowing if you've brought your edge around enough before the back inside rockers, the same principal applies as on the back outside rockers. If your chest is facing down the long axis, and your shoulders are parallel to the end of the rink, it means your edge has come around far enough, and it's time to turn.

PROBLEM AREAS:

- Control problems (wobbly edges) after the forward and back turns.
- Putting the foot down on an outside edge when starting the back inside rolls, and then rocking over to an inside edge.

Pattern 3

POWER PULLS

PRIMARY FOCUS: POWER

SECONDARY FOCUS: QUICKNESS

Power Pulls

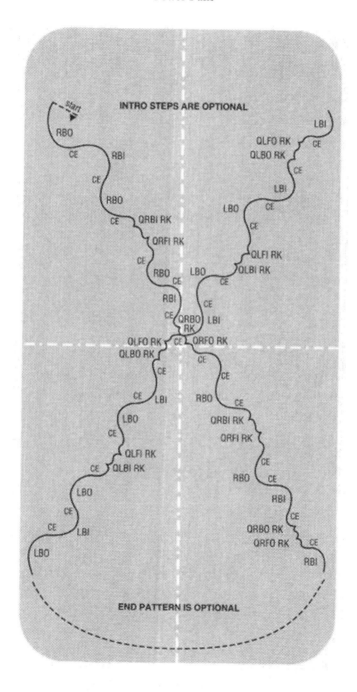

RECOMMENDED INTRODUCTORY STEPS:

This move can be started on either foot. I'll describe it starting on the right foot.

Starting on the mid-line of the rink between the red hockey circles, skate an edge on the left foot (can be flat), a right forward inside Mohawk around the end of the rink, followed by two back crossovers. This should bring you around enough to help you set up the Power Pulls in a diagonal direction, through the middle of the rink.

COMMENT

For a high-level move, this is one of the easier ones to perform. By the time a skater reaches this level, they have probably skated some pull change-rocker-rocker steps in a freestyle program or, at the very least, consecutive rocker-rocker turns.

The power should come from the power pulls between the rockers, and the necessary 'quickness' applies to the rockers, themselves. You don't have to rush the power pulls, just make them nice and 'edgy' by using your skating knee strongly, and controlling your hips. (Thank you, Savannah, for showing how Power Pulls should be skated in a test).

The free foot doesn't need to be close to the skating foot on the power pulls - maybe 6 to 12 inches behind the skating heel, over the tracing - but should be drawn in closer to the heel of the skating foot for the quick rockers. That way, it won't flap around loosely when you turn.

THE MOVE

After the last back crossover of the introductory steps - *and while you're still on a circle made by the crossovers* - step onto your right foot on an outside edge (first edge of the move), switch your arms so that your skating arm is now in front, your free arm behind, and take your free leg back behind you before you change edge onto the first power pull. Your arms and free leg will now be in the right position for the natural power pull movement.

Technically, the move starts with three power pulls, followed by two quick consecutive rocker turns. This sequence is to be repeated for the diagonal length of the rink. These pulls and turns are then repeated on the other diagonal on the other foot. There should be three or four sequences on each foot, but if they are skated with good flow, you may only need three.

Your body movement on the power pulls should feel exactly the same as it did on the Pre-Juvenile Power Pulls, but, hopefully, a lot stronger. And this is another move where you need to feel your that body is perfectly aligned over your skate.

Before you start the pulls you'll be on a back outside edge, so you'll pull onto an inside edge, then outside, then inside again for the two quick consecutive rockers. These will be inside edge rockers.

Make sure you have completed the edge change before you turn your rockers. I've seen many skaters letting their foot turn as they're changing edge, and are not set for the turns, so give yourself a split second to 'set', and feel right over your skate, before you perform the rockers.

There is a useful timing that gives a nice rhythmic movement to this move. When you pull the third time, you're 'setting' for the first rocker, so skate it this way: And one, and two, and set, turn, turn, and one, and two, and set, turn, turn, for the entire diagonal length of the rink. When you 'set', it means you have changed onto the edge for the rocker, and have rotated the shoulders just enough to be prepared for the turn. Then, it just requires a controlled twisting action of the hips against the shoulders to make the rockers turn quickly. I like to see the skater draw in their free foot close to the skating heel as the blade turns the first rocker.

At the speed you'll be traveling, it's essential that you work the rocker of the blade correctly. From ball to heel, and back to ball.

Try not to twist your body around too much on the power pulls. Skate them just as you did on the Pre-Juvenile test, but obviously with more power from your skating leg, and then rotate your arms and shoulders a little more to prepare for the rocker turns. So, on the power pulls, you should find yourself facing back down the diagonal line you've been skating along, and as you 'set' your upper body for the first rocker turns, you'll be facing a little more to the right.

After the consecutive back inside rockers, pull onto an outside edge, then inside, then outside for the consecutive outside rocker turns. Now you'll be facing a little to the left. Same principals again. Draw in the free foot, make a quick (but not too violent) twisting action of the hips against the shoulders, and use the rocker of the blade correctly.

Repeat the sequence of power pulls-rocker-rocker for the remainder of the diagonal line, and if you're skating in a rink with hockey markings, make sure you're at least inside the red circle at the end of the rink before you finish the first side.

It's optional whether you skate forward or backward across the end of the rink to start the move on the other foot, but I would recommend skating two backward crossovers (right over left) to come out of the corner, and then a push onto a strong right back outside edge to take you back to the corner on the other side of the rink. Follow this with two more backward crossovers to bring you around to perform the move on the opposite diagonal on the other foot.

Having described this move starting on the right foot, the second half of this move is performed on the left foot, and is a mirror image of the first side.

Use exactly the same technique as you did on the right foot. Just before the inside rockers you'll be facing slightly to the left, and just before the outside rockers, to the right.

PROBLEM AREAS:

Losing speed due to the following:

- Lack of strength in the skating leg
- Poor co-ordination of the twisting action of the body
- Tilting on the turns (not staying directly over the skate)
- Scraping the turns, by not using the rocker of the Blade correctly. You need to lift quickly to the heel on the turn to forwards, and quickly back to the ball of the foot to turn again to backwards. It's what is referred to as 'heel-ball'.

Pattern 4

CHOCTAW SEQUENCE

PRIMARY FOCUS: EDGE QUALITY

SECONDARY FOCUS: POWER

Choctaw Sequence

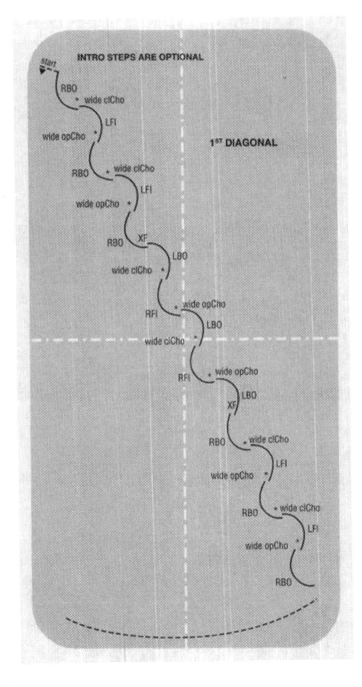

RECOMMENDED INTRODUCTORY STEPS:

This move can be started on either foot. I'll describe it starting on the right foot.

I would recommend using exactly the same introduction steps as on the Power Pulls.

Starting on the mid-line of the rink between the red hockey circles, skate an edge on the left foot (can be flat), a right forward inside Mohawk around the end of the rink, followed by two back crossovers. This should bring you around enough to help you set up the Choctaw sequence in a diagonal direction, through the middle of the rink.

COMMENT

Basically, this move involves just four edges. A backward outside edge on each foot, and a forward inside edge on each foot. Doesn't sound too difficult, does it? And you wouldn't think a move that only incorporates four basic edges could be so dreaded by some skaters, but it *can* present a few problems. On paper it doesn't look too difficult, but then again, we don't skate on paper. What makes this move challenging – and Junior level – is having to make controlled turns from one foot to the other on quality edges, while maintaining good flow.

Before this move was revised, skaters were allowed to turn their Choctaws quickly, and on fairly straight edges, with their feet quite close together, toe to heel. This really didn't do much to test a skater's ability, so the Moves in the Field task force wisely decided to make some changes. You're now required to perform these turns with more edge quality, and no need for quickness. It must also be stressed that these are now wide Choctaws, which means there should be at least five or six inches between your feet as you turn.

This is one of the more unforgiving moves. If you get off-balance on one of the choctaws, it can take a lot of effort and control to get back on track again. And, good posture, with a nice straight back and alignment over the skating hip, makes this move *so* much easier!

Generally, if you keep the feet well turned out in relation to each other, they'll do the turning, and not the body, provided that you're in the right position before each turn. And if you turn onto a soft knee, checking as you turn, your blade should take the ice running on a clean edge.

The hips have to turn a little with the foot, but the free hip still needs to end up being open on each edge.

The required power comes from how we use our knees, so try to feel that you 'sink' into your new knee on each turn. Then, from being on a bent knee, you can press up a little against the edge as you are turning, either from forward or backward, but especially on the backward to forward turn. It's a subtle movement, but if you can master it, it will help you keep the move flowing.

The free leg should be extended on the forward edge, and bent on the back edge.

Earlier in the book I talked about compromises, and here we have another example.

If you hold each edge too long, you'll run out of room, and not be able to complete the usual three sets we skate on each diagonal, but if you skate them too quickly, you'll finish the three sets much too soon. Try to find a happy medium with your timing. I usually tell my skaters to count 'and one, and two, and three, and four' through the four Choctaws. (Thank you, Julia, for making me aware of this important aspect of the Choctaw move, and for the way you adjusted your timing on the edges so that the three sets of Choctaws fitted the ice surface perfectly.)

THE MOVE

The skater is required to perform alternating sequences of Choctaws that cover the entire diagonal length of the arena. The skater will then repeat them starting on the other foot, using the other diagonal length of the arena.

There has often been confusion about what constitutes a Choctaw, so let me make it quite clear. A Choctaw is just *one* turn, from either forward to backward, or backward to forward, on edges of a different character. It's as simple as that. So, on this move, you'll start by performing a sequence of four Choctaws, followed by a cross in front that will enable you to perform four Choctaws facing the other way. Then, you'll cross in front again to perform them the original way once more. The rulebook states that you must skate them 'to cover the entire diagonal direction of the arena', and most skaters will do this performing three sets of Choctaws on each diagonal.

As I explained earlier, I'm describing this move starting on the right foot, so, to get a good start, make sure that you set up a quality right back outside edge (first edge of the move) after the last back crossover of the introduction steps. This should also set up the diagonal direction of the move.

On the introductory crossovers you'll probably be holding your right arm and shoulder back, so when you get onto the right back outside edge to start the move, you'll need to rotate your upper body so that your free arm and shoulder are back on the tracing, and your skating arm is outside the tracing. The angle between your arms should be about 135 degrees, so that they are neither 'L' shaped (90 degrees), nor in line (180 degrees).

Your free leg can be straight at the beginning of this edge, but you'll have to bend it to place it on the ice correctly to turn the first Choctaw.

Turning a good back choctaw to forward depends a lot on how, and where, you place your new foot on the ice. The placement of the new foot in relation to the old foot is crucial in making smooth transitions from one foot to the other, whether you're turning to forwards or backwards.

Think of the back edge as part of a circle, and that you need to step back into the circle, with your free foot and knee well turned out, in order to place the new foot on a forward inside edge. The feeling should be that it's right underneath you. If you place it on the ice correctly, and transfer your weight onto it, the blade of your right foot can come off the ice from a running back outside edge, without a scrape. And, as you'll need to extend your free leg in front of you when you turn to forward, the foot that's going onto the ice needs to be out of the way of the foot that's coming off the ice. For a split second you'll be on two feet as you transition from one foot to the other. You can't pick up one foot until the other is on the ice, so try not to 'jump' or 'hop' the choctaws.

At the same time you turn to forward, make a strong checking movement so that your skating arm and shoulder are now leading, and your free arm is checked back a little.

At this point, take a good look at yourself. On this, and all the following Choctaws, you may be making a strong checking movement with your arms, but are your shoulders and hips checking enough? Don't just rely your arms.

I have found that the arms should start the checking movement before the new foot goes onto the ice. They need to be moving in advance of the turning foot, so that, *by the time the new foot has taken the ice, the upper body is already in the checked position.* It's a matter of, move the arms, turn, move the arms, turn. It's a rhythmic movement, and helps the turns not to be 'jerky'.

After you turn that first Choctaw to forward, you should be able to get into a rhythm that helps you through the remaining three, so take extra care that you are right over your skate, and prepared for the first turn.

To turn the left forward inside Choctaw, keep your free foot well turned out and draw it back a little so that there is still about five or six inches between the heel of the free foot and the toe of the skating foot. Try not to break forward on this edge, because when you turn, you'll need to feel that you're 'sitting back' over the next back outside edge.

A common fault on the forward to backward turn is to draw the free foot back too far, almost to the point of it being behind the skating foot. This can create a mini spread-eagle effect, which can make it almost impossible to pick up the left foot into the position it needs to be in when you turn onto the back outside edge.

The feeling should be that your right foot is held out ahead of you when you turn onto it, which should enable you to pick up your left foot and hold it behind you in preparation to repeat the two Choctaws again. Be careful, also, not to let the left foot slide off the ice as you turn to backward. Make sure you pick it up inside the new back outside edge.

You'll be making four turns on each set (to forward, backward, forward, backward), and then rotate your upper body to face the other way in order to cross in front to set the left back outside edge for the second set of Choctaws. The trick here is to check the last forward to backward Choctaw very strongly, and then immediately release the arms and shoulders, bringing the free leg in front to cross in front for the four Choctaws facing the other way. If you can cross a little wide, it will makes it easier to hit the required outside edge.

Although there is a natural lean on each edge, you'll find it helps on the changeover from one set of Choctaws to the next, if you increase the lean as you turn onto the back edge of the last Choctaw (forward to backward). You'll then find it easier to rock the body over from that strong lean, and cross over from one outside edge to the other.

Assuming you're performing three sets down each diagonal, be very careful to turn the last forward to backward Choctaw onto an outside edge. I've seen many skaters turn to an inside edge, either because they've run out of room and would crash into the barriers if they turned onto an outside edge, or because they're anticipating skating across the end of the rink, and are getting a head start.

To go from one diagonal to the other, I recommend skating one or two back crossovers (depending on your speed) out of the corner, and then bring the feet together to push onto a strong right back outside edge to take you back to the opposite corner. Following that, skate one or two crossovers around that corner to set up the diagonal direction for the second part of this move on the other foot.

The second diagonal will be starting on a left back outside edge for the first Choctaw, but use the same method for turning these Choctaws as you did on the first diagonal. Four Choctaws, cross in front, four Choctaws facing the other way, and then a final cross in front to perform four more Choctaws the first way again. As on the Power Pulls (previous move), the second side is a mirror image of the first side.

PROBLEM AREAS:

- General lack of control.
- Edges too flat. Not distinct outside and inside edges.
- Loss of flow during the move.
- Bringing the free foot back too far before the forward choctaw, causing it to turn onto an inside edge. It's so important to place the new foot on the ice correctly, in relation to the old foot.
- Backward Choctaws scraped.

EXERCISE:

Using the red or blue lines, skate the forward inside edge on one side of the line, and a back outside edge on the other side. Make sure you pre-rotate your arms and shoulders before the first turn, and keep your body over the line.

Another good thing about using these lines is that they are just about the right width to skate wide Choctaws, so you must try to place you feet on each side of them.

TRICKS OF THE TRADE:

- In the first part of this book I suggested a useful exercise whereby you have to follow a turn with another turn. The object of this exercise is to show that you will only be able to perform the second turn effortlessly if you've checked the first turn - in this case, a Choctaw - correctly. The torque will be there to help you. Therefore, when you've turned to forward, you should only have to bring your free foot back behind you skating foot to turn a forward inside three, or a forward inside rocker if you want to show off. And when you've turned to backward, you should be able to turn a back outside three immediately, or a back outside rocker if you want to show off again!
- Lean a little more strongly on the back outside edge of the last Choctaw of each set, so that you feel a definite change of lean from skating hip to skating hip as you cross in front to start the next set.
- If you check the forward to backward turn correctly, and get your body in the right position over the skating hip and edge, you should also be able to put your free toe on the ice, and skate a back pivot.

$\mathcal{P}$attern 5

BACKWARD LOOP PATTERN

FOCUS: EDGE QUALITY, CONTINUOUS FLOW

Backward Loop Pattern

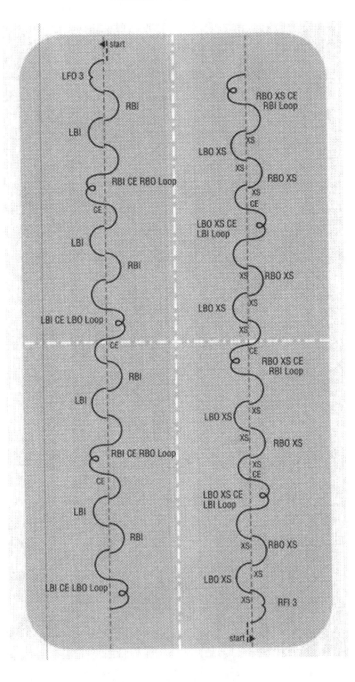

RECOMMENDED INTRODUCTORY STEPS:

This move starts from a standstill, with a three turn. It may also start in either direction, meaning that you can start with either the outside, or inside loops.

On USFigureskating's own website, the demonstration video shows the skater going straight into the second side without stopping, but I would advise going by the rulebook which states: 'Both sides start from a standstill'.

COMMENT

I think this is the most difficult Junior move, but many will disagree, and vote for the Choctaws.

From my experience, skaters find it harder to balance and hold their position on outside loops than they do on inside loops. This is because the free leg can swing out and around the skating leg on outside loops, and can often move too soon. On inside loops the free leg is not likely to swing around, so it's easier to hold it in the right position until you need to draw it back into the loop.

THE MOVE

BACKWARD OUTSIDE LOOPS

From a standstill, skate a left forward outside three turn into three back inside rolls, each starting on the long axis.

Talking of compromises once again, here we have another example. You need a certain amount of flow on this move, but if you go too fast, you may end up scraping your loops. Try to stay near the ball of the foot throughout this move, because if you get back on the blade in the loops, you're going to give yourself some problems.

Use the first back inside rolls to build up enough flow, and skate each one with your free arm in front, and your free foot held behind near the heel of the skating foot. One the third one (right back inside) you're going to be skating a change of edge to perform a right back outside loop. To do this, bring your edge around to the long axis, keeping your right shoulder back, and your free leg outside the tracing behind you. Simultaneously, rise on the knee, bring your free leg forward as you cross the long axis, and rotate your free arm and shoulder back, re-bending the knee after the change of edge. This 'bend–rise–bend' movement on the skating knee really helps.

You should now have completely reversed your upper body position so that you're facing out of the circle, with your skating arm in front of you. Your free leg should be slightly crossed over your skating leg, inside the tracing. Be patient, and hold this position until you reach the top of the loop. When you get there, start moving your free leg back, passing it close to your skating leg, and then extend it back as you switch your arms and shoulders to make a checking movement against it.

When you reach the long axis, change to an inside edge, and push onto three consecutive back inside rolls. From the last one (left back inside) you'll now skate a change of edge to left back outside to set up the left back outside loop. Use the same method to enter the loop as you did on the right back outside loop, but now you'll be skating on the other foot.

After you exit this loop and finish the lobe, skate a change of edge at the long axis, and repeat the back inside rolls and right and left back outside loops once more, making a total of four loops.

After each of the first three loops you need to skate a small change of edge to push onto the following back inside rolls, but after you've finished the lobe of the last loop (left back outside) you can step forward to skate across to the other side of the rink to perform the back inside loops.

The second half of this move starts with a forward inside three turn, and it would be much easier to skate into this turn if you were already moving, but the rule book says that both sides start from a standstill, so stop at the long axis and wait for the judges signal to commence the second half. I think the judges will appreciate this very short break because this is a high level move, and they may need a few seconds to comment on the first half.

BACKWARD INSIDE LOOPS

From a standing start, get a good push onto a right forward inside three so that you can start building up some flow. After the three turn, skate three back cross strokes (left, right, left). You should have no difficulty getting enough flow by the time you reach the first back inside loop if you skate these cross strokes with a little power.

At the end of the third cross stroke you need to skate a change of edge on the long axis to set up the back inside loop. If your arms and shoulders are in the same position as they would be after a basic back cross stroke, that is, with the skating arm in front, and the free arm back, you can now stretch your free leg back on the tracing, and then, simultaneously, bring it forward and switch your arms and shoulders as you cross the long axis, so that your skating arm is pressed back, and you free arm is held in front of you. Your arms should be in an 'L' position, and need to be held that way until just after the top of the loop.

Just before you enter the loop, press your skating shoulder back a little more, and move your free leg so that it's slightly outside the tracing. To enter the loop, bend both knees, drawing your free foot in close to your skating foot, with the toe still pointed. Hold your free foot still for an instant as you go around the top of the loop, and then draw it back along the tracing as you press up on the skating knee to exit the loop. I see many skaters 'whipping' their loop around too much, so try to perform this back inside loop as though you're skating in slow motion.

In the loop, you should still have your free arm in front of your chest, but as you exit the loop draw it back behind you, and move your skating arm onto the tracing.

When you reach the long axis, skate a short change of edge, and perform three cross strokes (right, left, right) to prepare for the change of edge into the right back inside loop.

Use exactly the same method to execute this loop as you did on the left foot.

After you exit the right back inside loop and finish the lobe, skate a change of edge at the long axis and repeat the cross strokes and left and right back inside loops one more time, making a total of four loops.

PROBLEM AREAS:

- Starting the loop too late on its lobe. The skate has to start entering the loop about a third of the way into the lobe (see diagram), therefore, start thinking of entering the loop soon after skating the change of edge.
- Releasing the position of the arms and shoulders before the top of the loop (especially on outside loops), making it difficult for the skate to exit the loop.
- Rocking up onto the toe pick on inside loops. This usually happens as the skater bends their skating knee and draws in their free foot. Try to stay near the ball of the foot.
- Falling into the circle (inside loops) because of your weight not being well over the skating hip. You almost have to feel like you're leaning outwards because your skating hip is on the outside of the circle.
- 'Whipping' the body around on back inside loops, making it look like a spin.

Pattern 6

STRAIGHT LINE STEP SEQUENCE

FOCUS: EDGE QUALITY, CONTINUOUS FLOW

Straight Line Step Sequence

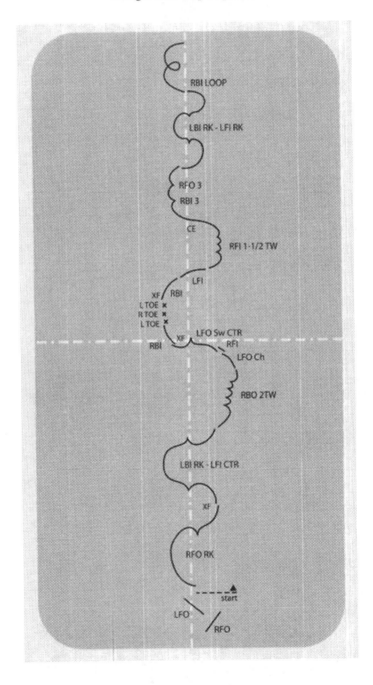

Straight Line Step Sequence-Repeat

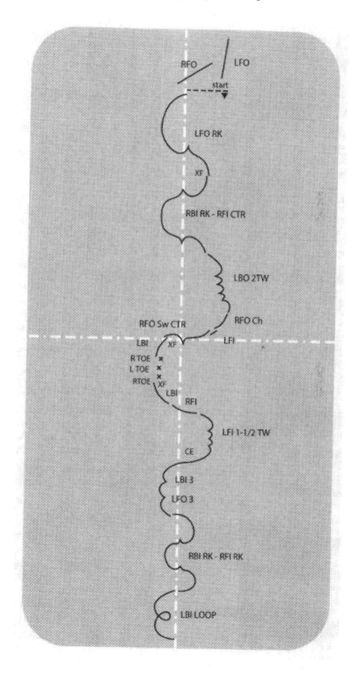

This move may start in either direction

RECOMMENDED INTRODUCTORY STEPS:

The introduction steps are set in the rule book. A left, right - or right, left - depending on which foot you start, followed by the first outside rocker.

I'll describe this move starting with the right forward outside rocker.

COMMENT

This move is probably the least serious of the Junior moves, and is just about the only move at this level that allows for some individual expression regarding arm movements, and arm and free leg positions on the twizzles and other parts of the move. It is also the only move that uses the midline as a continuous long axis, which sometimes makes it difficult to practice on a freestyle session. The good news is that you can practice it down the side of the rink, but it may not be so easy to maintain that long axis.

The focuses are edge quality and continuous flow, but there also needs to be continuity from one movement, turn, or twizzle, to the next, so that you give a pleasing performance.

The name 'Straight Line Step Sequence' only refers to the fact that it is *basically* a straight line pattern, as opposed to a circular step sequence, or serpentine step sequence, but it's anything but a straight line when you perform it. The required pattern demands that your edges are going to curve away from, and back to, the long axis all the way down the ice surface.

THE MOVE

Skate the two introduction strokes on a slight diagonal away from the long axis, so that you can then skate a strong right outside edge to turn the outside rocker on the long axis. This rocker can be skated as a swing rocker, or it can be skated in the same manner as I described in Pattern 1 of the Junior Moves, where you can bend your free knee before and after the turn, if that makes it more controllable. There are, actually, no set rules regarding the use of the free leg.

After you've turned and checked the rocker, you need to get a strong stroke from your right back outside edge as you cross in front in preparation for the following left back inside rocker. This shouldn't be turned until you reach the long axis, so wait until your edge curves around enough, and rotate your left arm and shoulder back, bringing your free arm slightly across your chest in preparation for the turn. To turn, simultaneously rise on your skating knee, draw your free foot in close to your skating foot, and lift to the heel, and then immediately back to just behind the middle of the blade as you exit.

It's essential that you have good control out of this rocker, so use the same method to prepare and turn as on the forward inside rocker in Pattern 2. The turn needs to be checked very strongly because you'll need to keep your skating arm and shoulder leading to help the edge curve back to the long axis. I've noticed a lot of skaters having trouble keeping their arms and shoulders in the right position after this rocker. You now need to prepare to turn a left forward inside counter on the long axis, so rotate your free arm and shoulder forward just as you did in the Forward Inside Counter (Novice Moves, Pattern 3).

Immediately after you've turned the counter, put your right foot down and push onto a right back outside two-revolution twizzle. If you hold the back inside edge of the counter too long, it may cause the twizzle to be too far around the lobe.

When you step forward out of this twizzle, make sure that you're facing down ice on a left forward outside edge, so that the next edges can then curve back toward the long axis. The left forward outside edge is followed by a short right forward inside edge (basically, a chasse), and that sets up the left forward outside swing counter. Stroke onto this edge with your free arm slightly leading, and then counter rotate your arms and shoulders as you swing your free leg forward. Swing your leg back and rise on your skating knee to turn the counter on the long axis. So, on the first four turns, you should have the feeling that you're crossing the long axis as you turn.

Immediately after the swing counter, cross in front and skate three toe steps, rotating your body one revolution clockwise (left toe, right toe, left toe), and then cross in front again (right back inside edge) immediately after you turn the last toe step to backward. Step forward on a left forward inside edge, which should take you back to the long axis. The cross in front, toe-toe-toe, cross in front, and step forward are all on the same lobe.

The next item is a more complex one, involving a twizzle, pull change of edge, back inside double three, all skated on the right foot. The twizzle is a one and a half revolution right forward inside twizzle, followed by a pull change of edge from the exit edge of the twizzle (right back outside edge), with the edge changing on the long axis. It's going to be important to use your arms and shoulders strongly to help you pull out of the twizzle and then make the change of edge to set up the back inside double three.

After you change onto the right back inside edge, I would recommend pulling in your arms and free foot close to your body to help turn the back inside double three. The free foot is usually held close to the skating foot during this turn.

Following the double three, you need to push onto a strong left back inside edge to prepare for a left back inside rocker. Make a strong checking movement out of this rocker because it's followed by a left forward inside rocker. Keep the lobes on these rockers fairly small, on tight edges, to show edge quality. These two rocker turns are also turned on the long axis. Use good knee bend into and out of these turns to help bring the edges around.

The remaining step is a right back inside loop, so push onto a right back inside edge with your weight well over your skating hip, your skating arm and shoulder pressed back, and your free leg held in front over the tracing so that it is trailing the skating foot. Hold your free arm in front of your chest, so that your arms are virtually in an 'L' position, and then bend your skating knee to tighten up the edge to make the loop. At the same time, bring your free foot inside the loop beside your skating foot, and then draw it out behind you as you exit the loop, rising up on your skating knee. Be patient while your blade goes around the top of the loop before you try to exit. It's the same advice for all loops - you have to wait until your blade has gone past the top of the loop before you try to get out of it.

We often associate footwork with quickness of movement, but that isn't required here – or, indeed, on any part of this move – so try not to rush your loop just to get it over with. If you do, it can end up as a tiny spin on a back inside edge, and you don't want your loop to qualify for inclusion in the Guinness Book of Records as 'the world's smallest loop'.

This completes the first half of this move, which should have used the full length of the ice surface. The move is now repeated from a standing start, on the other foot, skating back down the midline of the rink. This means that your introductory steps are now left, right, and then left forward outside rocker. Use exactly the same techniques as described on the first half.

PROBLEM AREAS:

- Not curving the edges enough (edge quality) to the long axis for the turns.
- Not checking the back inside rocker (second turn) well enough to help the edge curve back to the long axis for the forward inside counter.
- Lacking control from the back inside rocker to the forward inside rocker (before the final loop).
- Rushing the final loop, turning it into a spin.

Senior Moves in the Field Test

1. Sustained edge step
The skater will powerfully perform a BI three-turn to a sustained swing change of edge followed by a FI rocker, stepping to a BI double three-turn. Backward crossover steps follow this sequence. This pattern is then repeated to cover the entire surface of the rink. The skater will then repeat this step in the opposite direction. Introductory steps are optional. This move may start in either direction.
Focus: Edge Quality and Power

2. Spiral sequence
The skater begins with a series of spirals, transitioning from a RBO spiral to a RFI spiral through the use of a RBO3 that is parallel to the long barrier of the rink. The free leg is then lowered into a RFI open mohawk and steps wide a two-foot power push transition into two backward R over L crossovers. The skater steps onto a LFI and then immediately onto a RFI-RBO spiral sequence, again transitioning between spirals with a RFI3. The skater then does a cross stroke behind LBO swing

roll followed by a RFO triple three-turn. Then step LFI into a RFI3, followed by a step forward into a LFO crossover and finally a LFO spiral. The pattern is repeated in the opposite direction, and transition steps are optional. (NOTE: All spirals should be sustained with an extended free leg to demonstrate the skater's form and flexibility.) This move may start in either direction. Introductory steps are optional.
Focus: Extension and Edge quality

3. Backward Outside power double three-turns to power double inside rockers
The skater will perform BO power double three-turns, then complete a power pull to BI double rockers. These rockers are immediately followed by another power pull. This sequence is repeated consecutively down the entire diagonal of the rink. The skater will then perform the same step using the opposite foot down the opposite diagonal of the rink. Introductory steps are optional. This move may start on either foot.
Focus: Power and quickness

4. Backward inside power double three-turns to power double outside rockers
The skater will perform BI power double three-turns, then complete a power pull to BO double rockers. These rockers are immediately followed by another power pull and the sequence is then repeated consecutively down the entire diagonal of the rink. The skater will then perform the same step using the opposite foot down the opposite diagonal of the rink. Introductory steps are optional. This move may start on either foot.
Focus: Power and quickness

5. Serpentine step sequence
The skater begins with a RFO3 followed by a LBO double three-turn. The free leg then crossed in front for a RBI. This edge is followed by three clockwise toe steps and another cross

in the front RBI. Next the skater will step forward onto a LFO edge and perform a 2-1/2 revolution RFI twizzle, ending with a LBO cross stroke behind the three-turn. This turn will initiate a series of quick mohawk turns followed by a quick LBI then a step-wide into RBI rocker. The skater should then simultaneously cross behind and reverse arm position to do RFI bracket into RBO counter, followed by a LFO cross front, RFI cross behind. The final part of the sequence is an open RF/LBO double Choctaw followed immediately by a RFI counter, then push to LBI double twizzle, and finishes with a RBI loop. Optional steps take the skater to the repeat of the sequence in the opposite direction. The skater has the option of starting in either direction. Introductory steps are optional.

Focus: Edge quality and continuous flow

Revised 7/1/2010

And so we come to the final level of moves. By the time a skater gets to this test, they have demonstrated that they can execute all the different turns and movements, and shouldn't have too much trouble mastering the final challenges that this test presents.

You may think you're getting off easily only having to skate five moves instead of six, as on the two previous levels, but the judges will be expecting an even higher standard of skating. You'll have to demonstrate excellent control, good flow and presentation, with no scratchy turns!

You may well find the second and third moves (outside and inside back double threes to rocker/rocker) no more difficult than the Power Pull move on the Junior moves, because your blade will probably glide through more freely on the double threes than it would on the consecutive rocker/rocker turns.

Pattern 1

SUSTAINED EDGE STEP

PRIMARY FOCUS: EDGE QUALITY

SECONDARY FOCUS: POWER

Sustained Edge Step

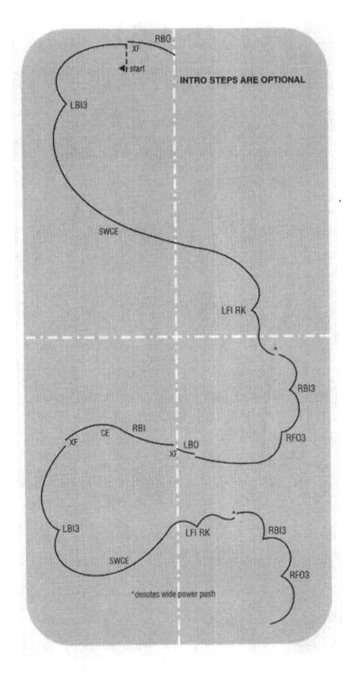

RECOMMENDED INTRODUCTORY STEPS:

As this move starts just after the midline of the rink, you'll need to set out your introductory steps so that they use the other half of the ice at the same end you're starting.

I recommend starting with a right edge, followed by a left forward outside three turn (which is only one step - a Mohawk is two), and then two back crossovers on a nice powerful curve to set up the right back outside edge that precedes the first edge of the move.

COMMENT

This move is all about drawing out your edges to cover a lot of ice, so take full advantage of the seven allowed introductory steps to build up some speed, otherwise you'll feel like you're on the sustained edge forever. If you don't apply power wherever possible throughout the move, you'll end up paying the price.

As this is a senior level move, it's important that you do everything to enhance the quality of your performance, so take advantage of the many places where you could add arm movements. As I go through the move, I'll point out where they could be added.

THE MOVE

Technically, the move starts with the sustained edge - a cross-in-front left back inside edge - but there is a necessary right back outside edge which must skated before it in order to perform the cross in front.

Just after the midline, skate a powerful left back inside crossover onto a well bent knee, and extend your free leg behind you, but outside the tracing. At the same time, pre-rotate your shoulders and arms a little in preparation for the turn, but not too much. This is all you will need to turn to forward, as your blade will turn very easily when you rise on the knee. Draw in your free foot for the turn, and then immediately extend your free leg again behind you after the turn, staying up on the knee. Check your arms and shoulders so that your skating arm and shoulder are leading, and your free arm is checked back. This can be a classic position if all your body lines are stretched nicely.

You can use your arms very effectively on this turn. I recommend bringing the arms in before the turn, crossing them in front of you just above the wrists, and then stretching your arms back out again as you turn. This is not only a nice arm movement, it also helps check the turn.

You now have at least two options with regard to the way you use your arms as you perform the change of edge on the midline. My preferred method is to keep the free leg held back while you switch the arms, bringing the free arm forward and the skating arm back. Then, bend the skating knee and, as you approach the midline of the rink, simultaneously rise up on the knee, which should gain you more flow - the principle of a power pull - swing your free leg forward along the tracing, at the same time counter-rotating your arms and shoulders so that your skating arm is now leading, and your free arm is checked back. That way, you have a nice coordinated movement as you rise on the knee.

An alternative method is to leave the arms where they are, and just bring the free leg through, keeping the skating arm and shoulder leading strongly to help you through the change of edge.

It's important that you stay well over your skating hip on a solid outside edge right up to the change, and then swing your free leg back, changing edge as you cross the midline. There should be the feeling of going from one big circle to another. Your edge should be going *across* the ice surface as you go into this change of edge, and end up running down ice afterward, whereas the second change of edge on the first half of this move should retrogress before the change, so that you come out traveling across ice.

You can make a nice arm movement through the change of edge by sweeping your skating arm upward as your free leg swings forward before the change, and then sweeping it out in front of you as your free leg swings back after the change.

You should now be on the other side of the rink, so wait until your blade is running down ice and then perform a left forward inside rocker turn, followed immediately by a wide step onto a right back inside double three turn, drawing the free foot in close during the turns.

Getting a good push onto the wide step will help you to maintain flow through the double three. As you exit the turn, extend your free leg back creating a nice line. This also lets the edge run a little further, which helps you cover more ice.

On this back inside double three, you can either leave your arms extended, or bring your hands in closer to your body as you turn, and then stretch your arms out again as you check out of the turn.

Staying on the same curve, push onto a left back outside edge and then skate a deep right back inside edge crossover, free arm in front, sinking well into the skating knee. Rise on the knee, changing edge and, simultaneously, switch your arms and bring your free leg forward to cross in front onto a strong left back inside edge.

The second half of this pattern is actually a repeat of the first half, but on stronger, tighter edges. This means that some edges are going to be heading in a different direction.

Skate a tighter circle on the repeat of the back inside three, and bring the exit edge around so that, instead of approaching the change of edge across ice - as on the first part of this pattern - you edge will actually be running back up ice near the midline before you change edge for the left forward inside rocker, which will be running *across* ice. You'll remember that the first forward inside rocker was running *down ice*.

After the change of edge, skate a left forward inside rocker, followed by another right back inside double three turn. This will now be the end of the first half of this move, so check out of the double three with your arms and free leg beautifully stretched, and take a deep breath in readiness for the second half.

The second half of this move is a complete mirror image of the first half, so, obviously, you'll need to have the same flow starting into it, but here we have a good news, bad news situation. The diagram in the rule book shows the first half of the move ending up fairly near to the end of the rink, and if you reach that point you've shown that you've utilized the ice surface well, with good coverage. The rule book actually states, 'This pattern is then repeated to cover the entire surface of the arena'. The bad news is that, on most moves, judges don't want to see a skater circling around on crossovers to get up speed, but if you're at the end of the rink you may have no other option but to do so. On this move, it wouldn't be a bad thing.

Having said this, on most tests I've witnessed, the skater usually ends up about four fifths of the way down the ice. This usually allows enough room for some for quick, powerful back crossovers without having to circle around, before setting a strong crossover to start the second half of the move.

The move is then repeated in the opposite direction with a right back inside crossover into a back inside three turn. Use the same technique as on the first side, but with everything on the opposite foot.

PROBLEM AREAS:

- Lack of flow through the first (sustained) edge, resulting in weak edges, and the probability of the change of edge taking place well before the midline.
- 'Kicking' the free leg forward before the change of edge, instead of swinging or stretching it forward.
- Turning a forward inside three turn instead of a rocker at the end of the sustained edge.
- Lacking control coming out of the following back inside double three turn.
- Skating the repeat of the first edges in the same direction, and not skating a stronger pattern into the repeat change of edge.
- Not having enough flow into the second half of the move.

Pattern 2

EXTENSION SPIRAL STEP

FOCUS: EXTENSION, EDGE QUALITY

Spiral Sequence

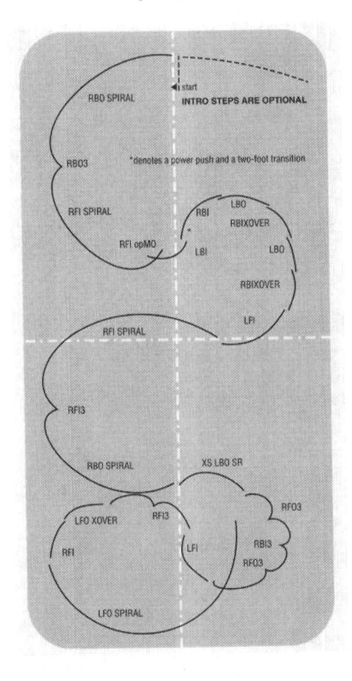

This move may start in either direction

RECOMMENDED INTRODUCTORY STEPS:

Left, right, left forward outside three turn, two back crossovers before getting a further push onto the back outside edge for the first spiral.

COMMENT

In my opinion, this revised move is now easier than the previous version. It makes sense that the Moves in the Field committee decided to take out the final back spiral - turn - spiral in favor of adding an extra new one, the forward outside spiral. This actually affords the skater the chance of a breather as they skate this spiral, as it will last for about five seconds, in one position.

The Extension Spiral Step move greatly favors skaters who can create beautiful spiral positions and, of the five senior moves, this one gives the best opportunity for the artistic skater to express themselves with pleasing arm movements, as well as demonstrating some classic body lines.

Although there are no rules about how high the free leg should be held, this *is* a senior move, so the judges will expect the free leg to be held well above hip level. Obviously, the spirals are the highlight of this move, but there are other places where the skater can take the opportunity to be quite artistic. Some effective arm movements can be incorporated on the triple-three turn and the following forward inside three.

I must also add, it's been my experience that most skaters find this quite a tiring move.

THE MOVE

This move takes a fair amount of time, so, as you don't want the judges to miss their bus home, you would be well advised to gain plenty of flow on the introductory steps that take you into the first spiral - turn - spiral. From here, you must do your best to maintain flow throughout the move. The cleaner you make the turn between the spirals, the more flow you'll maintain.

Start the right back outside edge spiral on the midline, raising your free leg immediately into spiral position. Obviously, the higher you can hold your free leg, the more impressive it will be. Keep your back slightly arched, and hold your head so that there is a beautiful line through your body from your head to your free foot. Make sure you are over your skating hip, and on a solid outside edge. The curve you're skating on must remain constant through the turn and onto the forward inside spiral so that you are, in effect, skating a large semi-circle (lobe).

Just before the top of the lobe, rise up out of spiral position and draw your free foot in to turn a back outside three turn to forward. Immediately after this, raise your free leg up again into a forward inside spiral position. Hold this position until just before the midline of the rink, where you need to rise up and bring your free leg down to turn a forward inside Mohawk from the spiral edge onto a wide step (right back inside edge). Make sure you get a good push onto this wide step, and off it, so that you can gain flow through the following two back crossovers. After the second crossover, step forward (but still get a push as you do so) and skate a left forward inside edge on the same curve. This should take you to the midline of the rink where you will start the right forward inside - turn - right back outside spiral.

On one side of the rink or the other, you'll probably be starting this spiral going toward the judges, so make a good impression by immediately raising up your free leg, arching your back a little, and keeping well over your skating hip, almost as though you're leaning out of the circle. 'Eyeball' those judges, and 'sell it'!

At the top of the lobe, rise up and lower your free leg, bringing your free foot close to your skating foot, and turn a forward inside three turn to start the back outside spiral. Keep on the same circle, well over your skating hip.

When you reach the midline, skate a back cross stroke onto a left back outside swing roll. As you push onto it, your free leg will extend forward. You can then make a nice swing back of the free leg, keeping on an outside edge, and prepare to step forward onto a right forward outside triple three turn. This triple three must be kept on a circle, and you should get a good push onto it. It works really well if you perform it with your skating shoulder and hip leading strongly, and your free side held back so that your shoulders are almost parallel to the tracing. If, on the previous back cross roll, you rotated your free shoulder back a little in preparation to step forward, you should find yourself in an ideal position to start the triple three.

The triple three will almost turn itself if you push onto a well-bent knee, on an outside edge, and then just rise on your skating knee, keeping your free leg in a beautifully stretched position behind you. You'll turn to backward, forward and backward again, as though your body is turning in 'one piece'. Here is another place where you can add beautiful arm movements. I like to see the skater raise their skating arm up gradually and continually as they start turning, while leaving their free arm parallel to the ice, but there are many nice arm movements that can be used. Experiment, and you'll find one you're comfortable with.

From the back inside edge at the end of the triple three, step forward on a left forward inside edge on the same circle, so that you end up momentarily facing down ice. This move has something of an 'S' pattern across the end of the rink, and you should now have completed the first part of the 'S', albeit in reverse.

The next step is a powerful right forward inside three turn, and is the perfect place for a big arm movement. I like to see the skater circle both arms up over the head as they turn the three, and then bring them down again. This turn is usually done with a well-extended free leg, and is then followed by an immediate step forward to stroke onto a left forward outside edge, and a crossover.

You should now have come around enough to be facing the end of the rink, where you will push onto a forward outside spiral on a large semi-circle, ending up facing down ice again. In normal sized ice rinks, I have found that this spiral can start on one red hockey 'dot', curve near the hockey goal, and up at the red hockey 'dot' in the circle on the other side of the rink. Red 'dot' to red 'dot', so to speak, on a big semi-circle. This is quite a long spiral, and generally takes about five seconds, so make sure you're in a good position throughout. Finish in a nicely presented position, and get a good lungful of air to start the second half of this move.

It works best to start both sides of this move from back crossovers, so after you finish the final spiral on the first side, either turn a forward outside three turn, or a Mohawk/wide step movement, to backward, in order to skate two or three back crossovers around to the midline of the rink to start the left back outside spiral – turn – spiral.

The pattern is repeated in the opposite direction, starting on the other foot, using the same technique I described for the first half.

PROBLEM AREAS:

- Obviously, a poor spiral position, with the free leg held too low, is unacceptable at this level. After all, this *is* a senior move, not a Senior Citizen move (and I'm certainly not making fun of Senior Citizens because I am one, myself!). You don't have to raise your free leg into the amazing position the great Sasha Cohen achieved, but the free leg should be held well above the level of the free hip.
- A 'rocky' triple three turn, with poor body position.
- Lack of flow throughout the move.

EXERCISE:

Alternating triple three turns down the ice. Check the third turn well so that you can step forward with your skating side leading, and your free side held well back. Your shoulders, hips, and free leg will be almost parallel to the tracing. You can incorporate any pleasing arm movements you like, but the thing is not to turn the body to make the turns, but merely rise on the skating knee. Keep your free hip very open as you go through the turns.

Pattern 3

BACKWARD OUTSIDE POWER DOUBLE THREE-TURNS TO POWER DOUBLE INSIDE ROCKERS

PRIMARY FOCUS: POWER
SECONDARY FOCUS: QUICKNESS

BO Power Double Three-Turns to Power Double Inside Rockers

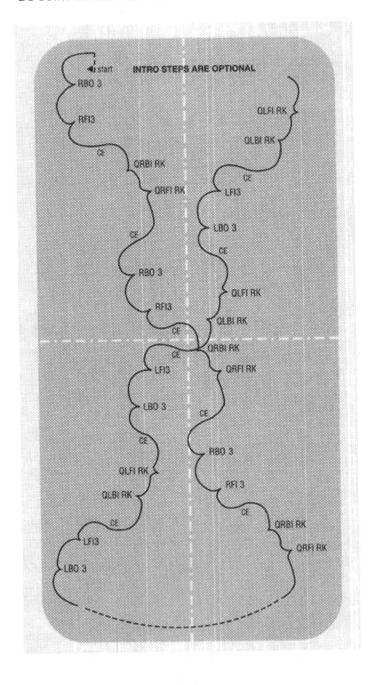

It doesn't seem to say this in the rule book, but you can start this move on either foot.

RECOMMENDED INTRODUCTORY STEPS:

The same as the Junior Power Pulls and Junior Choctaws.

Standing on the midline near the end of the rink, a left outside edge, followed by a right forward inside Mohawk to two back crossovers. This will set up the push onto a right back outside double three turn to start the move, which travels diagonally across the ice surface.

COMMENT

This is a move that needs to be skated strongly. In fact, when you've finished one diagonal you should have the feeling that your quad muscles have had a good workout. This will come from all that bending and pressing up on the knee to perform the power pulls between the turns. You'll also need to keep up a rhythmic movement throughout the diagonal line, and keep right over your skate, especially on the rocker/rocker turns. Any loss of balance on these turns will cause your blade to slow down, and make it difficult for you to maintain flow.

The pull change from the rockers to the double-threes is slightly more difficult than the threes to the rockers because the threes are on more of a circle, and therefore on an edge, whereas the rockers are on more of a flat-topped lobe, requiring you to get onto an edge to be able to make a pull change.

The 'quickness' on this move is expected on the rocker turns, not the power pulls or double threes.

THE MOVE

Let's make sure you get started correctly. The first part of this move is a power back outside double three turn, and as three turns are turned on part of a circle, make sure that you get over your skating hip in readiness to push onto a good outside edge for the first turn. I'm saying this because I see too many skaters step onto a straight line - often running parallel to the side of the rink – and turn flat three turns before getting onto an outside edge to make the pull change. Now, I'm not saying you have to set a strong edge, but at least try to feel that you're on a natural curve through the threes.

After you've skated the last crossover of the introductory steps, use the push onto the right back outside double three to start the rotation of the arms and shoulders. As you are, basically, getting a swizzle push onto the first back three turn, it's natural to go through this turn with your free leg extended in front – rather like most skaters do on the back power three turns in the Juvenile moves test – and then draw it in close to the heel of your skating foot to turn the forward inside three. On the remaining double threes, you have the choice of whether to extend your free leg forward as you skate the change of edge before the three turns, or just draw in your free foot close to your skating foot after the change of edge. Having said all this, you could also skate the first back outside three with your free foot immediately drawn in close to your skating foot.

Exit the double three turn with your free arm and shoulder back, your skating arm and shoulder in front, and then bend your skating knee so that you can press up to execute a strong change of edge from outside to inside. The body movement should feel the same as when you performed Power Pulls on the Pre-Juvenile moves, or Power Pulls (to rocker/rocker) on the Junior moves.

As you change edge, rotate your upper body so that your skating arm and shoulder are back, and your free arm and shoulder are forward. You should now feel that slight 'twist' at the waist, which means that your skating shoulder is further back than your skating hip. This will enable you to perform quick rocker/rocker turns by using a twisting action of your hips against your shoulders. It must be turn, turn. Not turn...yawn...turn. These rockers *are* on inside edges, but because of the skater's speed across the ice and the quickness of the turns, good edge quality is not expected.

When you come out of the rocker/rocker turns you should have some knee bend, with your free foot held behind you. You should also find your free arm in front of you, and your skating arm back, on an inside edge. You now have to perform a change of edge from inside to outside in order to repeat the sequence of back outside double three turn/change edge/back inside rocker, rocker.

To do this, three things are going to happen almost simultaneously. Press up on your skating knee, pull back your free arm and shoulder to change edge, and stretch your free leg back to help with the 'pull'. Having pressed up on the skating knee, re-bend it a little after the change of edge.

As I stated at the beginning of this book, different methods may be used on many of the moves, which is fine as long as we get the desired result. After this particular change of edge there are two different ways, that I know, of using the free leg. I think everyone is agreed that the free foot needs to be close as you turn the double threes, but before you draw in your free foot, my preferred technique is to make the same free leg movement I advised on the Junior Backward Loop Pattern (outside loops). That is, bringing the free leg forward, passing it close to the skating leg, as the free arm and shoulder rotate back. Then, by pressing up on the skating knee and drawing the free foot in close, the double three almost turns itself.

The alternative method is to simply draw your free foot in close to your skating foot after you've gone through the change of edge. As long as you make a strong movement of pre-rotating your upper body, your skating foot should go through the double three turns without much difficulty, because the hips and skating foot will follow that pre-rotation.

On the double threes, I recommend bringing the hands in close to the body, possibly with the fingers and thumb touching the thighs. This should make you turn more easily. Whatever you do, don't check the back three turn with your arms and shoulders. You could get stuck and not be able to turn the forward turn easily.

Repeat these back double threes to rocker/rocker twice more, making a total of three sets. If you can maintain good flow, by skating strong power pulls between the turns, you should easily complete the diagonal length of the arena. After you finish the final rocker/rocker turns, present yourself nicely, and then skate the same end pattern I recommended on the Power Pulls and Choctaws at the Junior level, i.e. two back crossovers, followed by a strong edge back to opposite corner, and then two crossovers to come out of that corner to set up the diagonal direction for the turns on the other foot.

Once again, get a good push onto the first back double three turn, and then perform three sets of back double three – rocker/rockers starting on the left back outside edge.

Throughout this move, you should feel as though you're 'weaving' your way each side of the diagonal line.

PROBLEM AREAS:

- Loss of flow toward the end of the sequences
- Scratchy rocker/rocker turns

Pattern 4

BACKWARD INSIDE POWER DOUBLE THREE-TURNS TO POWER DOUBLE OUTSIDE ROCKERS

PRIMARY FOCUS: POWER

SECONDARY FOCUS: QUICKNESS

BI Power Double Three-Turns to Power Double Outside Rockers

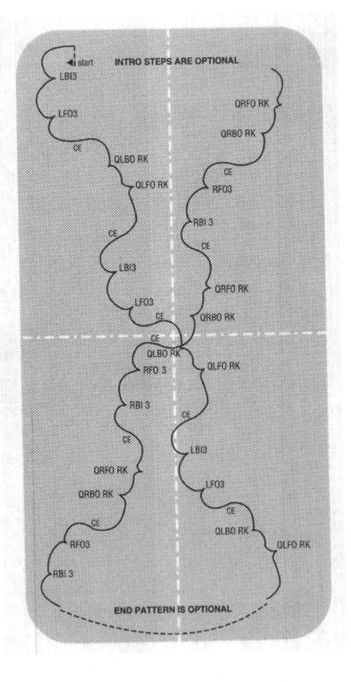

RECOMMENDED INTRODUCTORY STEPS:

Standing on the midline near the end of the rink, skate a right edge, and then a left forward outside three turn followed by three crossovers that should bring you around the corner. On the third crossover start the move with a left back inside double three.

COMMENT

This move is almost a carbon copy of the previous move, except that you'll now be skating back *inside* double threes, and *outside* edge rockers. Therefore, a lot of the comments and recommendations I made on the previous move will also apply to this one.

Personally, I think this is the easier of the two back double three moves because the pull changes seem more natural and coordinated, but that is only my opinion.

Once again, this is a diagonal move, so it's essential that you set up your first back inside double three to come out heading in a diagonal direction.

THE MOVE

After you've skated the introductory steps, prepare for the back inside double three by crossing over onto a good inside edge on a well-bent knee, extending your free leg back. Rotate your upper body so that your skating arm and shoulder are drawn back, and your free arm is in front of you. Rise up and draw you free foot in close for the double three turn, keeping your arms in the same position. Try not to check the turns. Just keep your shoulders rotating slightly ahead of your hips and foot.

If you can come out of the turn and bend your skating knee a little more – with your free arm still in front of you – you'll be able to press up on your knee and pull back your free arm and shoulder to make the change of edge to set you up for the rocker/rocker turns. As I stated on the previous move, when you've pulled back your free arm and shoulder in preparation for the rockers, you should feel a slight 'twist' at the waist. This will enable you to make quick rocker turns using a quick twisting action.

After you've made the second rocker turn, bend your skating knee and pull back your free arm and shoulder even more to skate the pull change of edge.

Once again, there are different ways of using your free leg through the change of edge into the back inside double threes. I prefer to see the skater first pull back their free leg, move it forward again as they change edge, and then draw the free foot in close to the skating foot for the turns. With your upper body pre-rotated, this method can make your foot turn more easily. The other method is to pull your free leg back into the change of edge, and then just bring your free foot close to your skating foot for the turns.

The sequence must now be repeated consecutively down the entire diagonal of the ice surface. It's usual for skaters to perform three sets of double three/rocker, rockers. You're not going to make it with two sets, and if you need four, then you're skating much too slowly.

After you've completed the first diagonal, perform the same steps on the other foot down the opposite diagonal of the ice surface.

PROBLEM AREAS:

- Loss of flow toward the end of the sequences
- Scratchy rocker/rocker turns
- Shallow changes of edge. Your edges should 'weave' their way across the diagonal.
- Lack of a rhythmic movement.

Pattern 5

SERPENTINE STEP SEQUENCE

FOCUS: EDGE QUALITY, CONTINUOUS FLOW

Serpentine Step Sequence

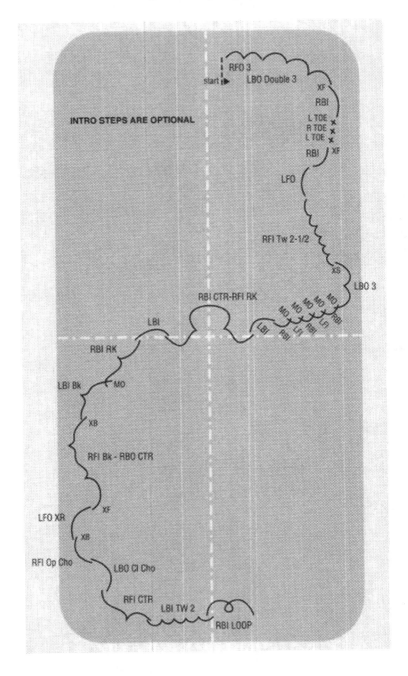

Serpentine Step Sequence – Repeat

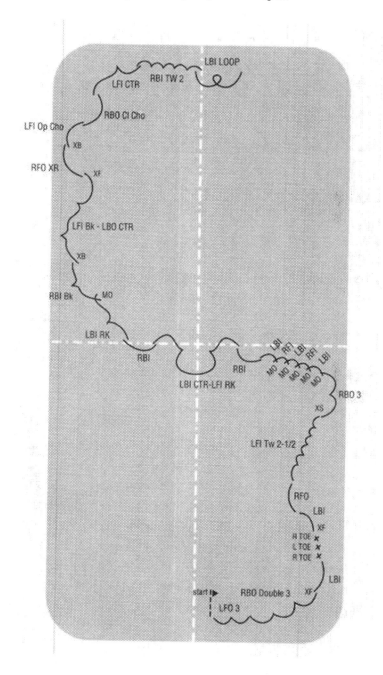

This move may start in either direction, but I'll describe it starting with the right forward outside three turn.

RECOMMENDED INTRODUCTORY STEPS:

Standing on the midline, between the red hockey circles, skate a bold right forward outside three to one or two back crossovers (one should be enough), and then present yourself nicely on a left back outside edge before stepping forward to start the move (right forward outside three).

The move starts just after the midline, so give yourself room for your introductory steps by facing the other side of the rink when you start. You can then skate a nice semi-circle on those steps, ending up near the midline.

COMMENT

So here we are. The last rung of the ladder, and I suppose it's fitting that this final move in the test schedule contains almost everything but the kitchen sink. Then again, this *is* a senior move, so it's not meant to be a stroll in the park. There are, approximately, twenty-seven steps (before you repeat them on the other foot), and many of the edges incorporate more than one turn.

This is not an easy move to practice because some of the sections will be going against the skating session traffic, so to speak.

Individually, each one of the turns and twizzles in this move should not present much difficulty to a skater testing at this level, but it's the way they're put together that makes them a little more difficult. You'll be expected to keep up a continuity of foot and body movement, with no hesitations, especially on the second half of this move.

I would say the most difficult section is 'bracket - bracket - back outside counter - cross stroke - cross behind - choctaw – Choctaw - inside counter'. Most move patterns have their difficulties, but getting through this section is about as awkward as carrying eight pounds of potatoes in a wet paper bag. There are, however, a few places in this move where you can incorporate some nice arm movements, so that your arms are not held in a plain position from start to finish.

This is quite an intricate move, so for explanation purposes, some knowledgeable people in the skating world advise dividing it into three sections. I'm not sure where they divide the sections, but I'll take advantage of their common sense and recommend the same thinking. I'll call them the 'easy section', the 'red line' section, and the 'twisty-turny' section.

THE MOVE

The 'easy' section

After the recommended introductory steps, step forward onto a right forward outside three and then onto a left back outside back double three, keeping the free leg over the tracing in front of the skating leg throughout the turn. You'll then be able to cross in front onto a right back inside edge to perform a toe-toe-toe step (left, right, left) rotating one revolution clockwise. Immediately after the third toe step, cross in front again on a right back inside edge and then step forward onto a left forward outside edge.

There are already at least two places where you can add arm movements and present yourself nicely. On the toe-toe-toe steps you could bring your arms and hands up over your head (a tried and trusted movement), and on the step forward you could stretch out your arms and free leg in line with the tracing, but only briefly.

These first steps should have brought you around the corner and about a quarter of the way down the ice. Think of skating the toe steps down ice because you're going to curve into the center a little when you cross in front coming out of them, and you don't want to get too far away from the barriers.

After stepping forward on the left forward outside edge, push onto a right forward inside two-and-a-half revolution twizzle, coming out on a right back outside edge. As you twizzle, you should be working your way back to the barrier. It will be helpful if you can come out of the twizzle on a strong edge, because you'll then be able to get a good push to cross-stroke onto a left back outside three. There's no need to check this turn because it's going to be followed by five consecutive forward and backward inside Mohawks that have a continual rotation, and it's actually a good thing that they're preceded by a three turn because that starts the rotation.

The back three turn also starts a steady curve, which continues with the consecutive Mohawks, so that you end up on the red line ready to travel across ice.

A word about these Mohawks. They are quite unique, and are also known as 'Scotties'. Although he may not have invented them - and I don't think he did because I remember my coach demonstrating them to me back in the late 1960's - Scott Hamilton frequently used them in his programs and exhibitions, and, at the speed he rotated, made them look quite spectacular.

Even at the lower levels, forward Mohawks are a piece of cake, but in all the moves you've skated, you've never had to perform a back inside Mohawk, so it's essential to know exactly what your feet are doing. You have to be nimble, and time it so that you change feet at precisely the right time, going forward on one foot, and backward on the other. Your feet are going to be quite close together as you turn these Mohawks, and, once the rotation starts, you have to go with it, rather like when you walk through a revolving door, and have to keep moving with the door so that it doesn't smack you in the back.

As you turn the back three, let your body continue to rotate to turn the first Mohawk to backward, picking up your free foot to be held near the skating foot. When your body has rotated to the point where you're facing out of the circle - and this will happen immediately - place your left foot parallel to your right foot. As you turn from backward to forward, your right foot must leave the ice *without turning a back inside three turn*. This means that, as your right foot is coming off the ice, your left foot is going onto the ice. You almost have to have the feeling of 'flipping' your right foot off the ice as you quickly transfer your weight onto your left foot.

I would also advise that you skate these Mohawks with a slight knee bend - without getting too bouncy - and hold your arms out nicely to help you balance, so that your whole body feels as though it's rotating in one piece. And don't think of extending your free leg on them. You're going to be turning five quick Mohawks, and they happen *very* quickly, so there's no time to extend. Just keep your feet right underneath you and keep your body turning, otherwise you'll probably trip yourself up.

It's really not that important, but if you look at the ice you should find the tracings crossing on these Mohawks, if you've kept your feet close and in the right position with each other.

These consecutive Mohawks curve around to the point where you end up on the red line, ready to travel across the rink.

The 'Red Line' Section

This section is relatively short, and should take you about three-quarters of the way across the rink, but you need to curve the edges strongly to demonstrate good edge quality.

From the right back inside edge of the last Mohawk, skate a plain left back inside edge starting, and finishing, on the red line. You now need to skate a right back inside counter using the red line as a long axis. When you exit the counter, bring the edge around to turn a right forward inside rocker, again on the line. After you've checked the rocker, let your edge come back to the line and then push onto a plain left back inside edge.

We now come to the more challenging section, which will be skated down the other side of the ice.

The 'Twisty-Turny' section

The beginning of this section travels toward the barrier, and the first three steps need a twisting action - the same hips against shoulders action you used on the rocker/Choctaws in the Novice moves test - to help check each turn and prepare the rotation for the next.

From the left back inside edge at the end of the 'red line section', push onto a right back inside rocker, aiming your heel a little toward the barrier, and pre-rotate your right arm and shoulder back on the tracing. As you turn the rocker, check your arms and shoulders, and immediately turn a right forward inside Mohawk, checking your right arm and shoulder back again. Check the Mohawk with your free foot held close to the heel of your skating foot, toe pointed and turned out. You're now prepared for the first bracket. This is a left back inside bracket, albeit on a shallow edge. In fact, the edges on this rocker/Mohawk/bracket/bracket section are not deep, but they should be correct edges. No matter what your feet are doing, just keep that twisting action going, and you'll get through these first three turns easily.

When you turn and check the first bracket, you can either keep your free foot close to your skating foot, or you can use my preferred method whereby you straighten your free knee and extend your free leg as you turn, and then immediately pull your free foot back to cross behind for the second (right forward inside) bracket. As soon as you start pulling your foot back, start switching your arms and shoulders so that your free arm and shoulder are leading for the second bracket. You need to switch your arms quickly, so it usually works best to lower the arms and pass them fairly close to the body.

Be careful that you don't get 'stuck' by checking the first bracket too strongly, or for too long, and then find that you can't rotate your shoulders easily enough to prepare for the second bracket. This is yet another place where continuity of movement is expected from one turn to the other, so the check on the first bracket can only be very brief because of the need to get straight into the second bracket.

The last part of this move is where it really gets interesting, and the back outside counter – cross stroke – cross behind – choctaw – choctaw – forward inside counter sequence can present some control problems.

As you exit the second bracket (on a right back outside edge) pull the edge with your free arm and shoulder before counter-rotating to turn a right back outside counter. After this turn skate a cross stroke onto a left forward outside edge, rotating your right arm and shoulder forward, and then cross behind onto a right forward inside edge.

The next two edges should look familiar to you if you remember your Junior moves test. They are two consecutive Choctaws, but these are not wide Choctaws, and are turned a little quicker. These Choctaws are skated slightly diagonally, so that you are working your way toward the midline to finish the move. It really helps if your right arm and shoulder are already leading on the cross behind, because you can now check them back as you turn the first Choctaw (right forward inside to left back outside). Remember to hold your free foot back inside the tracing as you turn to backward, so you can place it back on the ice correctly to turn to forward again. You should come out of the second Choctaw on a right forward inside edge with your skating arm leading, and your free arm checked back.

The next element is a right forward inside counter, which is best performed by pressing up on the knee, and switching your arms and shoulders so that your free arm and shoulder are leading into it. Skate it the same way I described on the Novice moves test.

From the exit edge of the counter, push onto a left back inside two-revolution twizzle, coming out on a left back inside edge, and then step onto a right back inside loop to finish the move. Try not to rush this loop, otherwise it can look like a scratchy one-revolution spin. These final steps should bring you just across the midline of the rink, so the move goes approximately from midline to midline, but makes a full serpentine pattern on the ice.

As for repeating the move the other way around starting on the other foot, the rule book states, 'Optional steps take the skater to the repeat of the sequence in the opposite direction'. Therefore, after skating the back inside loop, I would recommend the following connecting steps.

The loop should end up a little past the midline, curving around on it's own circle as you exit. You'll be checking out of the loop on a right back inside edge, so hold that edge and let it come back around toward the midline. Step forward on the same curve on a left forward inside edge that will take you away from the end of the rink. This should give you room to skate a right forward inside Mohawk, followed by one or two back crossovers that will circle around back to the midline of the rink. It's almost like a little 'S' pattern in reverse. When you get near the midline, present yourself on a nice right back outside edge before stepping forward to start the second half of this move with a left forward outside three turn.

Trick of the Trade:

- Take advantage of the fact that the rotation on the consecutive Mohawks starts with the preceding back three turn.

- Only make a slight check of the first bracket, and, while your arms help steady you, move the free foot quickly back for the cross behind step, *then* immediately change the arms and shoulders.

PROBLEM AREAS: (There are a few)

- Not getting a push on the back cross stroke after the first twizzle, which doesn't help the back three turn/consecutive Mohawks section.
- Not skating clear consecutive Mohawks, resulting in some back Mohawks becoming back inside three turns.
- Not keeping continuity through the rocker/Mohawk/bracket/ bracket section.
- Getting 'stuck' on the first bracket, and not being able to make a slick change of upper body position for the second bracket.
- Failing to turn the first Choctaw onto an outside edge, making it a Mohawk.
- Two-footing too much on the push into the back inside twizzle, giving the impression of steadying oneself. To remedy this, get a quick short push, and get that pushing foot off the ice.
- Whipping around on the final back inside loop, making it tiny, and often scratchy, too.

IN CONCLUSION

Ice skating is not the easiest sport to master, and there will be days when you'll feel that you're never going to get it right. But if you persevere, and have faith, you'll be surprised at how much you can achieve.

I'm sure many readers will wince when they read my final thought for this book, which is: Moves in the Field are like vegetables. Some of you may not like them, but they're good for you!

I welcome any comments or questions you may have about this book, and you may contact me at dalbywill@cs.com

Printed in the United States
By Bookmasters